Compact Cinematics

Compact Cinematics

*The Moving Image in the Age
of Bit-Sized Media*

Edited by
Pepita Hesselberth and Maria Poulaki

BLOOMSBURY ACADEMIC
NEW YORK • LONDON • OXFORD • NEW DELHI • SYDNEY

BLOOMSBURY ACADEMIC
Bloomsbury Publishing Inc
1385 Broadway, New York, NY 10018, USA
50 Bedford Square, London, WC1B 3DP, UK

BLOOMSBURY, BLOOMSBURY ACADEMIC and the Diana logo are
trademarks of Bloomsbury Publishing Plc

First published in the United States of America 2017
Paperback edition first published 2018

Cover design: Catherine Wood
Cover image © David Rokeby. A "slice" of Hand-held (2012),
commissioned by Le Fresnoy Studio National des Arts Contemporains.
Courtesy of the artist. http://www.davidrokeby.com/

IISBN: HB: 978-1-5013-2226-6
PB: 978-1-5013-4393-3
ePDF: 978-1-5013-2227-3
ePub: 978-1-5013-2228-0

A catalog record for this book is available from the Library of Congress.

Typeset by Deanta Global Publishing Services, Chennai, India

To find out more about our authors and books visit
www.bloomsbury.com and sign up for our newsletters.

Contents

Acknowledgments

This book is a follow-up to a special issue on "Short Film Experience," edited by Pepita Hesselberth and Carlos M. Roos (2015) for *Empedocles: European Journal of the Philosophy of Communication*. We are indebted to the contributors and coeditor of this special issue, some of whom have returned here in this book as well, for sparking off the discussion on the compact audiovisual form vis-à-vis cinematic experience. We want to thank our reviewers at Bloomsbury, Bruce Isaacs, Ruggero Eugeni, and Sarah Atkinson, as well as Yasco Horsman, for their valuable commentary on the book proposal and earlier drafts of the introduction. A preview of the introduction to this book was published in a special issue on "Small Data" of *NECSUS: European Journal for Media Studies* (Spring 2016). We thank *NECSUS* for the opportunity to share some of our thoughts ahead of this publication in their journal. On behalf of the authors, finally, we would like to thank the artists and institutions who kindly granted us permission to reprint their images; without them, the book would not have been the same.

About the Authors

Neta Alexander is a doctoral student in the Department of Cinema Studies at New York University, researching streaming technologies and digital spectatorship. She is the recipient of the Society of Cinema and Media Studies' Student Writing Award for 2016, and her articles have appeared in *Cinema Journal, Film Quarterly,* and *Media Fields Journal,* among other publications. She has also authored book chapters in the anthologies *The Netflix Effect: Technology and Entertainment in the 21st Century* (Bloomsbury, 2016) and *Anthropology and Film Festivals* (Cambridge Scholars Publishing, 2016).

Justin Ascott teaches film production at Norwich University of the Arts, and is also an experimental filmmaker whose work critically engages the mediated experience of urban space and place. His films have been screened internationally at venues such as Videotage (Hong Kong), Future of Buildings Congress (Munich), London Short Film Festival, and Festival of Contemporary Art (Slovenia). He is currently working on a film about high-rise roofscapes as symbolic thresholds.

Tina M. Bastajian is a media artist, researcher, essayist, and archival dramaturge originally from California and currently living in Amsterdam. Bastajian has taught at the Rietveld Art Academie and has been visiting faculty at the Dutch Art Institute, The Autonomy Summer School, and the Vrije Universiteit Amsterdam. In 2015, she was an artist in residence at TUMO-Center for Creative Technologies (Yerevan, Armenia) leading geo-located storytelling workshops. Alongside her own artistic research practice, she teaches documentary film at Amsterdam University College and leads thematic modules in artistic research at Piet Zwart Institute (Rotterdam) for the Masters in Media Design and Lens-Based/Networked Media.

Natalie Bookchin is an artist based in Brooklyn, New York. Her most recent film, *Long Story Short*, premiered at the Museum of Modern Art in February 2016 and won the Grand Prize at Cinema du Reel at the Pompidou in March 2016. Her work is exhibited widely including at PS1, the Walker Art Center, the Whitney

Museum, and the Tate. She has received numerous grants and awards, including from Creative Capital, the Guggenheim, and the MacArthur Foundation. Bookchin is a Associate Professor in Media and Associate Chair in the Visual Arts Department at Mason Gross School of the Arts at Rutgers University.

Jay David Bolter is the Wesley Chair of New Media and co-Director of the Augmented Environments Lab at the Georgia Institute of Technology. He is the author of *Remediation* (1999), with Richard Grusin; and *Windows and Mirrors* (2003), with Diane Gromala. In addition to writing about new media, Bolter collaborates in the construction of new digital media forms. With Michael Joyce, he created *Storyspace*, a hypertext authoring system. Bolter now works closely with Blair MacIntyre, Maria Engberg, and others on the use of augmented reality to create new media experiences for cultural heritage and entertainment.

Francesco Casetti is the Thomas E. Donnelley Professor of Humanities and Film and Media Studies at Yale University. He is the author of six books and more than sixty essays, including *Eye of the Century: Film, Experience, Modernity* (Columbia University Press, 2005) and *The Lumière Galaxy: Seven Key words for the Cinema to Come* (Columbia University Press, 2015). His current research focuses on three topics: early film theory, especially the cinephobic stances in the first half of the twentieth century; the relocation of cinema in new spaces and on new devices, and in general the persistence of an "idea of cinema" in the digital epoch; and screen as an optical apparatus and as a component of our "mediascapes."

Sean Cubitt is Professor of Film and Television at Goldsmiths, University of London, and Honorary Professorial Fellow at the University of Melbourne. Among his publications are *The Cinema Effect* (MIT Press, 2004), *The Practice of Light: A Genealogy of Visual Technologies from Prints to Pixels* (MIT Press, 2014), and *Finite Media: Environmental Implications of Digital Technology* (Duke University Press, 2016). He is the series editor for Leonardo Books at MIT Press.

Ulrik Ekman is Associate Professor at the Department of Arts and Cultural Studies, University of Copenhagen. Ekman's main research interests are in the fields of cybernetics and ICT, the network society, new media art, critical design and aesthetics, as well as recent cultural theory. Ekman is behind the publication of *Ubiquitous Computing, Complexity and Culture* (Routledge, 2015), and the editor of *Throughout: Art and Culture Emerging with Ubiquitous Computing* (MIT Press, 2013). Research articles have appeared in books and journals like *Fibreculture*, *C-Theory*, *Postmodern Culture*, and *Parallax*.

Maria Engberg is an Assistant Professor at the Department of Media Technology and Product Development at Malmö University and an Affiliate Researcher at the Augmented Environments Lab at Georgia Institute of Technology (US). Her research interests include digital aesthetics, locative media, and media studies. She is the coeditor of *Ubiquitous Computing, Complexity, and Culture* (Ekman, Bolter, Diaz, Søndergaard, and Engberg, Routledge, 2015), and the author of several articles on digital aesthetics and literature, locative media, and augmented and mixed reality. Engberg designs mobile media experiences for augmented and mixed reality (AR/MR) for cultural heritage and informal learning experiences.

Tom Gunning is Distinguished Service Professor in the Department on Cinema and Media at the University of Chicago, and author of *D.W. Griffith and the Origins of American Narrative Film* (University of Illinois Press), *The Films of Fritz Lang; Allegories of Vision and Modernity* (British Film Institute), and over a hundred articles.

Pepita Hesselberth is Assistant Professor Film and Literary Studies at Leiden University, and research fellow at the Department of Arts and Cultural Studies at the University of Copenhagen. She is the author of *Cinematic Chonotopes: Here, Now, Me* (Bloomsbury, 2014) and coeditor of a special issue on "Short Film Experience" for *Empedocles: European Journal of Philosophy of Communication* (Intellect, 2015). She is currently working on her project on *Disconnectivity in the Digital Age,* for which she received a fellowship from the Danish Council for Independent Research.

Yasco Horsman is Assistant Professor of Film and Literary Studies at Leiden University. He holds a PhD in comparative literature from Yale University. He is the author of *Theaters of Justice. Judging Staging and Working Through in Arendt, Brecht and Delbo* (Stanford University Press 2010) and the coeditor of a special issue of *Law and Literature* on "Legal Bodies: Corpus, Persona, Communitas" (Routledge, 2016). He has published essays on literature (Kafka, Beckett, Coetzee), cinema (Resnais), graphic novels (Spiegelman, Ware, Clowes), animation (Mickey), and flipbooks. He is currently working on a book on Radio and Modernism and collecting notes for a genealogy of the "funny animal" figure in early animation and comic strips.

Geli Mademli is a doctoral candidate at the Amsterdam School of Cultural Analysis at the University of Amsterdam, working on the intersection of media studies, archival studies, and film museology. For the last few years, she has been working for the Thessaloniki International Film Festival as a program assistant, catalogue coordinator, and editor of its annual publications. She is also a freelance journalist, specializing in film and media, and a member of the editorial board of the Journal of Greek Film Studies *FilmIcon*.

Anna McCarthy is Professor of Cinema Studies at New York University. She is the author of the books *Ambient Television* (2001) and *The Citizen Machine* (2010) and coeditor of the anthology *MediaSpace* (2004). For eight years she served as a coeditor of *Social Text*. She is a 2016–2017 Fellow at the Institute of Advanced Study, Durham University.

Todd McGowan is Associate Professor at the University of Vermont where he teaches theory and film. He is the author of *Capitalism and Desire: The Psychic Cost of Free Markets* (Columbia University Press, 2016), *Enjoying What We Don't Have: The Political Project of Psychoanalysis* (University of Nebraska Press, 2013), *The Impossible David Lynch* (Columbia University Press, 2007), and other works.

Maria Poulaki is Lecturer in Film and Digital Media Arts at the University of Surrey. She has an interdisciplinary background in Media and Culture (PhD), Psychology and Media (MA), and Psychology (BA). Her research outputs have been published in various international journals (*Screen, Projections, Cinema et Cie, Necsus*, and others) and edited volumes (*Ubiquitous Computing, Complexity and Culture; Hollywood Puzzle Films*). She is coeditor of *Narrative Complexity and Cognition* (University of Nebraska Press, 2017) and has advocated a complex systemic approach to the study of cinematic media and the dynamics of the mind perceiving them.

Richard Raskin is Associate Professor at Aarhus University, where he teaches screenwriting and video production. He is the founding editor of Short Film Studies, published by Intellect Journals in the UK. His books include *The Art of* *the Short Fiction Film: A Shot-by-Shot Study of Nine Modern Classics* (2002) and his articles have appeared in many peer-reviewed journals. A frequent lecturer on the short film at festivals and film schools, he has often served on juries at international festivals. Short films based on his screenplays have been funded by New Danish Screen and have won a number of awards.

Gillian Rose is Professor of Cultural Geography at The Open University and a Fellow of the British Academy. Her current research interests focus on contemporary digital visual culture and on so-called "smart cities." She is the author of *Doing Family Photography: The Domestic, The Public and The Politics of Sentiment* (Ashgate, 2010) and *Visual Methodologies* (Sage, fourth edition 2016), as well as a number of papers on images and ways of seeing in urban and domestic spaces. Gillian blogs at visual/method/culture, and a full list of her publications can be found at oro.open.ac.uk.

Alexandra Schneider is Professor of Film and Media Studies at the Johannes Gutenberg-University of Mainz. Her fields of expertise include amateur film and media practices, media archaeology, digital storytelling, children and media, and world cinema. She is the author of '*Die Stars sind wir': Heimkino als filmische Praxis* (Marburg: Schüren, 2004) and has coedited several volumes. Her work has been published in *Necsus, Projections, Film History, Bianco e Nero,* and *Visual Anthropology.*

Wanda Strauven is Privatdozentin of Media Studies at the Goethe University Frankfurt and Affiliate Associate Professor of Film Studies at the University of Amsterdam. Her research interests include early and avant-garde cinema, media archaeology, media screens, tactile media, and children and media. She is the author of *Marinetti e il Cinema* (Udine: Campanotto, 2006) and has (co)edited several volumes including *The Cinema of Attractions Reloaded* (Amsterdam: Amsterdam University Press, 2006). Her essays have been published in *Cinémas, Cinéma & Cie, Iluminace, Maske und Kothurn, Necsus,* and *New Review of Film and Television Studies.*

Pasi Väliaho teaches and writes on theory and history of film and screen media. He has a PhD in Media Studies from the University of Turku, Finland, and is Reader in Film and Screen Studies at the Department of Media and Communications, Goldsmiths, University of London. His books include

Biopolitical Screens: Image, Power and the Neoliberal Brain (MIT Press, 2014) and *Mapping the Moving Image: Gesture, Thought and Cinema circa 1900* (Amsterdam University Press, 2010).

Peter Verstraten is Assistant Professor Film and Literary Studies at Leiden University. He is the coeditor of *Shooting Time: Cinematographers on Cinematography* (2012) and the author of, among others, *Humour and Irony in Dutch Post-war Fiction Film* (Amsterdam University Press, 2016) and *Film Narratology* (University of Toronto Press, 2009).

Kim Louise Walden is Senior Lecturer in Film and TV Cultures at University of Hertfordshire. She has a long held interest in how digital technologies have shaped film and her published work includes "Run, Lara, Run: The impact of videogames on cinema's action heroine" in *Femme Fatalities: Representations of Strong Women in the Media* edited by Rikke Schubart and Anne Gjelsvik (Nordicom, 2004); "Rotoscoping and the Processing of Performance" in *Refractory: A Journal of Entertainment Media* (2008); and "Nostalgia for the Future: How *Tron: Legacy's* Paratexual Campaign rebooted the Franchise" in *The Politics of Ephemeral Digital Media*, edited by Sara Pesce and Paolo Noto (Routledge, 2016).

Introduction: Screen | Capture | Attention

Pepita Hesselberth and Maria Poulaki

With tremendous force, and against all odds, a laboring woman shoots out a baby from her body like a cannonball, the umbilical cord torn as it rockets through the hospital window into the orbit. As the screaming child arches through the skies it rapidly degenerates from a bald pink baby, through the various stages of physical maturation, into a gray-haired old man, his eyes wide open in fear. The latter shape is only barely assumed when the projectile hurls toward planet Earth, where it violently crashes into its grave, leaving of the tombstone nothing but smoke and crumbles. This 52-second clip grabs the viewer's attention like a dog sensing a squirrel. Its message is clear: in the age of omnipresent electronic and visual media we can no longer "Rest in Peace," but are forever reminded of the fact that "Life is Fast," and we need to "Play More."[1]

Though made for television, this soon-to-be-banned advert for the very first X-Box game console from 2002 (now watched on YouTube) arrests the viewer's attention, we argue, on account of specific cinematic qualities: the movement of the images, its affective appeal, the attempt at narrative, and the thickening of time.[2] Using one of the most interesting cinematic techniques of the time, i.e. that of the digital morph, the clip can easily be linked to both the effects-oriented cinema of postclassical Hollywood and the so-called early "cinema of attractions" (Gunning 1990) as it de-emphasizes techniques of narrative integration in favor of a different type of magical transformation. At once providing a pleasant experience and posing the threat of a disruption of that experience, the fragment is compelling, moreover, we would like to argue, because it is short and compact, sufficient unto itself, somehow recognizably different from the assemblage of mediated sounds and images of which it is nonetheless intricately part.

Screen

Since the advent and standardization of the theatrical feature-length film, compact audiovisual artifacts have been more or less marginalized in the discussions on the aesthetics, techniques, and experience of the cinematic. Whereas cinema is often considered a "larger-than-life" phenomenon, associated with the "big screen"— attracting special attention of mass audiences with disproportionate images of out-of-the-ordinary characters and subject matters—by contrast, and perhaps by contrast only, the notion of the "small screen" is more commonly reserved for another (then) emerging new medium, that is, that of television, which has come to be associated with the domestic, with immediacy, and with the discourses of the everyday.[3] Though the distinction between the big and the small screen has been put to productive use to differentiate the aesthetics and social appeal of television (and later the internet) from that of cinema, and has engendered valuable insights into the particularity of divergent media technologies, forms, and modes of spectatorship, it is also suggestive of an opposition that, we would like to argue, is in fact false, a claim to which a rich body of media-archaeological research into the many prehistories of cinema of the last two decades attests.[4]

Historically stretching from pre-cinematic toys (like thaumatropes and flip books), penny arcades, early cinema's actualities, and the flickering shadows of the vaudeville, to short films, avant-garde film, video art, QuickTime movies, machinima, and animated GIFs, the widespread use and consumption of compact cinematic forms, practices, and artifacts suggests that compactness is not an unwonted curiosity at the margins of cinema, but has existed from even before cinema's standardization in theatrical form, and in recent years has multiplied and proliferated, taking up an increasingly important part of our everyday multimedia environment. We feel that, in this context, the disciplinary contest over screen size and modes of spectatorship tends to be counterproductive, as it is prone to fall prey to a boundary fetishism that may in fact hinder our understanding of the role and function of the moving image in our bit-sized media culture today.

In this book we propose the term *compact cinematics* for the study of the various compact, short, compressed, and miniature (audio)visual artifacts, forms, and practices that circulate in our everyday multimedia environment, across technologies, genres, and disciplines. With its roots in *cine* (from Greek –*kinesis,* meaning movement or motion), the notion of *cinematics,* like that of cinema and the cinematic, alludes to the moving image. The suffix -*ics* (from Latin -*ica* and Greek -*ikos*) indicates at once a field of knowledge or area of study (like in mathematics, (meta)physics, robotics, politics, classics, aesthetics, or, in our case, cinematics), as well as referring, in its plural construction, to a category of characteristic activity (like gymnastics and athletics), or to qualities and operations relating to a particular subject (like acoustics or phonetics). In using the term *cinematics,* we thus wish to refer to matters relevant, or pertaining, to (the study of) the moving image, that is, to what it *is* as much as to what it *does*—as material form, praxis, and encounter: an activity. The notion of *cinematics* transcends the rigidity of the disciplinary limits of film, television, and digital media studies, and emphasizes the movement between disciplines and technologies, challenging us to situate the moving image in a constellation of humans, technologies, and environments that is by definition context-specific, and from which particular time, space, and agency formations emerge.

What happens when the compact form, instead of being considered a derivative or incomplete or less developed form of cinema, becomes the framework to rethink the cinematic in all its dimensions (time, space, agency), its uses and affordances, as artifacts as well as ecologies? We posit that format, content, technology, and use are inseparable, and suggest *compactness* as a theoretical framework to rethink the cinematic within our present-day bit-sized media culture. *Compactness*, here, is thus decisively used to refer to the shortening of the distance between the various components of the cinematic configuration, like the cinematic *dispositif,* which necessarily results in changes of the configuration as a whole. It is this changed (and ever-changing) configuration of the cinematic, and its corresponding field of practices and theories, *cinematics*, that the chapters in this book seek to address.

Short films or micro-narratives, cinematic pieces or units reassembled into image archives and looping themes are among the most common forms that compact cinematic content takes. These forms and practices challenge the concepts that have traditionally been used to understand the moving image, and call attention to complex and modular forms of expression and perception of which the cinematic partakes. Such forms, in turn, meet the requirements of digital convergence, which seems to have pushed the development of more compact and mobile hardware for the display and use of audiovisual content on laptops, smartphones, and tablets, necessitating new forms of content and an adjusted spatial and bodily interaction with them.

Meanwhile, contemporary economies of digital content acquisition, filing, and sharing equally require the shrinking of cinematic content for it to be recorded, played, projected, distributed, and installed with ease and speed. Our engagement with this content is usually ad hoc and casual, itself compact one could argue, concentrated so that it can be completed quickly and most likely feed into yet another bit of content, rebooted without an experience of break or discontinuation. Attributes such as the "giffiness" or "glueyness" of online videos (in this book discussed by Anna McCarthy) and the possibility of "speed-watching" (illuminated in Neta Alexander's piece) expose the cinematic character of compact audiovisual artifacts and practices, not just in terms of their moving image nature and their remediation (Bolter and Grusin 1999) of film, but mainly also in terms of the kinds of viewer engagement they afford, giving rise to new modes of engagement and forms of spectatorship, whether they be solitary, contingent, accelerated, fragmented, procrastinating, and/or productive. Manipulability seems to be a fundamental quality of such engagement, as small size devices nowadays afford extensive play with, and manipulation of, even typically large-scale cinematic phenomena like the panorama (an argument developed in Jay Bolter and Maria Engberg's chapter on Mobile Cinematics).

Moreover, the products and practices of filmmaking seem to be adjusting to a smaller scale as well, giving rise to new kinds of mobile films and pocket shorts (media archaeologically explored in Kim Walden's contribution), including the "little thumb films" of our children (as discussed by Alexandra Schneider and Wanda Strauven). These new media practices, in turn, build on and enrich the miniature aesthetics already fostered in precinematic optical toys, like the flipbook, early cinema, and animation (addressed by Yasco Horsman). In this process, the traditional chain of production, distribution, and reception of content also gets contracted, its links folding back upon one another, taking place almost simultaneously (addressed here in Geli Mademli's piece). By the same token, cinematic experience is shortened and condensed as well, so as to fit the late-capitalist conditions of time, space, and energy distribution characteristic of (and generating) the current attention economy. This brings us to a second aspect we wish to address here, and that is the linkage between compact cinematics and the new economy of attention.

Attention

Compact cinematic phenomena, it seems, have a differential effect on cinema's acclaimed relationship with the mental faculty of attention. As early as 1916,

Hugo Münsterberg (2002) posited the claim that the photoplay, as he called cinema, offers a hyperfocused view of the world by visualizing the mental act of attention (87). Cinema, moreover, offers a cropped image of the world using devices such as the close-up, and, as such, attracts our attention to elements that might slip our attention under everyday conditions.

The Photoplay was published at a crucial point in the history of the moving image, as 1916 is often considered the year in which cinema entered its "mature" phase of narrative integration, establishing its identity as a medium through the feature-length format and the system of continuity editing. The continuity system evolved, as some have argued,[5] through a process of trial and error, in which filmmakers, exercising their intuition, sought to develop and refine the craft of grabbing and retaining the viewer's attention across a series of cinematic fragments (the film shots) that capture and crop the world for us, using devices such as match-on-action and point-of-view shots, and also of "rebooting" the viewer's attention across scenes.[6]

How is this classical function of cinema, to drive and guide attention across a series of images, still pertinent in light of these emerging compact cinematic phenomena? On the one hand, even feature-length films nowadays seem to have internalized the tendency of the cinematic to disperse in multiple smaller units, for example, by containing modular or micro-narratives and mise-en-abyme plot structures (as reflected in Peter Verstraten's chapter in this book); or by being composed of shorter shots and faster cuts—a tendency foreseen by David Bordwell (2002) in his essay on "intensified continuity," and more recently demonstrated through a software program called "cinemetrics."[7] On the other hand, as the cinematic no longer seems to be contained by the (feature-length) film format but has become dispersed across a proliferating variety of screens—from the microscale of the mobile screens in our pockets (here discussed by Walden, Bolter, and Engberg), to the macroscale of the urban façade (dealt with in Ulrik Ekman's and Gillian Rose's pieces), there seems to be an ongoing competition, not only to capture the best possible image, but also for the image to capture our own attentional "snippets" in turn.

The attention that is needed to connect frames and audiovisual scenes into meaningful assemblages is the mind's "cinematic labor," and also the labor of the cinematic, which enables such linking of experience, both on the level of perception (through the connection of still images into a "moving" sequence), and through editing. As a distinctly modern and Fordist phenomenon itself, early cinema participated in the standardization of time (Doane 2004) and attracted the crowds in the city by satisfying the need for the integration of an alienated and fragmented urban experience. A mechanized process par excellence, cinema has been said to have employed, and therewith "trained," the physiology of visual perception and attention in the aftermath of the second Industrial Revolution. Promising the reward of a well-rounded and coherent world, a narrative resolution as well as a spectacle worth being looked at, cinema—so the argument goes—offered a form of labor that was much more engaging and fulfilling than the one offered by industrialized labor.

Walter Benjamin (1968 [orig. 1936]) described cinema's system of perception—or this "work of cinema"—with ambivalent feelings, concerned as he was about the uses to which such a powerful tool could be put. A similar ambivalence cannot escape us when considering his view on cinematic labor as a model for understanding the equivalent, yet divergent, ways in which compact cinematic phenomena engage contemporary "contingent" or "solitary" viewers (discussed in Francesco Casetti's and Pasi Väliaho's contributions to this book, respectively), in acts of speed watching (Alexander) or productive procrastination (McCarthy), directing and arguably distributing his or her attention across a continuous, yet intermittent, surge of audiovisual materials. These developments show that the cinematic's "attentional machine," indeed, may work not just in the context of movie-watching but also in that of watching-on-the-move, that is, in the process of assembling discontinuous audiovisual bits, linking our attention to them into a compacted, yet plural, dispersed and heterogeneous cinematic experience.

Within our contemporary bit-sized media culture, viewers have become prosumers (Leadbetter and Miller 2004) or pro-ams (Manovich 2009) who are invited to stitch together their own personalized cinematic "spectacles" by linking compact bits and short samples to other bits, chunks, and segments of moving images, sharing and collecting them in online platforms, blogs, social media archives, and profiles, as if this stitching process is an acquired competency to keep our attention dispersed yet continuously flowing. The Fordist task of recycling labor through cinematic leisure has become the personalized task of post-Fordist subjects, who, living constantly on the margins of leisure and labor, willingly and proactively accept the challenge of recycling their own attention by attaching it to a multiplicity of available objects—short but self-contained, in other words, compact, audiovisual units, to be combined and recombined into a plurality of possible sequences.[8]

Movement, here, is an inherent quality of not just images alone, but also of the mode of their capture, reception, and combination. This is perhaps the cinematic effect par excellence: images set in motion by way of their linking. Throughout this process, attention needs to be anchored. Contemporary cinematics, we argue, retain the function of gluing attention between the fragments of everyday experience, even as the "suture" of classical cinematic continuity is transformed into a "stickiness" that demands the viewer to attune and respond to the loading and buffering of images in real time. Ironically, a certain sense of anxiety in this process still seems to be linked to the threat of discontinuation, albeit in a different form. Whereas in classical cinema, suture is achieved through the interlocking of shots so as to secure the continuity of time and space and therewith the position of the subject within discourse—thus diverting the viewer's anxiety over the discontinuation of the story world—within our present-day bit-sized media culture the viewer's anxiety seems to coincide with the prospect of "missing out" or losing access (the frustrations of buffering,[9] of no access to the internet), while continuation is secured through ever-accelerating broadband widths, constant updates,[10] the precipitation of portable devices, and the accompanying upsurge of compact cinematic phenomena that assure the viewer the possibility to glue (or be glued) to the screen.

The experience of discontinuity, unavoidable in our contemporary hypermediated environments, thus persists as a threat, we argue, as a sense of void, or "dead time," a term used in systems theory to describe the time after a discrete event during which a system is not able to detect or record another event, a moment when nothing is happening except for the constant attempt to reboot (think of the flash of a camera that has to recharge after taking a photograph). This is what makes contemporary cinematics sticky (and the serial form such a persuasive trend): in our response to the rhythms of our everyday media environment we find ourselves "spellbound by tidbits" (Väliaho's phrasing in this book) of images, as each discontinuation potentially pulls us into a mental experience of void that needs to be filled in, and therewith a-voided no matter what, and a bodily experience of strain that needs to be released into a new feedback cycle.[11] Compact cinematic bits and pieces, thus, are useful, productive even, in the sense that they allow for the (potentially seamless) filling up of voids, thus recharging the interaction that sustains the system.

This brings us to a third angle that we wish to broach in relation to contemporary cinematics, besides screen theory and attention economy, and that is the human-technology angle, which we will address through the notion of capture.

Capture

The way in which images move in our contemporary media-saturated landscape is indicative of the cinematic's transformation from a mechanical technology to a systemic, or cybernetic, one.[12] In his well-known essay "Surveillance and Capture," information theorist Phillip Agre (1994) provides a useful distinction that can help us understand this transformation. Referring to what would be now called ubiquitous computing, Agre signals a shift from what he describes as the centralized and optical model of "surveillance" toward the decentralized model of "capture," which, he argues, is more neutral in the sense that it requires the complicity of all its components, both sentient and nonsentient. Agre uses the term *capture* to refer to the (computational) models on the bases of which computers process information. Information, Agre argues, is captured in accordance with the ontological categories of the computer program that are at once predetermined (i.e., they are programmed) and yet can continuously (be) adjust(ed) to accommodate new elements and situations, thus making the system increasingly more complex. Whereas the classical cinematic apparatus has often been theorized in terms of voyeurism and panoptic surveillance, we feel the term capture, in Agre's nuanced terminology, is more apt to describe the present situation in which compact cinematic phenomena partake of an increasingly more complex ubiquitous network of (audiovisual) capturing technologies.[13]

The coupling of the psychic and technological apparatuses of compact cinematics forces us to take into consideration the mutual cycle, or loop, of interaction that sustains this dynamics. Here, both Münsterberg's conceptualization of cinema as visualizing thought, and the Benjaminian understanding of film's potential to (either or both) attune the modern subject to industrial capitalism and/or preserve humanity in the face of modernity's uniforming apparatuses return with a difference (and all the more political urgency), as we are now constantly invited to externalize our faculties of thought and perception in audiovisual units of content that we link and share in the online or physical realm in acts of precarious labor.

Whereas early cinema's relation to labor is perhaps best captured in the satirical figure of Charlie Chaplin's Little Tramp—whose sensory-motor scheme in *Modern Times* (1936) runs amok after suffering from a nervous breakdown from screwing nuts onto pieces of machinery at the ever-accelerating speed of the assembly line[14]—the contemporary cinematic laborer willingly offers himself or herself to be captured in turn, posing or adjusting his or her movement and position, like a minimalist Little Tramp, to match the machine's various checkpoints and sensors, with selfies, vines, tags, and check-ins being among the more obvious examples. A dramatic change of scale is certainly noted as the huge machinery of the conveyor belt, demanding the "Little" Tramp's standardized bodily adjustment to it, has now dispersed into small, friendly, and almost invisible gadgets that allow the contemporary Tramp, or Rube (Elsaesser 2006), ultimate flexibility. Minimal bodily gestures are sufficient to both capture and be captured, fed into the system without strain, in an almost seamless matching, and a much less standardized but arguably equally anxious pursuit of nuts to be screwed (life is short, play more).

As part of cyber-cinematic systems, contemporary view(s)ers are always alert to capture the next bit of audiovisual stimulation, which will find its place in personal or shared databases and archives. In so doing they enable their embodied "gaze" (Mulvey 1975), "glance" (Ellis 1982), or "graze" (Creeber 2013, 124) to be captured in turn, prolonging the interactive loop between them as viewers and their viewing apparatuses.[15] This loop is further amplified by the web's mass connectivity where the capturing behavior of humans and algorithms comes together, extending its dynamics by expanding in time and space into what Manuel Castells has called a "space of flows."[16] The search engines through which we often access and reassemble compact cinematic bits and pieces invite the redistribution of every successive thought, perception, memory, or imagination with every search, generating a line of assembled tags and possible screens contained within a larger screen (and a soon-to-be [de-]personalized algorithm), each one of which can be accessed and "screened" nonlinearly, and archived in search histories as a discontinuous series of past thoughts; a testament of distraction, which, within a day's use, might not even make sense to its own user.

Just as capture in the context of computer ontologies is concerned solely with information that can be mathematically represented (and manipulated), capture in the context of human perception refers to our ability to select from all the affordances in a given environment only those that are relevant for our survival (much like the car driver's scope is selective perforce, registering only that which is directly relevant to his or her purposeful action, a sort of instrumental viewing).[17] This begs the question, however, of how "relevance" can have any

bearing under the conditions of the surplus of mediated sounds and images that
we are confronted with in our present-day media-saturated environments, in
which we are constantly sidetracked by scraps of information, narrative probings,
and audiovisual attractions. In such environments, we suspect, users do not
only capture what is directly relevant for their immediate survival. Rather, we
survive postindustrial capitalism in constant distraction, attaching our attention
to the audiovisual apparatuses that turn leisure activity, as Bill Nichols has put
it, into "commodity experience" (1988, 30). The time of leisure, thus, becomes
commodified, as we lend our time and faculties to its cause. *Compact cinematics*
calls attention to such packaging of attention into audiovisual content rejoinders
and sets out to question the social and political ramifications of such packaging.

As the regulatory system of cybernetics has gradually progressed into a new type
of governmentality, a position held in more recent critical theory,[18] a question
that arises is what kinds of strategies compact cinematics can adopt within our
present-day hyper-mediated realm to generate envelopes of time, space, and affect
that are not complicit with the overarching ideology of the (media-consuming)
system that generates them—a system, we might add, in which discourses of
connectivity, quantification, self-tracking, and bio-sensing technology prevail.[19]

Historically, short and compact film formats have offered fertile ground
for filmmakers to experiment with the conventions of (cinematic) time and
space, calling forth new ways of world-building, time compression, and viewer
engagement (taken up by Todd McGowan, Tom Gunning, and Richard Raskin
in this book, respectively), that arguably have the potential to escape and subvert
the rational and (neo)liberal discourses of time, space, and agency formation.
While it may be argued that in the present-day context it is not so much the
compact form, but rather its counterpart—that is, the slow contemplative cinema
of protracted minimalist narrative and no attractions to speak of—that holds the
promise of denting the system, the various cases dealt with in this book demand
a more nuanced view.

Sure enough, while many filmmakers, media artists, and viewers nowadays
fully (though not necessarily uncritically) embrace the possibilities offered by
the cybernetic media system in which the cinematic participates, others have
found ways to scrutinize its constraints, for example by making intensified use
of its potential at the risk of "over-heating," or exhausting, it (e.g., the "good"
hacker's ethic; or political memes[20] gone viral); or by adopting a more disengaged
nostalgic view (this would be the stance of the cinephiliac who rejoices in the use

of analogue technologies, a position eloquently discussed in Yasco Horsman's reflections on the linkage between the tactility of the flipbook, the game console, and contemporary "cinematic" cartoon drawing).

Sidestepping the cases dealt with in this book for a second, a case in point here would be the work of David Rokeby, who has kindly lent us permission to use a slice of his installation *Hand-held* (2013) for the cover of this book. Though by no means intended as cinematic, and indeed rarely classified as such, much of Rokeby's work is invested in exposing the merciless judgment schemes (or capture) at work in computational systems that by default turn qualitative features into quantifiable data, and exploring the possibility of ambiguity within these systems. With suggestive titles like *Seen* (2002), *Taken* (2002), *Sorting Deamon* (2003), and *Machine for Taking Time* (2001, 2007) his work often combines complex hybrid interfaces of screen technologies, image and/or sound databases, (smart) algorithms that render these images or sounds in particular ways, and user-responsive environments that prompt the algorithm (or user) to adapt in response.

What is interesting about Rokeby's experimental work is how it challenges the computational technologies of which it makes use on at least three different levels: first, in the often mesmerizing compact cinematic images in which he exposes the computational logic at hand; second, in the confrontation these manifestations enable between the user and, on the one hand, the technological environment in which he or she is present, and, on the other hand, his or her bodily engagement with it; and third, on the level of the algorithm itself. In an interesting twist to the current discussion on beautiful data (Segaran and Hammerbacher 2009), as well as to the ancient discussion on the aesthetization of politics, Rokeby's work can be said to be at once critical in its aesthetization of capture, and political in its prioritization of source code as a tool for critical inquiry; he has often staked a claim for the proliferation of (code) literacy.

This strategy of using the available techniques against the logic of technology so as to circumvent or expose (and therewith possibly destabilize) its regulatory workings can take on many different forms, so the cases discussed in the present volume attest. We see it for example reflected in the "ethics of repair" enabled by the repurposing of archival footage as discussed by Sean Cubitt. We see it also in Justin Ascott and Tina Bastajian's work, in praxis and theory, on, respectively, the codification of urban space, and the interactive documentary as a reflexive threshold; in Ulrik Ekman's deliberations on the disorganized complexity of screen-transcoded milieux; and in Natalie Bookchin's adaptation of the aesthetics of social media to counterbalance, in a tactical move, contemporary media's erosion of the social. Though by no means restricted to the field of compact cinematics alone, such strategies are interesting within the present context, as they give pertinence to the question what other function the moving image can (still) fulfill within our present-day bit-sized media culture.

Compact cinematics, we argue, challenges us to reconsider object-oriented approaches to the moving image, and, while encouraging us to revisit early (film) theory's interest in the faculty of attention vis-à-vis moving image technology, it coerces us to rethink (with some political urgency) the processes of subjectivation of which the cinematic partakes. A focus on compact cinematics requires taking into account the specific context in which something can be viewed as compact, as well as the conditions and spatiotemporal configurations of the environment that renders it compact. Compact cinematics, thus, requires an ecological approach.[21] As a particular configuration of time, space, and agency, the cinematic creates an ecology for itself; but it also functions within larger ecologies of social, mental, physical, and technological infrastructures that make up our everyday-lived environment. Within this larger environment, (our engagement with) the moving image is increasingly dictated by the economic conditions of late capitalism and the decentralization that digital networks have brought about, as well as by the mobility and portability of new "connected" viewing technologies and the modes of engagement they afford. It is within this wider scope, we maintain, that the moving image demands our attention from the point of view of the compact. A focus on compactness not only encourages us to reconsider the moving image in light of the short, condensed, compressed, miniature, and compacted cinematic artifacts, practices, and modes of engagement that challenge traditional models for its theorization. It also offers a framework to critically examine the politics of subjectivation, specific to this historical moment, of which the moving image partakes, as well as to address the strategies used to defy it, in the hope, perhaps, of turning today's solitary screens, so powerfully addressed in Pasi Väliaho's piece, into tomorrow's solidary screens.

Notes

1   The clip is available at: https://www.youtube.com/watch?v=kNccPX03XaY (accessed May 10, 2016).
2   For a reflection on the cinematic in these terms, see Hesselberth (2012, 2014).

3   See, for example, Bennett (2016); Creeber (2013); Morley (1988); Palmer (2010); Spigel (1992); Thomson (2013); and Thumim (2002).

4   Carels (2015); Crary (1990); Gunning (2015); Zielinski (1999, 2006), to name but a few.

5   See Anderson (1996, 11).

6   Since Münsterberg, different accounts of how cinema visualizes or replicates the mind's processes of perception and attention have preoccupied film psychology. Tim Smith (2005) has, for example, recently suggested an "attentional theory of continuity editing" to give a scientific account of continuity in film, which explains the effect of continuity editing on attention by what in developmental psychology has been described as "existence constancy" (Michotte 1995). For a critical approach on certain premises of (contemporary) film psychology, especially regarding its tendency to naturalize continuity editing, see Poulaki (2015).

7   CineMetrics is a software program written by Gunars Civjans that allows for the online or offline calculation of average shot lengths of films. CineMetrics can be accessed on the relevant website (cinemetrics.lv), which at the same time functions as a database of shot lengths for movies users have parsed.

8   There has been a surge of publications in the last couple of years that link the emergence of a so-called participatory (digital) media culture to questions concerning immaterial labor, social and affective capital, and measurable attention. See, for example, Dyer-Witheford (2015); Fuchs (2014); Huws (2014); and Scholz (2012, 2016).

9   For a brilliant essay on buffering, see Alexander (fc. 2017).

10 For a thought-provoking reflection on the update, see Chun (2016).

11 A similar argument is made in relation to machine gambling in a thought-provoking study by anthropologist Natasha Schüll entitled *Addiction by Design* (2012). Schüll demonstrates that players find themselves pulled into a trancelike state they call the "machine zone," where the aim is not so much to win but to stay there, "in the zone," for as long as possible, "where nothing else matters" (12).

12 For our understanding of this development, we draw on Nichols (1988).

13 While the focus of this book is on the audiovisual components of capture and captured content, it is important to note that capture is not per se audiovisual but, rather, computational, thus accommodating a variety of different modalities, such as textual, haptic, kinaesthetic etc. The predominance of visual and audiovisual content is, however, something that makes more pertinent the discussion of the particular cinematic qualities of capture, within a larger multimodal and polyaesthetic (Engberg 2014) context of mediation.

14 If it seems hard to come up with a present-day counterpart of a canonical figure that embodies the relation between cinema and labor equally well, it is perhaps because, as Bergson (1998, orig. 1911) has argued, for the one who laughs from the position of *élan vital,* laughter is explicitly linked to automation, that is, comical relief, or laughter,

in Chaplin, is invoked by something mechanic encrusted upon the human body (We thank Yasco Horsman for this observation). In a time and age in which we so willingly allow for the exploitation of our *Élan vital* in acts of liking, clicking, (re)assembling, and sharing, we can wonder what such a position to laugh critically from would look like. As we have become part and parcel of the cinematic cybernetic system—and digital labor has largely substituted manual labor within our post-Fordist economies— it can be argued that it is perhaps not so much the human figure's internalization of machinic manners, but the computerized rendering of humanoid gestures that triggers this kind of laughter, albeit with a difference. As a running gag in the course of writing this introduction, for example, we kept on sending back and forth animated GIFs to comment on our progression (or lack thereof) and procrastinations. Typically, these GIFs would originate from a site called PhD Stress, and comment on the highs and lows of academic writing, with clips of human activity cut short and endlessly repeated in loops with suggestive titles like "writing a joint article" (first one, then two people, slipping on a bowling alley, over and over again); "starting writing that analysis" (two GIFs, "how I plan it" (acrobatic turner), "what normally happens" (crashing paraglider)); "researching" (Segway takes off with clinging man, legs all tied up); "writing" (endless attempts of a car to leave its parking spot); "when meeting the deadline for submitting an article" (high jumper misses mat); and "when finally getting that article finished and emailed" (American football player running like an eight-year-old schoolgirl in chase of the ball, successively overlaid with flickering words "OMG," "lol," "cool," "yay," "wut," and "Luvit"). If we would have been asked to make a short film of our endeavor, this is probably what it would have looked like. (At the risk of stretching matters too far, we ask ourselves while writing down these words if the reader's perusing of them constitutes what might be called a compact cinematic experience?). Available at: http://phdstress.com/ (accessed May 23, 2016).

15   This links to Lev Manovich's argument on the parallelism between cinema and the computer when it comes to their trajectories as capture/inscription and projection/ entertainment technologies. He argues that computers and new media are cinematic in that sense. See Manovich (2001, 21).

16   Castells (2000, 2004). Castells describes the "space of flows" as the material arrangement "made up first of all of a technological infrastructure of information systems, telecommunications, and transportation lines" (2000, 19).

17   Originally coined by J. J. Gibson (1982 [orig. 1977]) in his ecological psychology of visual perception, the term affordance was appropriated to the field of human– machine interaction by Donald Norman (1990), who used it to refer to the possibilities for action perceptible to the interactant.

18   See, for example, Galloway and Thacker (2007); The Invisible Committee (2015).

19 See, for example, Terranova (2004); Van Dijck (2013); Lupton (2016); Neff and Nafus (2016); and Nafus (2016).
20 On memes, see Shifman (2013).
21 The reference, here, is not to the aforementioned ecological psychology but to, for example, Matthew Fuller's *Media Ecologies* (2005), Isabelle Stengers "Ecology of Practice" (2005), and the more environment-oriented approaches to the cinematic as developed in, for example, Hesselberth (2014), and taken a (major) step further in Ulrik Ekman's piece in this book.

Part One

[Short]
Minimal Narratives

1

Countdown to Zero: Compressing Cinema Time

Tom Gunning

A compressed history of cinematic time

Cinema is a time medium. It emerged at the end of the nineteenth century with Edison's Kinetoscope, Lumière's Cinématographe, Armat and Jenkins's Vitascope—all machines that could visually record and replay events that take time. Edison's phonograph, unveiled in 1877, offered the ability to replay not only sounds (voices, music) but also a moment of the past, inscribed and replayed with amazing fidelity. Edison's patent caveat had announced that his Kinetoscope would "do for the eye what the phonograph did for the ear," visually recording and replaying a passing moment. Both cinema and the phonograph preserved time, not simply in individual memory or through synecdochic souvenirs, but by creating a technical process that allowed a passing moment to be re-experienced.

But it was soon discovered that cinematically recorded time was also malleable. By means of cinema, time could be shaped and rearranged as well as preserved. For instance, Georges Méliès and other early filmmakers discovered the magical possibilities of the "substitution splice." The filmstrip could be cut and spliced together so smoothly that the viewer would not notice the manipulation, producing the appearance of continuous time when the time of filming had actually been discontinuous. By cutting the filmstrip and manipulating action, Méliès could instantly transform a woman into a skeleton, a man into a woman, or make lunar extraterrestrials disappear in a puff of smoke (see Gunning 1989). Cutting together shots of continuous action in early chase films created a new synthetic flow of action across cuts that formed the basis of fictional filmic time (see Gunning 1984). Manipulating the rate of filming an event (the literal speed of the film passing through the camera) could speed up action in impossible ways. The 1901 Biograph film *Star Theater* used time-lapse cinematography (filming a few frames every day) to compress the floor-by-floor destruction of this New York City theater, which actually took about a month, into a film of about two minutes.

Viewers of the new phenomenon of the movies in the early twentieth century often saw them as an emblem of the heightened pace of modern life. Viewed with concern by social conservatives anxious over the psychological and physical effects this new lifestyle might bring, the new medium was denounced as nervous, over stimulated, and—most obviously—too fast. As Scott Curtis (2015) has shown, focusing his research on Germany before the First World War, these concerns were international and became an issue in countries undergoing industrialization and urbanization. Sociologists, such as Max Nordau in his influential 1892 book *Degeneration (Entartung)*, warned that the tempo of modern life threatened not only health and peace of mind but the very foundations of traditional human culture. Nordau claimed that the frenzied demands of the modern urban environment and industrial work would create a new culture of hysteria and degeneration (Curtis 2015, 128). Such beliefs were widespread, and cinema was seen as the exemplar of this dangerous culture of speed and brevity. Curtis quotes a German social commentator warning specifically about the effects of the fast pace of cinema images: "The mere habituation to the darting, convulsive, twitching images of the flickering screen slowly and surely corrodes man's mental and, ultimately, moral strength" (134).

During its second decade cinema moved from its initial fascination with the uncanny or magical effects that the manipulation of cinematic time could create, such as the time-lapse filming of *Star Theater* or the magical metamorphoses of trick films, toward more narrative forms. If new narrative genres seemed to corral cinema's temporal possibilities into familiar patterns, nonetheless specifically cinematic temporal manipulation continued to play a key role. The cinema's first psychological theorist, Hugo Münsterberg, in his 1916 book *The Photoplay: A Psychological Study* claimed that the narrative form of cinema reproduced the subjective processes of human psychology. Thus filmic time was not only malleable through technical manipulation of recording and editing; the relation it forged with viewers through cinematic conventions of narrative form also reshaped basic categories of human experience, including time.

Münsterberg summarized his argument toward the end of this pioneering work of film theory:

> The photoplay tells us the human story by overcoming the forms of the outer world, namely, space, time and causality, and by adjusting the events to the forms of the inner world, namely, attention, memory, imagination, and emotion. (Münsterberg 1916, 129)

Cinema's mastery of time became channeled into narrative patterns, many of which had parallels in traditional narrative forms. Münsterberg showed how flashbacks portrayed memories, flash-forward anticipated future events, and vision scenes opened up the unspecified time of dreams or reveries. Narrative films especially employ devices of temporal compression, both through ellipsis and editing strategies that can accelerate the tempo of action. Through cinema, the flow of time can be shortened, squeezed, compressed.

Can avant-garde films deal with narrative time?

In a previous essay on the short form in cinema, I explored the intensity of time that brevity can create by breaking up or ignoring narrative patterns, seeking out precisely the defamiliarizing effects of noncontinuous time, including the ecstatic experience achieved by the films of Austrian experimental filmmaker Peter Kubelka, most of which last for less than ten minutes (Gunning 2015). Avant-garde alternatives to the feature-length films explored a variety of the nonnarrative temporal forms. Pioneer American avant-garde filmmaker Maya Deren in the 1950s made a famous opposition between the "vertical" form of the poetic film, which she claimed explores the resonance of a moment, and the "horizontal" attack of the dramatic film, which plays out situations in time. The horizontal approach employs a continuous sense of narrative causality and the synthetic processes of memory and anticipation, creating a temporal sense of unfolding action and suspense. In sharp contrast, the vertical dimension seeks to escape from linear temporal development, pursuing either an ascent or a plunge into realms of experience beyond ordinary time. Deren (1963) associates this escape from time with the realm of poetry and specifically with the poetic tradition of avant-garde cinema.

However, as useful as Deren's schema can be in exploring the way that attitudes toward time define genres or modes of filmmaking, we should not assert that avant-garde cinema can never engage the action-based time of narrative. Russian Formalist critic Viktor Shklovsky offered a somewhat different understanding of the "poetic." Shklovsky claims that poetic literature directs our attention to the role of language, its sound and associations, rather than simply transparently conveying information, which he sees as role of prose. From this perspective, avant-garde or poetic films focus viewers' attention on cinematic form and conventions rather than simply narrating a coherent story (Shklovsky 1965, esp. 22–24). One can therefore conceive of an avant-garde film that would make narrative strategies and their use of suspenseful time visible, making narrative form an avant-garde theme by defamiliarizing it. A few avant-garde films have explored narrative form in this highly reflexive manner. If Kubelka's films primarily explore liberation from the linear progression of time, other experimental films invoke—and transform—the almost demonic onrush of narrative progression. Such films invoke narrative temporality and yet direct our attention as viewers away from simply following the unfolding of a tale; instead these avant-garde films make us consider the way that narrative structures our sense of time.

The classical art of storytelling in the feature films labors to distract viewers from focusing on narrative mechanisms and become involved in the story rather than its forms. In contrast, certain experimental films expose these mechanisms, refusing to naturalize them by facilitating and satisfying our desire to follow a plot. Michael Snow's 1967 film *Wavelength* with its relentless 45-minute zoom, and the scraps of a narrative it offers through the occurrence and discovery of an unexplained death, provides such a meditation on temporal protentions and retentions, as Annette Michelson's famous essay on the film demonstrates (1971). A possibly dramatic incident takes place, but rather than focusing the viewer's attention on it, the film's dominant formal device, the ongoing progressive zoom, actually ignores it, moving past it serenely. Ken Jacob's extraordinary 1978 film *The Doctor's Dream* systematically reedits the footage of a conventional short narrative film from the 1940s or 1950s, rearranging its shots in a way that both breaks down its natural narrative progression and calls attention to the energies and conventions such a film story routinely employs (I discuss Jacobs's film in Gunning 1981). As a complex engagement with the powers of narrative time, I want to discuss a recent avant-garde film by one of the most powerful current American avant-garde filmmakers, Lewis Klahr's *Two Minutes to Zero Trilogy*. Klahr's trilogy exposes and explores the role of narrative compression with a succession of three short films, closely related in imagery and theme. Each film becomes progressively shorter, as if moving to a final climax in which narrative compression explodes into—nothing.

Count down to zero

Klahr's films frequently rework elements of popular and mass culture (cartoons, comic books, magazine illustrations, advertisements, textbooks, menus, family snapshots) into ambiguous, dream-like narratives. Although satire operates in Klahr's films, it does not provide the master key. He is less interested in deflating or critiquing popular imagery than in re-imagining—sometimes even re-enchanting—this material. His collage films evoke the oneiric work of Max Ernst or Joseph Cornell, more than the social or political satires of John Heartfield or Stan Vanderbeek. Klahr's films dwell upon the material and sensual aspects of this imagery (color, textures of wear, mysterious fragments) discovering moments of unintended formal abstraction and beauty. However, Klahr's films provide other pleasures than these formal alternatives to narrative absorption. His collages also trigger highly associative scenarios, as viewers drift off in pursuit of stories and fantasies sparked by, yet not specifically narrated by, the images and their juxtaposition. Rather than ignoring narrative Klahr's films engage it in an ambiguous and essentially? experimental manner.

The films that make up the *Two Minute to Zero* trilogy (2004) mine images from a 1950s comic book based on the television series *77 Sunset Strip*. Re-mediation (to use Jay Bolter and Richard Grusin's [1999] term for the way new media adapt and transform the material of previous media) here becomes dizzying, especially when one factors in the fact that the original television series itself recycled aspects of earlier noir and cop films, and the comic book adaptation added its own medium specificity. Klahr's complete trilogy consists of three films of descending lengths. The first, entitled *Two Days to Zero* is approximately twenty-three minutes; the second, *One Hour to Zero* clocks in at eight-and-a-half minutes, while the concluding film, *Two Minutes to Zero* lasts just about a minute. One senses the material becoming compressed as in a vice, its progressive truncation creating a strange urgency and coming to a sudden climax. Klahr rapidly scans his handheld camera over the surface of the comic book pages, sometimes focusing on a fragment of a frame (the film rarely, if ever, shows the entirety of a comic book panel, offering, instead, a suite of disorientating close-ups and fragments). This mobile barrage of images seems to fulfill the early German film reformer's nightmare quoted earlier of "darting, convulsive, twitching" film images that defy comprehension and perhaps even perception. Staccato, the film pulses on the screen, alternatively swishing and pausing with a manic energy that makes it nearly impossible to distinguish edited juxtapositions from those achieved through camera movement. The images are occasionally slightly out of focus, but more often appear sharply detailed, revealing the materiality of the comic book printing—its matrix of Benday dots, saturated and sometimes overlapping blocks of pure colors—and the often highly schematic drawing of recognizable iconic elements redolent with narrative associations: guns, cars, telephones, and especially gesturing hands and contorted faces.

One is very aware that these images are taken from a story whose full sense we are never given. We recognize genre icons of the urban crime drama, and depictions of its paradigmatic actions: violence, robbery, car chases, erotic come-ons, and likely betrayals. But it would be impossible in any of the three films to reconstruct the specifics of the underlying narrative with any degree of confidence. One could conceivably watch the images purely for their formal play: the richness of color; the odd, almost hieroglyphic rendering of objects; the humor with which clichés or emblems of American life in the fifties are displayed. In this way Klahr's films might recall American Pop Art, most obviously the paintings of Roy Lichtenstein with their enlargement of comic strip images and looming Benday dots. Indeed, as he sweeps his handheld camera over these images, Klahr seems to reprocess Pop Art through the gestural practices of its stylistic predecessor, Abstract Expressionism.

But Klahr's film possesses a dimension such paintings lack—that of temporality, essential to the compression of the short film experience. The images that the film remediates remain in a certain sense frozen: motionless drawings taken from a comic book. However, even the static images of the comic book genre portrayed action and motion through a variety of devices, including the layout of panels and the drawing of the figures themselves (for a discussion of comic book portrayal of motion see: Bukatman 2014). Klahr's film literalizes (and in effect brings to life—animates) this potential motion with his quick cinematic pans and scans of the pages, which seem to be following the comic book's continuous action with a handheld camera, rather than dividing up an immobile layout. These rapid juxtapositions create a jagged sense of rhythm—underscored in all the three films by the sound track. Paradoxically Klahr's film, like Kubelka's (albeit in a very different manner and tone), offers a meditation on cinematic motion precisely by undercutting or suspending the cinema's common illusion of motion, while at the same time making us very aware of the film's essential relation to movement through the rapid succession of individual frames.

Whereas in a brief abstract film like *Schwechater* (1958) Kubelka seeks the intensity of ecstasy and an escape from time's demands modeled on cyclical natural and cosmic processes, Klahr never lets us forget the manic onrush of modern human time dominated by a sense of purpose and urgency. Rather than the release of ecstasy, his films evoke the compression of suspense and, even more, anxiety over time running out. Even in the ending of *Two Hours*, which cuts off the soundtrack and turns its final images upside down, seemingly favoring formal abstraction over narrative drive, these final moments still vibrate with high anxiety, rather than ecstatic release or transcendence. As commentators such as David Bordwell have noted, classical films often focus viewers' attention on the outcome of the story by setting up temporal deadlines, reinforced through shots of clocks or calendars that count them down, and situations that delay or propel them (for instance pp. 157–64).

The titles of Klahr's films chart the progression of his deadline very literally. The succession of titles in the trilogy mimes a countdown to a deadline with diminishing temporal units: Two Days, Two Hours, Two Minutes . . . converging toward zero. Although the genre iconography fills in some possible storylines around this deadline (a bank robbery and perhaps a getaway?), Klahr's minimal narratives allow only a schematic trajectory: in essence, time is running out. As each film becomes shorter, the drive toward a deadline tightens, and imagery becomes more frenetic. Although his complex form raises essential issues about the compression of time in narrative film, Klahr's film never assumes a critical or theoretical tone. The films pull out all the sensual stops to compel a visceral involvement by the viewer: rich colors; recognizable images evoking violent or erotic associations; an overpowering rhythm driving the rapid change of images and music; and the manic pace of camera movements zipping across the pages of the comic book. But the overdrive of this sensual immersion in urgent action (with an outcome that remains vague and undefined) precisely underscores its manic and underdetermined nature. Rather than naturalizing, motivating, and complicating this linear progression by immersing it in a story world, Klahr's film strips it naked, rendering it palpable and harsh.

The titles for the films of the trilogy focus on the progressive countdown, but they also name and declare its terminus: Zero. Zero marks both the end and the beginning of a numerical series. But it also represents nothingness, zilch, zip, nada. This hopeless title recalls both actual titles and the mood of films noir (there is a 1952 Hollywood film called *One Minute to Zero* [Garnett], a rather vicious Korean war film, although Robert Aldrich's tense *Ten Seconds to Hell* [1959] may be closer to Klahr's iconography). The nihilistic endings of many noir films, especially heist films, such as *The Asphalt Jungle* (Huston, 1950), *The Killing* (Kubrick, 1956), or *Odds Against Tomorrow* (Wise, 1959) in which stolen money is rendered ultimately irrelevant through apocalyptic endings, could all be nicely described as countdowns to zero. Film noir's fatal conclusions worked against the dominant Hollywood resolution of the happy ending, providing instead scenarios of loss, defeat, and death. The brief image of dollar bills flying through the air that ends *Two Hours* and comes near the end in *Two Minutes* recalls the ending of a number of failed heist films in which the money that the crooks died for blows aimlessly away.

Klahr's films engineer a confluence between the formal constraint of closure, the simple need to end a film (the numerical logic of reaching zero), and the fateful finality that comes with total defeat (what we could call the death drive of film noir). But Klahr's work, while hardly distanced, carries the force of a logical demonstration, rendering linear narrative visible in a way that emotional involvement in a clearly told story with fully developed characters would only naturalize and camouflage. While films by Kubelka and other filmmakers within Deren's tradition of poetic films reach an ending primarily through formal means, the dominant impression often remains that the film goes on continually (indeed Kubelka frequently circulates the film as multiple prints spliced together, so that once a film ends it can begin again almost immediately). In contrast Klahr's sense of ever-shortening closure as we move from film to film carries a sense of an ever-tightening temporal compression, like a tensely coiled spring. Klahr's film could never be described as a classical narrative, but the *Two Minute to Zero* trilogy would be almost incomprehensible without a reference to Hollywood crime films and the finality of narrative closure. That reference, however, never becomes a simple nostalgic recycling, and certainly not an instance of neo-noir or neoclassicism, but rather a critical act—a reflection—one that not only examines the structure of time but also immerses us in its sensual affects.

Emerging in the sixteenth century, the clock as a measure of time eventually served not simply to mark, but also to regulate, human behavior. As a key instrument of a disciplinary society the clock determined the rhythms of labor, and coordinated the networks of the modern metropolis, increasing the precision of timetables and quickening the pace of interactions. Cinema emerged not as only the result of temporally precise machinery, but from a new conception of time based in the instant. Yet if cinema reflects the accelerated and systematic nature of modern temporality, it may also offer a means to transcend it, to offer experiences that either escape or subvert the rational course of time. Klahr shows that cinema can even examine its own temporality. In all its forms cinema offers the possibility to play with time, to manipulate and display its structures. As time becomes squeezed into ever more compressed forms we might ask: are we playing with time—or is time, in fact, playing with us?

2

On Conflict in Short Film Storytelling

Richard Raskin

If you can find something everyone agrees on, it's wrong.

Mo Udall

Introduction

Virtually all screenwriting manuals categorically assert that "all drama is conflict" (Field 1994, 12); that "without conflict a film story cannot come to life" (Howard and Mabley 1993, 46); that conflict is "the heart *and* soul of screenwriting" (Hunter 1994, 19) and "the central feature of the screen story" (Dancyger and Rush 2002, 3). McKee goes so far as to proclaim "the Law of Conflict," which he formulates this way: "*Nothing moves forward in a story except through conflict*" (1997, 210).

Essentially the same view is held in short film manuals, where we find for example that "the central role of conflict in the development of your story cannot be over-emphasized" (Cooper and Dancyger 2000, 117) and that

> the importance of conflict in dramatic writing can hardly be overstated. Without conflict there is no drama. … Never put two people in a scene who agree with one another. If you do your scene will have no conflict. And a scene with no conflict is almost always a snooze. (Beairsto 1998, 29–30)

The only manual that stands out from the others in this respect is Claudia Hunter Johnson's *Crafting Short Screenplays that Connect* (2000). Here conflict is viewed as only "half the story"—the other half being the *connectedness* that gets to "the heart of the matter, to that level of story that engages us most deeply" (2):

> The conflict and surface events are like waves, but underneath is an emotional tide—the ebb and flow of human emotion. It's just as essential to story as conflict but it has been essentially overlooked. (3)

For Johnson, connection and conflict are "woven together like strands of deoxyribonucleic acid, the double helix of drama" and constitute the *yin* and *yang* of storytelling—with connection, the *yin*, involving the "closeness, relatedness and intimacy" that she considers more typical of a woman's sensibility, and conflict, the *yang*, representing what she sees as essentially the male component of narratives (6–7).

Although Johnson presents connectedness as being equally important, she still regards conflict as a necessary part of short film storytelling.

A more radical position will be proposed in the present chapter: that in the short film, conflict is *not* in fact a necessity. But before proposing an alternative model, I would like to preclude some possible misunderstandings by clarifying how the terms "short film" and "conflict" will be defined in this context.

Definitions

The term "short film" will be used here to refer to films that are typically under ten minutes in length and have a maximum run time of fifteen minutes. A sharp distinction is made here between the short film and a format which in Scandinavia is called the *novellefilm*—the 25–40 minute format used for graduation films at film schools and which is essentially a miniature feature film in the way it tells its stories, while the short film is an art form in its own right. A discussion of the narrative properties in question can be found in Raskin (2014). In the present context, only the short *fiction* film will be considered, both in its live-action and animation forms, since fiction is the primary focus for discussions of conflict in cinematic storytelling.

The term "conflict" is often used loosely by commentators who take it for granted that there must be conflict in all stories, and who therefore define the term in so broad a manner that they can always find what they are calling conflict in any narrative. Some commentators would say for example that whenever a character can't immediately get what he or she wants, then conflict is in play (Phillips 2012, 57, 59). For other commentators who are equally inclined to discover conflict in any narrative, all that is needed is for a character to have important choices to make, as though decision-making and conflict are necessarily intertwined (Flattum 2013; Duncan 2006, 32, 34). Yet others confuse conflict with tension, which is why there are so many recent attempts on the web to distinguish between the two concepts (Weiland 2012; Bottcher 2013; Puglisi 2013; Tagg 2015; Colburn 2016).

In this chapter, the word "conflict" will refer to a high-stake opposition between characters, one or each of whom seeks to thwart the other's goals and who are engaged in a zero-sum contest, meaning that any gain enjoyed by the one equals a loss for the other (Baron 1990, 199). It is this *interpersonal* form of conflict that will concern us here, because when internal conflict arises in a short film, as is the case for example in Jonas Bergergård and Jonas Holmström's *Natan* (Sweden, 2003, 12 min.), the fleeting moments of inner turmoil experienced by the main character invariably derive from an overriding interpersonal conflict that occupies the foreground of the film and is what justifies viewing it as conflict-driven. The same is true of conflict with the setting, as in César Días Meléndez's award-winning animation film *Zepo* (Spain, 2014, 3 min.) when the little girl struggles desperately to free herself from the icy water in which she is drowning, as the fascist soldiers who had arranged to drown her stand by and observe her futile efforts to save herself. Here once again the interpersonal conflict is primary.

With these definitions of the terms "short film" and "conflict" in place, we can now proceed.

Two arguments

If it is conflict that captures the viewer's interest in short film storytelling, then we should expect to find conflict in the opening scene of a film, since that is when the viewer must be drawn compellingly into the story. Yet those short films in which conflict plays a central role often open with a scene that is entirely devoid of conflict.

For example, in David Greenspan's *Bean Cake* (US, 2001, 12 min.) set in Tokyo in 1933, a boy is sternly punished by his teacher for answering "bean cakes" instead of "the Emperor" when demonstrably asked in class: "What is most important to you in this world?" But in this film, which won the Palme d'Or for Best Short Film at Cannes in 2001, there isn't a trace of conflict in the opening scene running a minute and a half, in which a mother gives her son a plate of bean cakes to his utter delight, and there is perfect harmony between the two characters.

Likewise in John Lawlor's *Sunday* (Ireland, 1988, 8 min.), which is set in a Catholic working-class home as indicated by the décor and props, a young boy is slapped in the face by his father at the dinner table for innocently asking his mother: "Have you ever had an orgasm?" But in this film, which opened the Uppsala and Cork Film Festivals, winning the award for Best Director at Cork, there isn't a hint of conflict until the boy asks his startling question, four-and-a-half minutes into the film, when *Sunday* is more than half over.

In both cases, it should be obvious that something other than conflict must be responsible for drawing the viewer into the film.

Furthermore, there are exemplary short films that are conflict-free from start to finish. An example of this is Marianne Olsen Ulrichsen's *Come/Kom* (Norway, 1995, 5 min.), which won a Special Jury Mention for Best Debut Film at the Aspen Filmfest and the prize for Best Short Film at Cinema delle Donne in Torino. Here, an elderly woman touches a pocket watch, which triggers a memory of herself as a girl. In this flashback, we see her holding the watch that apparently belonged to the young man she has chosen. She dangles it like bait to draw him away from his friends, then places it in his breast pocket and presses his chest with her hand, saying "come" and leading him to a more private place where she touches his face, thereby initiating their lovemaking. In our return to the present, she reenacts something of that past event by placing the watch in the breast pocket of her now elderly spouse and saying "come."

In Unni Straume's *Derailment/Avsporing* (Norway, 1993, 7 min.), there is likewise no conflict driving the storytelling. In this short film, which was included in the official selection at Cannes in 1993, a woman taking her seat in the Paris metro makes room for her legs by inserting her knees between those of the man sleeping on the seat opposite hers. She then falls asleep and either dreams or remembers a scene of lovemaking with him. When she opens her eyes she sees that the man, now awake, is smiling at her, and a moment later on seeing him look back at her as he prepares to leave the train, she decides to get off at the same stop and to follow him, which will presumably lead to a scene of lovemaking like the one she had already dreamed or remembered.

In both of these films, an interaction initiated by a woman—strategically in the first case and without premeditation in the second—eventually leads to a romantic union and sexual fulfillment and the storytelling unfolds and reaches completion with no conflict whatsoever.

This means that in a short film, something other than conflict can attract and hold the viewer's interest, before conflict finally appears as in *Bean Cake* or *Sunday* among others, or throughout a film that remains conflict-free through to the very end, such as *Come* and *Derailment,* among others.

E. M. Forster's model

The reader is asked to bear with me while I describe a particular conception of story and plot that will at first appear to have no connection to the issue of conflict in short film storytelling but that will soon turn out to be useful in that context.

E. M. Forster's seminal work, *Aspects of the Novel,* originally published in 1927, contains this passage that is frequently quoted and widely assumed to be all that Forster had to say about the differences between story and plot (2002, 61):

> We have defined a story as a narrative of events arranged in their time-sequence. A plot is also a narrative of events, the emphasis falling on causality. "The king died and then the queen dies," is a story. "The king died, and then the queen died of grief" is a plot.

However even more importantly for our purposes, Forster's discussion continues in this way (61):

> Consider the death of the queen. If it is in a story we say "and then?" If it is in a plot we ask "why?" That is the fundamental difference between these two aspects of the novel. A plot cannot be told to a gaping audience of cave men or to a tyrannical sultan or to their modern descendant the movie-public. They can only be kept awake by "and then—and then." They can only supply curiosity. But a plot demands intelligence and memory also.

If we tweak Forster's model just a bit, we can say that reading a novel for story is driven by curiosity, which Forster regards as "one of the lowest of the human faculties" (61). In that case, the reading process is motivated by a wish to know what happens next. However reading the same novel for plot means using our higher faculties of intelligence and memory in an effort to understand the causality in play, to understand why things are happening as they do. Forster's discussion might further suggest that when reading a novel, we are driven simultaneously by a lower, more primitive motivation to find out what happens next, and by a higher, more refined incentive to understand the causality in play.

Conflict and performance

Returning now to the subject of this chapter and inspired by Forster's model, I suggest that experiencing a short film can engage two ongoing processes: a lower or more primitive responsiveness to *conflict,* activated whenever and if ever conflict appears in the film; and a higher, more refined responsiveness to *performances* that is continuously active from the opening to the final shot of the film.

In this way, the role of conflict in a short film can be acknowledged without our having to accept the widespread and in my view erroneous assumption that conflict is necessary in short film storytelling; and we can explain what it is that fascinates the viewer while experiencing those scenes when the storytelling is conflict-free.

The viewer's responsiveness to performance is of course a highly multifaceted process, with performance consisting of two main components: (1) *character performance,* by which I mean the performance of the fictional characters in managing their interactions with one another as each carries out his or her own agenda or responds to the actions of other characters; and (2) *filmmaker performance,* by which I mean the performance of cast and crew, and which in turn might be broken down to such factors as (a) the achievements of the screenwriter in designing vital and unpredictable characters and their behavior as components of the plot while meeting the special challenges of short film storytelling with less-is-more as a major principle; (b) the appropriateness of the casting; (c) the convincingness and vitality of the actors' performances; (d) the director's competence in directing the actors, staging the action, coordinating the work of everyone on the set, etc.; (e) the cinematographer's ability in lighting the set and framing the actors; (f) the sound crew's proficiency in recording and editing the audio; (g) the film editor's competence in cutting the film in a way that serves the story to the fullest; and so on. Though not necessarily aware of it, viewers are continuously responsive to the skill, resourcefulness, and originality of all of these performances, and it is their quality that keeps viewers glued to the screen.

Borrowing Claudia Johnson's double helix metaphor but giving it new meaning, I will suggest that the two ongoing, interrelated processes of character and filmmaker performance are the double helix of drama in short film storytelling, its DNA, and that these intertwined forms of performance are what genuinely fascinate the viewer, whether or not the viewer is aware of their power, and whether or not any conflict is in play within the film.

On the variability of character performance

In any short film, there may be fleeting moments when no characters appear on screen, for example when all we see in a shot in *Sunday* are the tubes inside a radio, or in *Derailment* a curtain fluttering in a window or over a broken flower pot lying on the floor. At these moments, the only performance to engage the viewer is that of the filmmakers who designed and executed those shots in the service of their story. The rest of the time, whatever the characters do in a quality short film serves to sustain the viewer's interest, though to varying degrees and most particularly at moments when the main character actively shapes his or her own story by taking initiatives and making choices. This happens for example when the boy in *Sunday* asks his mother whether she has ever had an orgasm; in *Derailment*, when the woman pushes her legs between the knees of the male passenger sleeping in the seat opposite hers; in *Eating Out*, when Parka wipes the sniveling nose of the robber's girlfriend with his coat sleeve.

What I am suggesting is that the degree to which the characters in a short film engage the viewer's interest may vary somewhat from one moment to another, depending on how unexpected or significant or game-changing the characters' behavior is at any given time. But with the exception of rare shots in which no characters appear, there will always be some degree of character performance in play and thereby some measure of viewer engagement in the ways the characters manage their roles and relations with one another.

On the variability of filmmaker performance

At every point in a short film, the skillfulness of filmmaker performances in play will more or less consciously be gauged by the viewer. This might be most evident when there is a lack of skill for example in the writing if a beat in the storytelling leaves the viewer thinking "No, that character would never do such a thing," or "That event makes no sense in this story." Or it might involve a faltering performance on the part of an otherwise competent actor. But the gauging of filmmaker performance may also be particularly evident when the writing or acting are of a quality that earns a surge of admiration on the part of the viewer; or in the case of animation, when the skillfulness or originality of the execution is breathtaking. In any event, in a well-crafted short film, every shot will meet the high standards of storytelling and production values, thereby providing a flow of esthetic pleasure on a level that sustains the viewer's appreciation of and engagement in the film, whether or not any of the storytelling is conflict-driven.

Conclusions

In response to widespread claims in screenwriting manuals that conflict is necessary for a short film to tell an engaging story, I have argued that in a quality short film the combination of character and filmmaker performance is what earns the viewer's interest throughout the film, while conflict—if and when present in a short film—may add a further, and somewhat more primitive and intermittent, appeal.

This would help explain (1) how a short film in which conflict first arises half way into the film has not lost the viewer's interest during the opening minutes; and (2) how there can be award-winning short films that are entirely free of conflict.

The performative model proposed here should be seen as an alternative to a conflict-based model solely for short film storytelling. That conflict is merely optional rather than necessary in the short film is an important way in which the narrative properties of the short film and feature film differ. It is doubtful that a film running ninety minutes could sustain the viewer's interest if the storytelling were entirely conflict-free, regardless of its performative qualities.

However, as a final note, I will mention that in his *Art of Poetry*, Aristotle—the undisputed father of dramaturgy—describes the basic structure of any tragedy as consisting of *desis,* generally translated as Complication and literally meaning the "binding together" of narrative threads, followed by *lusis,* the "loosening" of those threads, which is appropriately translated as Dénouement (Bywater 1990, 63; Walker 2014). Nothing in Aristotle's chosen metaphor of the tying and untying of narrative threads suggests conflict, though it is sometimes erroneously assumed that conflict plays a central role in his dramaturgy (Smith 2007).

Returning now to the Mo Udall quote used as an epigraph for this chapter, the "everyone" agreeing on the necessity of conflict in *all* drama does not include Aristotle.

Short films cited

Bergergård, Jonas and Holmström, Jonas, Dir. (2003), *Natan,* Sweden, 12 min.
Greenspan, David, Dir. (2001), *Bean Cake,* USA, 12 min.
Lawlor, John, Dir. (1988), *Sunday,* Ireland, 8 min.
Meléndez, César Díaz, Dir. (2014), *Zepo,* Spain, 3 min.
Straume, Unni (1993), *Derailment/Avsporing,* Norway, 7 min.
Ulrichsen, Marianne Olsen, Dir. (1995), *Come/Kom,* Norway, 5 min.

3

Accelerated Gestures: Play Time in Agnès Varda's *Cléo de 5 à 7*

Peter Verstraten

In the second scene of the Spanish art-house success *Hable con Ella [Talk to Her]* (Pedro Almodóvar, 2002), the male nurse Benigno tells the comatose patient Alicia how he had enjoyed a modern ballet performance by Pina Bausch, shown to us in the film's opening. His words may seem like a soliloquy to deaf ears, but, as Benigno will later disclose, he believes that narrating remarkable experiences to patients is essential to their therapy. In the four years since Alicia's accident, he has attended many dance performances and silent movies, since doing so was among the patient's favorite pastimes. Hence, it is no surprise that, almost one hour into *Hable con Ella*, he begins describing to his patient a love story he had seen a few days earlier at the movies. While we are hearing Benigno's voice-over commentary, there is a cut to the silent black-and-white short film *Amante Menguante [Shrinking Lover]*, a title we had seen on a poster in the preceding scene. Since, as Benigno has said earlier, he is not particular about silent movies—"German, American, Italian, I watch them all"—*Amante Menguante* has no special (narrative) significance in *Hable con Ella*: it's just one of those movies he has happened upon and enjoyed. Or at least it seems so initially.

The way the short film format is integrated into Almodóvar's film bears a formal resemblance to the screening of a short silent slapstick comedy in Agnès Varda's famously vibrant *Cléo de 5 à 7 [Cleo from 5 to 7]* (1962). Almost one hour into the movie, *Les Fiancés du Pont MacDonald, ou (Méfiez-vous des Lunettes Noires) [Lovers of MacDonald Bridge or (Beware of Dark Sunglasses)]* is presented as an enjoyable intermezzo, meant to distract and elicit a smile from protagonist Florence Victoire, nicknamed Cléo. After the projectionist Raoul has been informed that she might be afflicted by a serious disease, he playfully alludes to the possible therapeutic effects of a short comedy: "A laugh's good for any illness." The short film makes Cléo smile, indeed.

Though the short film format is used in both films to interrupt the main story as apparently delightful and perhaps even beneficial distractions, my aim here in this chapter is to articulate the different functions of these embedded short films, respectively, in these two feature-length movies. In the Almodóvar film, the "attraction," to coin Tom Gunning's term, is ultimately contained by narrativization, hence causality is prioritized; but in Varda's film, the gag spectacle will remain excessive to the story. Because of this undigested textual excess, the short film format in Varda's movie surpasses the conventional function of mirror miniature film. Rather, the format works as a guide to reading that both downplays causality in favor of contingency and offers a reflection upon cinematic time.

(Not) a *mise en abyme* for Cléo's transformation

Before Benigno in *Hable con Ella* starts recapitulating the plot of *Amante Menguante*, he mentions in passing that the male protagonist Alfredo is a "bit chubby like myself, but quite handsome nonetheless." Accompanied by Benigno's voice-over, we see black-and-white images and additional intertitles about Alfredo, who seeks to prove his love to his girlfriend Amparo, a female scientist, by drinking an experimental potion she has prepared. The short film is then interrupted for twenty-six seconds by a shot in the diegetic present. We see Benigno massage the patient's body while he keeps on narrating the film's developments. The short film then continues and we see how Alfredo starts to shrink as a result of the potion. When he gets to be very small, he undresses and enters Amparo's vagina.

The brief interruption is a sign here that the link between the short film and the main story is not arbitrary, but intentional and significant—as is hinted by Benigno's identification with Alfredo on the basis of their similar physical appearance. The definitive clue, however, that we should regard *Amante Menguante* as a mirror-text for *Hable con Ella*'s plotline becomes evident in the subsequent scenes. When it turns out that Alicia is pregnant, Benigno is accused of having raped the comatose patient. Through a series of flashbacks, told to his friend Marco, it has already been revealed to us that Benigno had been infatuated with Alicia even before she was hospitalized. In retrospect, the embedded episode about Alfredo is not some distracting story, but the short film helps the viewer to fill in a structural absence in *Hable con Ella* as such: no wonder Benigno was so touched by the love story. At the same time, it should be noted that as an instance of European narrative art cinema, Almodóvar's film remains shrouded in mystery. Definitive proof that Benigno has raped the comatose woman is withheld, and his later suicide cannot be taken as certain admission of his guilt.

Unlike the obvious signs of a feedback loop between primary diegesis and the embedded short film in *Hable con Ella*, such indications are clearly missing from Varda's *Cléo de 5 à 7*. Whereas *Amante Menguante* appears only as an integral part of *Hable con Ella*, by contrast *Les Fiancés du Pont MacDonald* was released as a separate film in 1961, a year earlier than *Cléo de 5 à 7*. Originally, the farcical short film of almost five minutes contained credits, but when the film was made part of Varda's feature, these were omitted. Moreover, though some of its shots are slightly longer in its original version, the brief story in both versions is similar: a Buster Keaton lookalike (played by, of all people, Jean-Luc Godard) waves goodbye to his white-clad blonde girlfriend (Anna Karina). As he puts on his sunglasses, the scenery turns dark: now dressed in black and with black hair, the girlfriend (now played by Emilienne Caille) waves goodbye to him from the other side of the riverbank, where she stumbles over a fire hose and is knocked down by its jet of water. She is instantly carried off into a hearse, much to her lover's distress and sorrow. He buys her a funeral wreath, and takes off his glasses to wipe away his tears (see Figure 3.1). He then realizes that these glasses are what have caused all the misery. As he observes his girlfriend in the "original" white dress descending the staircase, this time on the right side of the riverbank, she once again stumbles, this time over a ship's rope. Before she can be transported into the ambulance that turns up too quickly, her lover knocks down the eager male nurse and puts the funeral wreath on the latter's belly. The text reads "À ma poupée d'amour" (To my baby doll). The film ends after the lover has thrown away his "damned sunglasses" and finally kisses his girlfriend, punctuated with an iris-in.

Although the short film within *Cléo de 5 à 7* is often noted in writings on Varda's so-called *cinécriture*, it has hardly ever been analyzed, which is all the more surprising, Phil Powrie observes, because the short film in his view clearly "functions as a *mise en abyme* of the whole film" (2011, 76). To understand Powrie's argument, as well as my counterargument to it, it is useful to look at how the story of *Cléo de 5 à 7* is structured. In the few color shots that open the otherwise black-and-white film at 5:00 p.m., the blonde pop singer Cléo visits a

Figure 3.1 The Buster Keaton lookalike takes off his glasses to wipe away his tears. Still from *Les fiancés du pont Mac Donald, ou (Méfiez-vous des lunettes noires)* [*The Lovers of the Bridge Mac Donald, or (Beware of Sunglasses)*] (5 min., 1961) in Agnès Varda's *Cléo de 5 à 7* [*Cléo from 5 to 7*] (1962). Ciné Tamaris.

tarot reader. While the cards only aggravate her fear of having stomach cancer, by the end of the film, at 6:30 p.m., when her doctor informs her that her disease is curable, her fear seems to have already subsided. In between, there are only some apparently mundane events and ordinary encounters: Cléo buys a hat with her secretary, takes a cab back home, rehearses a song with two composers, walks the streets of Paris, goes to see a friend (a studio model for art students), and, after the screening of the short film by Raoul, meets a soldier on furlough from the Algerian War who decides to accompany her to the hospital. In essence, the film offers little more than a representation of a woman who is wandering aimlessly, anxiously awaiting the medical results she is dreading to hear.

A number of readings of the film point out that Cléo undergoes a significant transformation within the film's ninety minutes. In the first half, Cléo feels nauseous and behaves in a capricious and narcissistic fashion, which is emphasized by the numerous times she looks into mirrors and is moreover formally underscored by swervy camera movements. However, as she dons her wig halfway through the movie and changes her white attire for a simpler black dress, she develops into a woman who is becoming more attentive to her surroundings. Thus, while she is undertaking a voyage of self-discovery, Janice Mouton for example argues, Cléo swaps fear and superstition for curiosity, as she begins to become part of the cityscape, as befits a true flâneuse.

It is not my aim to take issue with dominant interpretations of Cléo's transformation, but rather with the suggestion that the inserted short *Les Fiancés du Pont MacDonald* functions as a mirror-text of the whole film on a thematic level, which seems too easy an option to me. For Powrie, the slapstick pastiche marks a key moment, because Cléo, who herself happens to be wearing dark sunglasses prior to watching the short film, loosens up only after she has seen the silent film about the boyfriend's darkened look and its effects. Serving as a "metaphor for Cléo's dilemma of perception," Steven Ungar argues, the short film punctuates the change from the world of tarot readers and "dark" superstition into the "white" domain of reason, embodied by the doctor (2008, 77–78). In a similar vein, Roy Jay Nelson has stated that the short film serves to teach her the lesson that she should break free from her enslavement by deceptive mirrors (1983, 740). This point is hammered home when Cléo's friend Dorothée shatters her hand-mirror by accident on the stairs upon leaving the theater. Still, the main pitfall of taking the short film as a mirroring of Cléo's transformation and a revelation of the importance of "the theme of the gaze" (Powrie 2011, 76) is that this interpretation aligns Varda's film too tightly with the logics of linear (real-time) causality, while at the same time reducing the embedded short film to nothing more than its thematic content.

In the case of *Hable con Ella*, I argued that the short film fills in a gap in the story that is too atrocious to represent. Such a reading finds support in *Amante Menguante* being inextricably interwoven with the film's primary diegesis, both visually (the silent love story is alternated with a relative lengthy scene in the diegetic present) and on the level of the audio track (as the black-and-white images are overlaid with Benigno's voice-over). Any such formal clues to read *Les Fiancés du Pont MacDonald* as thematically and/or narratively integrated with *Cléo de 5 à 7* are conspicuously absent, however. The slapstick comedy, which the protagonist and her friend watch through a hole, clearly stands apart from Cléo's series of brief encounters. The short film, therefore, does not operate metaphorically, but can be seen as a guide to reading *Cléo de 5 à 7* as a whole, and so compels us to take seriously its nature as a gag spectacle.

Calculated rupture

In his article "Pie and Chase," Donald Crafton criticizes the tendency to dismiss gag elements in slapstick comedies, which cannot be contained by the film's narrative. By considering these elements as "textual excess" (Crafton 2006 [orig. 1987], 359), story is implicitly valorized over slapstick (355). Crafton, however, argues that gags in silent film comedy are a "calculated rupture": these spectacular remainders, such as the thrown pie and the pratfalls, are designed to be kept antagonistically apart from the "story—the arena of the chase" (356). Gags are "specific forms of intrusions" (357) that resist absorption into an overall plot, and hence they should be appreciated as "'attractions,' elements of pure spectacle" (358).

In his response to Crafton's article, Gunning maintains that gags are recovered by narrativization, but he adds that this assimilation is deceptive. Only through an integration with narrative can gags become the parodic subversion of storytelling logic. Gunning's claim that in slapstick comedy the "absurdity" of the principle of narrative integration is revealed (1995, 122) does not so much concern the absurd gestures the characters are making. There are several such examples in Varda's short film: the lovers wave goodbye in an overly affectionate manner; the male nurse treats his patient brusquely, and, most striking, several characters blink their eyes rapidly in frontal close-ups. Here, then, narrative logic is exposed by the short film as absurd because slapstick cinema, unlike classical narrative feature films, "points no moral" (Brett Page, quoted in Crafton 2006 [1987], 357); or, if it draws some conclusion, as in Varda's short film, its lesson is obviously silly and hence not a lesson at all. In *Les Fiancés du Pont MacDonald*, causality as the seminal building block of narrative cinema is parodied in its bare, overt logic. A guy sees how his girlfriend meets a gloomy fate and, in a streak of childish naïveté, his sunglasses prove to be the single cause of all the misery—so simply get rid of them, and the world looks fine.

If causality as a reigning narrative principle is comically undermined in Varda's pastiche of a slapstick comedy, then it makes sense to ignore the concomitant principle of psychological motivation. Those scholars who take the short film in *Cléo de 5 à 7* to be emblematic of the protagonist's mental transformation unduly activate the very principles that the slapstick comedy pokes fun at. Insofar as *Les Fiancés du Pont MacDonald* can be interpreted as a *mise en abyme* for the film, it is a call to downplay causality and "tight plot construction" and to favor "narrative intransivity" as their opposite. "Narrative intransivity," one of the "virtues" of counter-cinema according to Peter Wollen in his famous article on Jean-Luc Godard's *Vent d'Est [Wind from the East]* (1969), is marked by "gaps and interruptions, episodic construction, [and] undigested digression" (2004 [orig. 1972], 525). The episodic nature of the main story of Varda's film is much in line with Patricia Mellencamp's characterization of the flâneur/flâneuse, for Cléo's main occupation is to just float "freely in the present" (Mellencamp 1988, 60). She takes a walk without having any particular destination, and she visits the hospital only because the soldier urges her not to wait until the evening when she is supposed to telephone the doctor for the laboratory results. Adventures in a movie could not be "more whimsically selected" (Biró and Portuges 1997, 3) than in *Cléo de 5 à 7*.

In Allan Cameron's definition, the scenes in episodic narration follow one another in no inevitable sequence and thereby "critically weaken or disable the causal connections of classical narrative" (2008, 13), foregrounding contingent links. Unlike many contemporary episodic narratives, which tend to juggle the order of past, present, and future, *Cléo de 5 à 7* remains restricted to a linear temporal flow. It seems as if Varda's film does not make an attempt to compress time, even to such an extreme degree that, as narratologist Mieke Bal would assert, the time of the *fabula* and the time of the story (more or less) coincide. This marked collapse of the story's progress and its duration on screen is emphasized by the thirteen chapter headings that constantly remind us of the minutes about to unfold: "Chapitre V: Cléo de 17h.25 à 17h.31" or "Chapitre XIII: Cléo et Antoine de 18h.15 à 18h.30." Although potentially disruptive, these headings are superimposed over the images, so that they do not arrest the flow of movement, thus intensifying the impression of the film's strict chronological and continuous unfolding, in the vein of a "real-time" documentary about a Parisian woman.

The slapstick comedy in Varda's film is so striking because it belies the conception of temporal continuity, for two reasons. First, the comedy is structured around a repetition: the girl in white descends the stairs, and after the boyfriend has realized that the girl in black is a *trompe l'oeil* (or a *trompe les lunettes noires*, actually), he sees the girl in white descend the very same stairs, once again. Second, time is out of joint due to the overtly accelerated movements in the short film. Shot at sixteen frames per second while projected at twenty-four, the gestures of the actors in *Les Fiancés du Pont MacDonald* are comically rapid. If I were to consider the original release of this short film, I would be inclined to regard this replay of a slapstick short as a nostalgic reference to the silent era of comic actors, when such accelerated movements were not uncommon. As part of the feature film, however, the projection of a short film at a speed of sixteen frames per second alerts us to the fact that cinema is founded upon "false movements," to cite Alain Badiou's phrase.

As proponents of the apparatus theory have stressed time and again, there is no continuity in cinema, for film consists of a series of still frames that give only the impression of movement. The slapstick here lays bare the falsity of this impression by showing that any "natural" flow is a product of projection. Moreover, if cinema is "nothing but takes and montage," as Badiou's definition has it (2013, 97), the edits in a film are false in terms of temporality, for they are inherently immeasurable: the viewer often does not know how much time has passed from one shot to another or even whether time has passed at all. *Cléo de 5 à 7* had apparently solved this problem by giving exact indications of time in an attempt to make the time of the *fabula* coincide with the time of the story. But if we bear in mind that the slapstick comedy lightheartedly exposes that cinematic time is malleable via the accelerated gestures of characters and the crucial repetition of a descent on the stairs, an early scene in Varda's film now becomes relevant in retrospect. After her visit to the tarot reader, Cléo descends the staircase, which is shown in a series of jump cuts, as if Cléo were coming down three times, "in an editing loop" (Martin 2008). It is tempting to disqualify the jump cuts as a mere glitch, because they are not only narratively unmotivated but also at odds with the continuous unfolding of time. In other words, the formal device of the jump cuts gets lost in the temporality of the narrative. The inserted slapstick comedy makes us realize, however, that temporal manipulation is at the heart of cinema. Taking this short film into account, it becomes evident that the series of jump cuts is not some minor detail that erroneously sticks out—to the contrary. The idea of presenting *Cléo de 5 à 7* in the guise of a documentary record of time is only a willful lure to the spectator. Thanks to this guise, the formal devices that disturb a "natural" temporal flow—jump cuts, repetition, accelerated gestures—gain increased significance, revealing that movements in cinema, echoing Badiou, are temporally false and deceptive.

Although I started this chapter by noting a formal resemblance between the use of short films in both *Hable con Ella* and *Cléo de 5 à 7*, the format is ultimately explored in opposing ways. The comically vulgar *Amante Menguante* had a "shocking" dénouement, and since the story represents what could not be represented, this integrated short film tells by suggestion, hinting at a structural gap in the narrative. The "excessive" short silent film in *Hable con Ella* is meant to be assimilated via narrativization. By contrast, I have argued that Varda's pastiche of a slapstick comedy resists narrative absorption. To note and stress this resistance is to oppose those scholars who attempt to yoke meaning to contingency by claiming that *Les Fiancés du Pont MacDonald* teaches Cléo a lesson—about the "potentially transformative power of looking" (Mouton 2001, 13). Further than seeing thematic parallels between the film's main story and its embedded short comedy, I have pointed here to a highly significant formal similarity. Varda's episodic narration makes its viewers believe in clock time, as if the time of the *fabula* and the time of the story (can) coincide. The insertion of the slapstick sequence, however, exposes the fallacy of this supposed coincidence and thus makes us read *Cléo de 5 à 7* differently. The short film, with its remarkable projection speed, is not just some amusing intermezzo. Rather it illustrates, in tandem with the jump cuts, that the bigger charm of this (and any) film is ultimately to "play time."

Films cited

Almodóvar, Pedro, Dir. (2002), *Hable con Ella*, Spain: El Deseo.

Varda, Agnès, Dir. (1961), *Les Fiancés du Pont MacDonald, ou (Méfiez-vous des Lunettes Noires)*, France: Ciné Tamaris.

Varda, Agnès, Dir. (1962), *Cléo de 5 à 7*, France: Ciné Tamaris.

4

Lynch on the Run: The Proximity of Trauma in the Short Film

Todd McGowan

The virtues of brevity

David Lynch's filmic style seems to require a large canvas. Though he does not make epics like Cecil B. Demille or David Lean, his films always create two distinctive worlds and use the length of the feature to elaborate these competing worlds. This technique reaches its zenith in *Lost Highway* (1997) and *Mulholland Drive* (2001), in which the two competing filmic worlds have their own definite logic. The logic of one world flies in the face of the logic of the other. The key to Lynch's films lies in what occurs when these worlds collide: we see a moment in which an impossible event happens on the screen. In order to elaborate the existence of two different worlds and their collision within a single film, Lynch needs time. And yet, Lynch began his career as a filmmaker, like many do, with short films. The short film format restricts Lynch's possibilities for elaborating two opposing worlds, and the result is that his early short films are stylistically distinct from his features. But in the four films that Lynch made prior to *Eraserhead* (1975), one can see his later aesthetic commitment nonetheless begin to emerge.

One could make the claim that even Lynch's shortest film (which was also his first), entitled *Six Men Getting Sick* (1967, 40 sec.), hints at the existence of two distinct filmic worlds that interact in a way that anticipates *Lost Highway* and *Mulholland Drive*. But this interaction operates differently in the early short films than in the features. In contrast to the features, the opposing worlds in *Six Men Getting Sick* and *The Alphabet* (1967, 4 min.) are not fully developed or fully distinct. It is not until his (significantly longer) short film *The Grandmother* (1970, 33 min.) that Lynch becomes Lynch and takes up the formal approach that would come to define him as a filmmaker. In this sense, *The Grandmother* is the first Lynch film. The additional running time of *The Grandmother*—it is more than thirty minutes, whereas both *Six Men Getting Sick* and *The Alphabet* are less than five minutes—enables Lynch to elaborate a fantasy world that exists in opposition to the primary world of the film. But after discovering this form in *The Grandmother*, he applies it to a shorter film, *The Amputee* (1974), which runs roughly as long as *The Alphabet*.

The larger canvas of the feature permits the filmmaker to use narrative to structure the opposition or contradiction that the film addresses. While short films also employ narrative, the lack of time at the filmmaker's disposal forces her or him to probe the film's central opposition through some other aspect of the form. Of course, a filmmaker can avoid formal inventiveness, but the short structure places a premium on it. The compactness of narrative time tends to push the filmmaker's exploration away from narrative and into editing, sound, mise-en-scène, and so on (see Raskin on the performative dimension in short film aesthetics in Chapter 2).

In Lynch's filmic universe, the division between worlds correlates to the opposition between lack and plenitude, or to that between desire and fantasy. Absence defines one of the worlds, and this absence constitutes a regime of desire, in which the spectator finds herself or himself constantly deprived of any satisfying object. The other world is fantasmatic and overly burdened with satisfying objects (or with the over presence of a specific satisfying object). Even though fantasy typically provides respite from desire and its lacking, both of Lynch's worlds traumatize the subject and the spectator, albeit in opposing ways. Lynch draws the contrast between filmic worlds in order to show that the escape always leads back to the trauma that the subject flees, and actually extends the trauma further.[1]

By making clear to spectators that the fantasmatic escape from the impossibility of our desire is no escape at all, Lynch is not creating a cinema opposed to fantasy. To the contrary, he illustrates that fantasy enables us to recognize that even our satisfaction involves trauma. This is what Jacques Lacan is getting at when he states that "fantasy has a role [in the subject] of the signification of truth" (Lacan 1966–67, session of June 21, 1967). Obviously, fantasy doesn't involve what really happens, but it does signify the truth of the subject by translating the loss that defines the subject into a narrative scenario. Lynch's films indicate fantasy's revelatory power, its ability to show how even the perfect object fails.

But in the short films, these filmic worlds, simply by virtue of the films' length, occur in a much closer temporal proximity. Though Lynch uses different filmic styles to emphasize the contrast between these worlds as he does in the features, the compact time prevents him from creating the sense of separation between the worlds that exists in the longer films. As a result, the spectator sees the proximity of desire and fantasy—how each world intrudes on the other. Though this also becomes apparent in Lynch's features, the proximity of desire and fantasy is clearest in the early short films.

A chronic illness

Though *Six Men Getting Sick* does not have a clear narrative, the spectator can make out two distinct events that occur in the brief film: the construction of the figures on the screen and their vomiting. Though Lynch separates these two events, he does so in order to indicate how they are tied together. Because the film runs on a loop, the two events lose any sense of temporal linearity and come to exist side by side in time. Three figures initially appear on the left side of the screen, and as the film starts, two additional heads appear on the right side. During the first half of the film, the throats and stomachs of all the figures appear, while at the same time another head forms out of the two on the right side, so that there are six in all. *Six Men Getting Sick* begins not with sickness but with the construction of the figures.

Lynch announces the divide between the first half of the film and the second by turning the entire image red, and the red tint obscures everything in the image except for the three heads on the left side. Soon after the moment of redness, the word "sick" appears in the bottom of the image, and the figures begin to evince distress, as their stomachs fill with liquid that ultimately travels up their throats. The film concludes by depicting the stomachs disappearing followed by a massive outburst of vomiting that fills the entire screen.

The first half of *Six Men Getting Sick* depicts the construction of the sixth figure and the filling out of the others. The absences in this part of the film suggest a future moment of satiation—a time when the figures will be completed.[2] But when the moment of satiation comes in the second half, it is excessive and leads to the nausea that ends the film. Rather than depicting a satisfying completion of the construction that occupies the first part of the film, Lynch portrays the figures as if they have had too much of a good thing. The sequence then repeats.

Lynch places these events on a loop in order to indicate that, despite their radical distinctiveness, the logic of each part leads inexorably to the other. The excess that defines the second half of the film mirrors the absence that defines the first half rather than providing relief from it.

Six Men Getting Sick lacks the fully elaborated contrasting worlds of Lynch's later (feature-length) films, and yet, the structure of all his films already appears here in an embryonic form. The object's presence traumatizes the subject even more than its absence, which is why fantasy is not a flight from trauma but the path, as Lynch sees it, to recognizing the constitutive status of trauma for the subject. As the figures vomit, the spectator sees that all satisfaction is always too little or too much satisfaction.

The perils of alphabetic order

After viewing *The Alphabet*, everyone remembers the second sequence of the film that depicts the bloody violence of the alphabet as experienced by an unnamed girl (Peggy Lynch). The film shows in a direct fashion the trauma that the individual undergoes as it submits to imposition of the signifier. As a girl sings the "ABC" song, each letter appears on the screen in a way that tortures the girl who is lying awake in her bed, and the film ends with the girl spitting up blood. Lynch makes clear that the violence of this final shot is that of the signifier itself, but this violence is nowhere evident in the first part of the film, despite the fact that it also depicts images of the alphabet.

It is significant that Lynch does not devote the entire film to the horrific concluding sequence of the "ABC" song and the terrified girl. This is what separates *The Alphabet* from simply being an avant-garde horror film. After an opening shot of the girl lying in bed (with an audio track of children repeating a chant of "a, b, c") and shots of a woman in dark sunglasses, the first part of the film's running time is devoted to an animated sequence with an operatic audio track and a singer practicing. This first part bears no relationship to the horrors that follow. There is nothing threatening about this sequence: instead, the music and animation together reveal the playfulness of the signifier, and this creates a stark contrast with the depiction of the terrified girl.

The film shifts toward the sinister dimension of the signifier when the letter "A" begins to relate to the human body. As we see the "A" reproduce itself on the screen, the audio track turns to the sound of a baby crying. Lynch then shows a human body with the letter "a" in the place of the head, a scene that anticipates the famous decapitation scene in *Eraserhead* (1975) where an eraser replaces a man's head. In the next moments, a distorted human head forms from this initial letter, which suggests the structuring power of the signifier for the subject. Our thinking, the film suggests, is the result not of our psychological make-up but of the violent imposition of the signifier on our physical being. The letter ends up shaping an entire human body, even though it creates a distorted body that resembles a surrealist artwork. It is this power that we see traumatically impacting the girl in the final sequence, as she responds with horror to the enunciation of each letter of the alphabet.

The contrast between the innocent first part of *The Alphabet* and the terrifying conclusion is extreme, but the film forces the spectator to recognize that the moments of innocence are only a brief respite from the horror that is always implicit in them. Though the sequences are distinct, the short running time of the film—it is only four minutes long—demands that we connect the disparate sequences that it presents. In this way, Lynch adds to the horror of the conclusion. There is no interaction with the signifier that avoids the trauma that we see the girl enduring. Even the moments of play always lead back to the trauma.

Growing a relative

With *The Grandmother* (1970), Lynch provides the first indication of the insight that would drive his entire filmic career—that our turn to fantasy allows us to experience the trauma of the fundamental loss that defines us in a way that ordinary social reality obscures.[3] After an opening animated sequence, the film depicts a father (Robert Chadwick) and mother (Virginia Maitland) emotionally abusing their boy (Richard White). This abuse manifests itself in the mise-en-scène of the boy's bedroom. Only the bed is lit, and darkness surrounds it. No other furniture is visible, so it seems as if the boy lives in the equivalent of a darkened prison cell. The parents berate their son with exaggerated gestures but otherwise display indifference toward him. But the abuse reaches its high point when the boy wets the bed one night. Lynch registers the bed wetting through a large spot of orange paint in the middle of the bed, and the lack of realism indicates the psychic impact of this event. Just as the orange spot remains (unlike urine that would dry), the trauma continues to define the boy's existence. When the father sees it, a close-up of him screaming reveals his anger and confirms the isolation of the boy.

In response to his parents' abusive treatment, the boy searches in the attic of the house, where he finds a bag of seeds. On a bed in the attic, the boy places a mound of dirt on the same spot as the orange spot on his own bed, and after he plants the seeds, he waters and tends to the odd-shaped plant that grows. The attic is here a distinct and separate world from the rest of the house, but its look exactly mirrors the look of the boy's bedroom except for the absence of the prominent urine stain. Eventually, the fruit of this plant turns out to be a loving grandmother, who contrasts completely with the boy's parents. She is the perfect fantasy object, providing love where it was entirely absent.

In a scene that anticipates the key point in *Mulholland Drive* to a remarkable extent, the boy and the grandmother engage in what appears to be a romantic kiss. It is clearly a fantasmatic moment, a moment in which the subject attains a union with the perfectly satisfying object that is impossible in the social reality. In order to signal the perfection of the moment, Lynch preserves it in a freeze frame. But soon this image of perfect enjoyment becomes troubled. Even though the boy and the grandmother are inside the house, snow begins to disturb the image. After an extended animated sequence, we see the grandmother in her bed grasping at her throat and unable to breathe. As the grandmother suffocates, the boy begs his parents for assistance, but they simply laugh at him because they don't believe that the grandmother exists. The boy is unable to prevent her death, and the film ends with him again alone on his own bed. Just before this conclusion, however, the boy sees the grandmother's grave and the grandmother herself nearby. When he approaches her, rather than kissing him, the grandmother denies him, indicating his isolation even within the fantasy.

The fantasy of the grandmother provides the boy respite from his loveless childhood and abusive parents, but it also introduces him to the trauma of loss. While enduring his parents' abuse in the beginning of the film, the boy was alone and experienced a profound absence. Loss defined his existence, but the boy had no experience of this loss. Because it creates the satisfying object that ultimately disappears, the fantasy of the grandmother enables the boy to have an experience of loss. Rather than offering an escape from a traumatic reality, fantasy shows the subject the connection between enjoyment—the kiss with the grandmother—and trauma. Fantasy points toward what our everyday reality obscures. As Richard Boothby puts it in *Freud as Philosopher*: "Phantasy is always a picturing, an imaginal figuration, yet also aims toward something unimaginable" (2001, 275). This is what all of Lynch's features accomplish, and *The Grandmother* is his first experiment with a longer format, which is perhaps why it is his first film to take up this structure. But his subsequent short film, which like his first two is less than five minutes long, reveals that this structure is possible even without much filmic time.

An amputated structure

Lynch made two versions of *The Amputee* just to test videotape stock for the American Film Institute. The two versions don't differ substantially, though the first is shorter and slightly more comical. Both films depict a woman (Catherine Coulson) with two amputated legs narrating a letter that she's writing to a friend while sitting in a chair. As her voice-over articulates a series of statements surrounding various relationships, a nurse (David Lynch dressed as a woman) enters the room and attends to one of her legs. The only action of the film occurs when the dressing of the wound goes awry and results in blood gushing from one of the amputated legs as the nurse flees the room.

It is difficult to sustain the idea that Lynch depicts contrasting worlds in *The Amputee* since the entire film takes place in a single shot with no camera movement. The absence of variation in the image does not leave any space or time for opposition. But Lynch manages to introduce variation through the contrast between the audio track, which is nothing but the woman's voice-over narration, and the visual image. While voice-over traditionally orients the spectator relative to the image, it sometimes serves as a counterpoint to the film's visuals in order to reveal, for example, the psychic state of the character speaking, as most famously occurs at the conclusion of *Psycho* (Alfred Hitchcock, 1960). Neither strategy is at work in Lynch's film.

In *The Amputee*, Lynch handles the voice-over in a way that initially appears straightforward, but ultimately proves almost uniquely distinctive. In the visual track, a woman sits in a chair and writes a letter, while on the audio track, she articulates the content of the letter. A simple correspondence between the visual and audio tracks is immediately evident. But when one examines the correspondence closely, its straightforwardness becomes questionable.

It soon becomes apparent that there is no relationship at all between what the woman says in the voice-over and what she writes. Though we don't see the words that she writes, her hands never move in conjunction with what she says: she is neither reflecting what she says before writing it, nor saying what she says before writing it, nor reading what she has written. The woman writes much less than what she says and in a way that displays no correspondence to what she says. The opposing worlds of *The Amputee* are the one of the woman's voice and that of the visual image.

The visual world of *The Amputee* is the world of the desiring and lacking subject. Here the subject's lack has a clear visual analogue—the woman's amputated legs. On the audio track, however, the woman articulates an elaborate fantasy in which her obvious lack plays no part at all. In her voice-over, the woman attacks her unnamed correspondent for her failure to understand the woman herself as well as someone named "Jim." The woman also criticizes the correspondent's treatment of someone named Helen and concludes with a menacing question about the correspondent's whereabouts at 3:00 a.m. Though the spectator has no context for making sense of this attack or for any of the people the woman references, what stands out is the disconnection between the woman's image of herself in the audio track and how she looks in the visual image. The woman's fantasy world leaves her bodily limitations behind.

But the woman's body nonetheless makes itself evident during the course of the film as the nurse redressing the wound causes it to begin bleeding. When the blood spurts out of the amputated leg during the conclusion of the film, this is not an indication, as one might conclude, that the woman cannot transcend her body, that the fantasy of herself that she describes collapses on the weight of reality. Instead, it is a testament to the ability of the invective that she displays in her letter to obtrude on her actual body. Her leg bleeds out of control because it is not safe from the outrage articulated in the woman's letter. It is as if the disembodied voice causes the visual disturbance as the excess of the fantasy world disturbs the woman's lacking social reality.[4] Though the fantasy provides respite from the trauma of the amputation, it also introduces a further disturbance into the subject. In the letter, the woman can imagine herself as unamputated, but she also creates a narrative that engenders trauma. Like *The Grandmother*, the film makes clear that the fantasmatic escape is never simply an escape, but also a pathway to an experience of the trauma that defines the subject. The spectator sees the wound gushing at the moment she reaches the traumatic point in her fantasmatic narrative, which suggests that the narrative itself triggers the spurting blood. The *Amputee* is just an experiment that Lynch conducted, but it reveals that he can find a way to bring the aesthetic that he develops in his longer films into the format of an extremely short film.

Lynch's early short films are not his greatest achievements, and they are more important for what they foreshadow than they are in themselves. But the short form does enable Lynch to elaborate a distinct idea that is not as apparent in his later features. In a feature film like *Lost Highway* (1997), we see how the attempt to escape trauma through fantasy—Fred Madison (Bill Pullman) fantasizes himself as another person, Peter Dayton (Balthazzar Getty), to avoid the mystery of his wife's desire—leads the subject to an even more tangible trauma: he knows that his wife is enjoying sex with many other men. In Lynch's features, the escape always fails and returns the subject to a trauma. This same dynamic informs the short films, but the compression of time in these films brings the escape and the trauma closer together. The features allow for a temporal respite from trauma that doesn't exist in the short films.

Though the features all suggest the link between our flight from trauma and the trauma itself, in the short film we see more clearly the inescapability of trauma for the subject. The compactness of the temporality in the short film format forces Lynch to show the trauma intruding itself throughout the fantasmatic sequences. The short film format reveals that narrative is not an escape but rather a way of constituting trauma. Trauma occurs in the form of an encounter, and the duration of the feature film has the effect of creating a time in which the spectator can lose herself or himself in the fantasy of evading this encounter altogether. The absence of time in the short film creates the possibility of trauma more conspicuously intruding on the filmic fantasy. The short film format has the potential to not give the spectator time for respite. As narrative time shrinks, narrative's relation to trauma sharpens.

Notes

1 For a detailed elaboration of this idea, see McGowan (2007).

2 Martha Nochimson sees the fundamental opposition in *Six Men Getting Sick* not between construction and vomiting, but between stasis and flux. She writes, "*Six Men* is a genuinely wonderful collision of the static forms of control with the plasticity of the flux of movement" (1997, 150). Nochimson's point here reveals the extent to which Lynch utilizes extreme oppositions even in his shortest film in order to explore the connection between these oppositions.

3 Michel Chion makes a related point about the turn to the fantasy world in *The Grandmother*. He notes that *The Grandmother* contains "the first expression in Lynch's work of a parallel world, culminating in the Red Room of *Twin Peaks*" (1995, 18).

4 The disembodied voice of the woman in *The Amputee* resembles what Michel Chion calls the *acousmetre*, a voice detached from any character within the visual field and yet not a voice-over narration, like the voice of Norman Bates' mother in *Psycho* (Alfred Hitchcock, 1960). The difference is that the disembodied voice in *The Amputee* is clearly attached to a character within the visual field, even though we don't see her mouth moving. Lynch creates a voice existing somewhere between the *acousmetre* and the voice-over. For more on Chion's concept, see Chion (1999).

Part Two

[Condensed]
Polyphonic Archives

5

The Ethics of Repair: Reanimating the Archive

Sean Cubitt

When we consider archives, we should consider not only how we recall the dead, but how they recall us.

Archive footage and found footage films are a significant subgenre of the compact cinema addressed in this book, from Len Lye's exquisitely overpainted library footage in *Trade Tattoo* (1937) and Joseph Cornell's *Rose Hobart* (1936) to Bruce Connor's *A Movie* (1958), Ken Jacobs' *Tom, Tom, the Piper's Son* (1969), the scratch videos of George Barber and the contemporary collages of Craig Baldwin, and many music video makers. In the intensity of their channeling of the past, these bursts of reworked history raise particular questions for compact cinematics.

How does ethical obligation operate across temporal disjuncture? How does archival obligation relate to the dominant regime governing time today: debt? Debt as gratitude is a universal of human experience binding us to each other and to the earth. Debt as universal economic peonage ejects us emotionally and legally from the social, and poisons our relations with nature. Debt ties us to a model of time: what we consume today has to be repaid in the future; or rather, the principal is never repaid, but we commit to perpetual payment of interest on it. In this, debt sublimates and perverts the principle of obligation. Archive ethics have a special role to play in urging us to consider ourselves as media through which the ancestral archives transmit themselves into a future other than that of perpetual indebtedness.

Archived works come toward us as alien, or at least as orphaned. We greet them not only as evidence of a lost world but also as technical artifacts. Their technicity confronts us. The otherness of the archival film or video comes toward us as a stranger, a technical thing: its substrates and its acquired damage.

This object presents itself as fragile. As a fragile, damaged object, it stands before us in need.

In Levinas' (1969) account of ethics as first philosophy, the encounter of human individuals is always already ethical: when I face the Other, the Other places on me a demand for recognition. In Simon Critchley's (2007) reworking of the thesis, the demand is infinite: I am obliged *beyond reason* to the Other. Something of this alterity drives the archival encounter. What I encounter is other than myself, yet has a life of its own that I feel bound to acknowledge. What confronts us is not just what is represented but the mediation, more physically present in archival material than in the ordinary media we tend to see *through*. Even more than the most formally self-reflexive works, archival encounters bring us face to face with fragile but living entities carrying freights both of the intentions of their makers and of the accidents that have occurred to them in their journeys through time. The archival thing is more than its freight of human motivations and symbols. It is a palimpsest of chemical and physical processes that occurred down the long years between its making and the meeting in the archive. The things we encounter are in this sense wholly technological.

Archives extend ethics beyond the interpersonal, humanist plane. For Levinas only the encounter with another human counts (and not for example with a film or televised representation), so that we only meet the other as a member of our species, a finally unknowable other who nonetheless shares with us a here and a now. The archival encounter, like the encounter with the recorded or broadcast image, is different in that the simultaneity and co-location are not guaranteed, and we do not meet our likeness in a member of our own species, but something other, ghostly, of another time and place. In preparatory work for his proposal of an ethics of encounter, Levinas addressed the artistic "obscuring of being in images" (1989, 142). Counter to Kracauer's or Bazin's redemption of physical reality, Levinas poses the image as stranded in a mythic "meanwhile," a time outside of becoming. Yet the archive image is always historical in this physical sense, vanishing or being remade. There is then an implication that archive footage has a privileged relation to becoming as forgetting and erasure, quite as much as an indexical relation to a once-real. Indeed, in witnessing the vanishing of the past in its own combination of recalling and losing, the archive trumps both humanist realism and formalist ontology in its encounter between human subjects and archival objects traveling in opposite directions through time, one acquiring memories, the other losing them.

Such is the encounter enacted for us in Marisol Trujillo's short film *Oración [Prayer]* (1984, 9 min.). Before the Revolution of 1959, Cuba was the major center for US film distribution into Latin America. The Insituto Cubano del Arte e Industria Cinematográficos (ICAIC), as combined film school, production house, and distributor, took over that archive and made it available for educational, critical, and study purposes. Trujillo's nine-minute film dips into features and newsreels for images of Marilyn Monroe, which are accompanied by a poem of the same title (*Oración*) by the Nicaraguan Sandinista poet Ernesto Cardenal, written and read, with great passion, by the Cuban actor José Rodríguez. Music video is typically commissioned to accompany a music track already recorded. Trujillo takes Rodriguez's reading as her source text, punctuating his plea to God to consider his servant Norma Jean Baker (Monroe's real name), and using images from the then recent Vietnam and Biafran wars to underpin the global reach of Cardenal's verse. In the opening stanza, instigating the practice of the whole film, Trujillo constantly reframes the found footage and stills, culminating in a rotation of the famous Monroe Playboy nude spread focusing on her face until it cross-fades to that of a starved victim of the Biafran genocide.

In the second stanza, after the title, Monroe disappears visually, even as Cardenal recounts and interprets a dream she recalled in a *Time* interview in which she steps carefully over the heads of her fans in order not to step on them. Trujillo here montages shots of colonial atrocities and fascism with protests against them, closing on the 20th Century Fox logo with US warplanes mapped against it (see Figure 5.1).

Figure 5.1 Still from Marisol Trujillo's short film *Oración* (*[Prayer]* 1984).

The third stanza reads the church of Monroe's dream as the temple of her body, turned into a den of thieves by Fox, from which Christ drives the moneylenders. "Señor," his voice intones between pauses, as the montage of war and horror gives way to an early starlet image of Monroe's face. Surely God will forgive a shopgirl's dreams that turned into a technicolor reality, dreams that are also ours. Forgive us, he asks, for our twentieth century, as Trujillo's montage moves across images of plenty that invariably include some corner of deprivation, and then a series of women's faces caught in anger, bewilderment, and mourning.

The fourth stanza takes us into Monroe's growing mental instability and the emptiness of the drugs and therapies offered her, which in Trujillo's montage, by identifying her made-up eye with the eye of a slum child, extends to the scale of a global event, surrounding Cardenal's account of her public celebrity with images of prostitution, drug addiction, begging, and scavenging. The most luminous capture of the film, from the sequence of her racing to the yacht in full torch-singer costume in *Some Like It Hot* (Wilder, 1959), is composited with footage of a bridge swaying surreally during an earthquake accompanying the line "Her life was unreal" (see Figure 5.2), a shot that gives way to a slightly slowed footage of nuclear testing in the Pacific, that threat of final war which weighed so heavily in the politics of Monroe's lifetime, the period in the 1980s when Trujillo was working, and with which the name of Cuba was almost synonymous since the missile crisis of 1962.

And in the final stanza, with paparazzi shots of the apartment bedroom where Monroe died of an overdose, and a comparison of shots of her face ambiguously

Figure 5.2 Still from Marisol Trujillo's short film *Oración ([Prayer]* 1984).

caught between sexual ecstasy and drug overdose with that of a newborn child in pain, Cardenal's poem asks who she was trying to call as she lay dying. While images of revolt and revolution mount, culminating in the image of a child reaching skyward, he demands "Señor, contesta Tu el telefono," "Lord, You answer the telephone." The strains of Blake's *Jerusalem*, in the setting by Parry (who assigned copyright in it to the National Union for Women's Suffrage), swell over images of children and revolutionaries, ending with a child in the pose of Blake's *Glad Day*. (According to an email from Michael Chanan, Trujillo knew nothing about the song, not even that the words were Blake's, but only that it simply sounded right: intuition is as significant to the archival encounter as scholarship in generating new possibilities and meanings.)

Aesthetics is the ethical matter of mediations through which we perceive and communicate our own happiness—or otherwise—and that of the worlds we inhabit, social, technological, and "natural." Therefore the ethical-political question of the good life, even before we extend it beyond the human, is already a question of mediations and thus aesthetic; and it is doubly so when the aesthetic is the first mediation through which we become aware of the unhappiness—or otherwise—of excluded and nonhuman others, the moment at which aesthetics ceases to be individual and becomes political. Because it deals with the natural physical and chemical decay as well as the constraints of antique technologies, the archive operates in this aesthetic-ethical-political zone as a special intersection between human and nonhuman, included and excluded, as an encounter between individuals and polities, and between them and technological and natural environments, the living and the dead.

Trujillo's encounter with the Monroe of the archive is not, and could never be, an encounter with the real Norma Jean Baker. Transformed and transfigured in her own encounter with Hollywood, Monroe, in Cardenal's account, has already lost sight of her own reality. The archival encounter, moreover, is not with Monroe but with the image, precisely that image which in Cardenal is already occupied by the moneylenders, and in Levinas is already a betrayal of the real. Yet in Trujillo's film, the reality of Monroe's archive is not of her body as immaculate origin of the image but on the contrary, the star-making machine itself. In her montage, Trujillo undermines the Technicolor dream to show the brutality inflicted on this woman and all women and their children. There is no real to encounter, but the traces, already fading, of a hegemony that is also fading, and in spite of which the dream of beauty and freedom survive their desecration.

The demand the archive places is the demand of the irreplaceable. The archival ethic, then, is to save this specific copy. Increasingly dealing with the constraints of storage and restoration costs, archivists are faced with the choice of what it is that they are trying to conserve, the question of canon-formation, and the balance between preservation and access. Caroline Frick (2011) argues that the industry has had the lion's share of preservation and access, while, as Jane Gaines (2007) points out, there has been a tendency to ignore or sideline women's work—in a province where sidelining is in effect a death sentence. Many colonial films, African-American films, and other marginalized practices have suffered equally. The work of the archive is as much one of systematic forgetting as it is of remembrance. In this, the archive participates in the logic of the image. Still photographs are ripped from the continuum of time. The moving image was invented as a way of healing that trauma, but can only do so on the principle that each frame is itself radically incomplete, necessitating the next image and the next. Every movie arrives in order to supplement and, eventually, to supplant every previous one.

It is not enough for Trujillo to preserve in this short film. The archive can in any case preserve only the current state of decay. Instead, Trujillo embraces and enacts the ethics of encounter, mediating the savage system that glorified and threw away Monroe for another generation to wonder at. That *Oración* is so difficult to find, with most copies now several electronic generations away from the cinema print, only emphasizes that core truth of decay. By the time of her death, Monroe had already achieved the status of myth, moving from sports hero's wife to wife of the best-known intellectual of her day to the mooted mistress of the most famous US president of her century. It is this myth that we see in its decay, rather than the woman or the star: the myth of 20th Century Fox, the mythical time of suspended reality apart from a history that always reclaims it. Trujillo cannot retrieve the sufferings of Norma Jean Baker, or make amends for them, but only reach back into the rift in the real that images leave as their lasting legacy.

Under financialization, debt spends today the earnings of the future, pledging us to repay, so committing us not only to work but to maintain the wage relation in perpetuity. In its very decay, the archive video that is its most commonly seen form demonstrates the morbidity, not of ephemerality, but of permanence, where permanence has become the permanence of finance. Because in each single frame we ineluctably miss the completion of flux in the present, Trujillo's handling of the archive footage seems to say, we owe our tremendous debt not to the future but to the past. If so, then the future owes us a debt, rather than us owing it. We are the ancestors who look to the future for our justification, the justification adumbrated in Trujillo's closing shots of children, symbols of hope and futurity. Just as we are the posterity who must somehow justify the massacres and atrocities evidenced in the newsreel footage, and the heroism of those who fought against them in other shots from demonstrations and battle scenes from Vietnam and Latin America. When the Playboy centerfold cuts to a child dead of malnutrition, the commerce of desire and of death begs us for a resolution. The aesthetics of archiving derive from this impossible task of bearing their truth to those for whom we also will in turn be ancestors.

The archivist's work is always melancholy, not because of nostalgia for an impossible original state of the archive object, but because the moving image's impetus to complete the rift in the real, instigated by the still image, inhabits the archive's impulse to return to its origin while knowing it is impossible. What remains is to recognize the fact, subjective and objective, of torn time; to encounter the infinitely demanding Other of decay; and to transform that inevitability into a talismanic promise that the future will not be an unending duplication of the past. What the present encounter with *Oración* now archives is not the record of Monroe but of this unrepeatable archival encounter in ICAIC in 1984.

Since there is no God, and our posterity will no doubt be as fallible as we have been in our role as posterity to the past, it is the present audience, hearing, who must answer the telephone, who must accept the repayment offered by the past for the debts of the present.

6

Long Story Short

Natalie Bookchin

Introduction

In this chapter, I reflect on *Long Story Short* (2016), an art project that takes form both as a 45-minute film and a multichannel video installation. In the project, over 100 people at homeless shelters, food banks, adult literacy programs, and job training centers in Los Angeles and the Bay Area in Northern California discuss their experiences of poverty—why they are poor, how it feels, how they cope, and what they think should be done. *Long Story Short* shortens many stories, which are then stitched together into a polyphonic account of poverty told from the inside. Instead of a single talking head filling the screen, many compact cells of talking heads fade in and out in choral-like formation across the screen in *Long Story Short* (see Figure 6.1). Brief phrases and single words at times are punctuated as voices overlap, speak in unison, or echo others, offering variations on themes, supplementing, and reinforcing each other's words. In this chapter I will discuss my use of the aesthetics of the small in the film: the multiple frames of miniature video fragments that appear on a single screen; the numerous condensed stories, short vignettes, as well as the small-scale production values; and, finally, the so-called "small" voices of ordinary citizens.

Long Story Short, which comes out of a nonfiction practice in the field of contemporary art,[1] positions itself against and in conversation with contemporary social media, while seeking to offer an alternative to dominant depictions of poverty and homelessness in popular media. I will reflect on the film's use of multiple minute frames of videos as a way to invoke collectivity and commonality among the films' many subjects as well as to suggest the social and iterative nature of poverty itself. I will also discuss the formal aspects

Figure 6.1 Still from *Long Story Short*. Courtesy of the artist.

described above as a means to grapple with, call attention to, and engage with the aesthetics, the tools, and the ideologies of social media, neoliberalism, and the so-called sharing economy, appropriating those same tools to make visible and highlight the voices, faces, and opinions of those disenfranchised by that same economy.

Footage for *Long Story Short* was collected at community centers and nonprofit organizations that provide services such as food, shelter, job training, and GED preparation, and anyone attending those programs was invited to participate in the film. The production of *Long Story Short* was extremely small scale, with a tiny crew of one or occasionally two. Video was shot with a simple webcam attached to a laptop. Rather than intruding on private moments or spaces, or reproducing stereotypical images of poverty (pictures of urban blight and its inhabitants: disheveled men and women roaming the streets with shopping carts filled with possessions, people congregating and sleeping under freeways, decrepit interiors with peeling walls) *Long Story Short* shows its subjects poised in offices and rooms in nonprofit community centers, speaking directly to the camera, framed as "talking heads" in the manner of a TV broadcast or an online video diary or "vlog." Subjects were asked to compose their own on-screen images, and to take their time describing and reflecting on their social and material realities and conditions, as well as the meanings and feelings they assign to those realities.

The video portraits produced by the webcams are stationary images, low in resolution, and slightly skewed, with faces lit by the glow of the computer screen, a form that is accessible in its familiarity from social media platforms and its amateur aesthetic, and clearly opposed to the large-format professional image typically seen in glossy documentary films. This small-screen aesthetics suggest the ease with which these compact cinematic images can be produced as well as transmitted across networks onto small screens. They address an audience whose interest and attention may be triggered by their slightly modified and altered familiarity, with faces and stories by people whose stories and opinions don't often appear in this form on our screens.

Popular media and poverty: The entrepreneurial self

Today, our small screens display continuous flows of media fragments, opinions, and rants about world events and local stories. Personalized and intimate, this flow addresses us directly, beckoning us to join in, comment, upload, and perpetuate its never-ending stream. The more we oblige and the more we click, the more the algorithms can adjust the content of our media streams, and we see a world reflected back to us, shaped by our preferences, the opinions we share, and the stories we like.

According to a report by the Pew Research Center, nearly half of web-using adults report getting news about politics and government from Facebook, about as many as those that get it from TV (Pew Research Center 2015). These "social" media shape and allow access to the world, but also screen out other parts of the world. Visibility depends on popular affirmation (likes, clicks, shares, remixes). Alexandra Juhasz, in her careful analysis of YouTube (2011), suggests the difficulty in finding less popular videos on YouTube, an aggregate platform that feeds videos into numerous media streams. YouTube's secret search engine algorithms appear to privilege popularity and commercially sponsored and produced videos over all other criteria. More critical or socially marginalized videos may, as a result, sink to the bottom or disappear, entirely out of reach.

Social media platforms like YouTube and Facebook are the well-lubricated tools of our current neoliberal condition. I define neoliberalism here following Wendy Brown (2015) and Michel Feher (2009), who discuss it not only as a set of political and government policies and tendencies that include a shrunken welfare state, unregulated markets, increased privatization, and increased temporary work and job precarity, but also as a condition that presupposes a particular form of subjectivity. Under the neoliberal condition, they both argue, human beings are redefined as human capital, and all aspects of existence are seen and understood in economic terms.[2] Many log in to social media in the hopes of connecting with others, only to find themselves isolated in an individualizing, atomizing, and cacophonous environment. Once online, individuals are transformed into entrepreneurs who vie for attention and social capital—more friends, more likes, more visibility.[3] This entrepreneurial self is consistent with current attitudes about the poor, who are often blamed for their supposed bad investments in themselves—for not working hard enough on themselves, for laziness, or for having bad morals.[4]

Hand in hand with the growth of the internet and its sharing economy, the gap between rich and poor has widened. In the United States, the income gap is now worse than in any other advanced industrial country (Alvaredo et al. 2013), and nearly 35 percent of the population has faced poverty at some point in their lives (National Center for Law and Economic Justice 2015). Yet despite the numbers, there is a striking absence of media coverage that specifically addresses poverty (Froomkin 2013) and the stories that do appear tend to depict it as an individual problem rather than a social one. A recent study on poverty coverage in the United States reveals how dramatically the narrative has shifted between 1970 and 2008, moving from a focus on structural causes to negative portrayals of the poor as cheaters, lazy, dysfunctional, and exploiting welfare programs.[5] In news stories, those actually facing poverty are rarely consulted for analysis, as if their very poverty seems to disqualify them from having an opinion worth considering. Instead, "experts" are typically brought in to explain and elucidate, a process that risks rendering the disenfranchised, already silenced or cast out of society, as mute or passive, scrutinized and analyzed by those who supposedly know better.[6]

The one genre in popular media that tends to take on the issues of the disenfranchised with any regularity is the conventional character-driven documentary film typically screened on the big screen and on cable and public television in the United States. This genre characteristically follows the model of conventional Hollywood filmmaking, using classic narrative arcs and one or a few charismatic characters, organizing real-life situations into easily digestible entertainment. Regardless of the subject matter, the form itself, with its emphasis on individual characters, risks reinforcing prevailing myths of individualism already pervasive under neoliberalism. Critiques about the political limitations of this genre and form are well known, beginning as early as the 1920s and 1930s in writings by Eisenstein,[7] and continuing through much critical writing after the 1970s by artists and writers influenced by feminist and post-structural critiques of representation.[8]

Multiplicity

There is a long tradition of filmmakers and artists who reject or push at the boundaries of mainstream cinematic forms, as well as a number of influential works exploring multiplicity in their depiction of groups of people living within particular geopolitical or social conditions. In the interest of brevity I'll mention just a few. In his cinema-vérité documentary, *Comizi d'amore (Love Meetings)* from 1965, Pier Paolo Pasolini traveled across Italy and interviewed groups of people on their views about sex. Speakers, organized by groupings such as gender, age, location, education, and class, crowd into the frame, speaking over each other, debating, arguing, and boasting as they respond to Pasolini's questions. The film reveals a cross-section of the population struggling over and negotiating meanings and definitions of words and ideas that shape and discipline bodies, while exposing the contradictory, but largely conservative, attitudes about sexuality that permeated Italy in the mid-1960s. A more recent example, Chantal Akerman's *Bordering on Fiction, D'Est,* a film reworked into an installation in 1995, consisted of twenty-five monitors with looping distant tracking shots of private and public spaces and people filmed in East Germany, Poland, and Russia just as the former Soviet Bloc was collapsing. The installation forsakes the authoritarian voice of the documentary, instead offering multiple simultaneous documents of everyday life during a time of major political and social transformation. Never privileging one view, viewers select and edit as they pause in front of one monitor or the next, mirroring the camera movement tracking and navigating through disparate locations. Lastly, in 2004, Turkish artist Kutluğ Ataman produced a video installation entitled *Küba* consisting of forty monitors, each displaying a portrait of a different resident of a mostly Kurdish shantytown on the outskirts of Istanbul. In front of each monitor is a comfortable chair, inviting viewers to settle in and watch. As viewers move between stations, the various links between the different portraits become increasingly apparent. Together, Ataman writes, "they construct a shared singular identity, namely being a Küban."[9] Each of these works described produces a composite portrait of a society, shifting focus away from individual characters and singular narrative arcs, and instead offering a multiplicity of views. Viewers are asked to consider their own role in the production of meaning as they navigate, select, and edit their way through the documents presented and shaped by the filmmaker.

Long Story Short

Long Story Short is carrying this body of theory and practice into the current context of social media. It borrows from the aesthetics of the database and social media, and—with its emphasis on multiplicity and experimental sonic and visual forms—from the avant-garde, using its idiosyncratic cinematic forms to politicize its content. By appropriating the tools and aesthetics of the sharing economy, the film aims to use those same forms to highlight and amplify the voices of those most displaced and dispossessed by them.

Instead of presenting the viewer with one larger-than-life hero, *Long Story Short* is comprised of video footage drawn from an accumulated archive in which many subjects relate their stories and views on living in poverty. Rather than allowing algorithms or popularity to determine who is seen and heard, all those who volunteered to participate in the film are included, no single perspective or voice privileged over others.[10] Subjects speak both as individuals and, through their accumulation in an edited assemblage, as part of a collective. Through this process, shared experiences and commonalities among strangers are highlighted, instigating unexpected links, and stipulating connections between and among strangers, revealing that poverty, much like social media, is viral, iterative, part of a web of connected experiences. The multitude is depicted as interconnected, not through competition, but rather through common struggles, hopes, and dignity in the face of tremendous obstacles.

The narrative structure of *Long Story Short* is episodic: the film is made up of many short vignettes that focus on topics as varied as money, neighborhoods, class, poverty, homelessness, unemployment, hunger, panhandling, and visibility. In each section, numerous small slices of individual narrations are composited together to create larger choruses. Anywhere from one to twelve video frames appear on the screen at any one time. Making use of jump cuts and looped footage, the film's spatial montage is composed of shots and countershots in adjacent frames, so as to provoke encounters among strangers in separate locations, who seem to acknowledge each other's presences, eyes miraculously matching, as they add to each other's words. Even while crowded together on the screen, people remain visible and legible in their singularity. Speakers lock viewers in their gaze, and speak about how it feels to not have money, to be judged by others, or to feel unseen. The direct address confronts viewers, suggesting that viewers are, have always been, implicated within the same social structures responsible for both their impoverishment and their lack of visibility. Often, a single speaker addresses the camera as others linger on the screen, appearing to glance over at the speaker or reach out to the viewer, as if witnessing, observing each other's words, sometimes adding a word or phrase, sometimes a gesture, a glance, or nod at the viewer or the speaker, as if acknowledging him, her, or us, too, in solidarity (see Figure 6.2).

Figure 6.2 Still from *Long Story Short*. Courtesy of the artist.

While individual video frames vary in size, they never occupy the full space of the screen. Even when a single frame is presented, it appears slightly off-center, and small in the context of the otherwise empty screen, suggesting that no one speaker can ever give the full picture of what it is to live in poverty under the conditions of neoliberalism and our omnipresent media culture (see Figure 6.3). There is always more to be told, always another person, another perspective, another experience to be recounted. The remaining empty black space on the screen is also a placeholder, suggesting the potential limitlessness of the archive, where, with the potentially ever-expanding scale of poverty, for every voice heard, there are hundreds of thousands more unheard.

It is through this modular and polyphonic compilation of short image fragments, condensed from a potentially limitless archive, that *Long Story Short* aims to reveal patterns without using abstractions, establishing links within and across the many small, singular, and short stories that in their collectivity make up the "big picture," yet without subordinating the small and the singular to the collective composition. In so doing, *Long Story Short* offers the possibility of a fragmentary imaginary collective, yet to materialize. While individuals in separate spaces appear in isolation, trapped within their own video frames and mirroring the isolating aspects of the media forms the film appropriates, words flow across the screen like a musical ensemble. This choral voice moves across a social body of common experiences and variations on shared themes, as narrators momentarily join together, and then splinter apart. In their conjunction, and without obscuring the singularity of each of its members, these many small and compacted frames of images and fragments of voices create something larger, and more akin to the social, than either one of the voices alone, or the affirmative

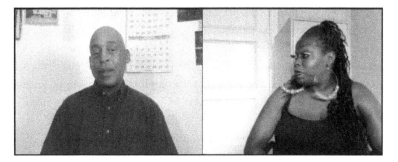

Figure 6.3 Still from *Long Story Short*. Courtesy of the artist.

stereotypes that circulate in mainstream and so-called "social" media. In this way, *Long Story Short* appeals to the most precious of human values—solidarity and compassion—with all their possibilities and potential still to be realized.

Notes

1 For a discussion on recent tendencies in the intersection of contemporary art and documentary, see Steyerl (2003) and Lind and Steyerl (2010).

2 See also Michel Feher's series of lectures at Goldsmith College "The Age of Appreciation: Lectures on the Neoliberal Condition," November 2013–May 2014, archived at https://vimeo.com/80882516 | https://vimeo.com/86138288 | https://vimeo.com/90220914 | https://vimeo.com/98656030 | https://vimeo.com/114709929 | https://vimeo.com/121149487 | https://vimeo.com/123325158 | and https://vimeo.com/128427841 (accessed February 21, 2016).

3 Jodi Dean writes about how in conditions "of intensive and extensive proliferation of media . . . messages get lost. They become mere contributions to the circulation of images, opinion, and information, to the billions of nuggets of information and affect trying to catch and hold attention, to push or sway opinion, taste and trends in one direction rather than other . . . submerge[ing] politics in a deluge of circulating, disintegrated spectacles and opinions" (2009: 24).

4 For current attitudes about the poor in the United States, see The Salvation Army (2012). The report found that half of the more than 1,000 Americans surveyed agreed that a good work ethic is all you need to escape poverty. Forty-three percent said that if poor people want a job, they could always find one. Twenty-seven percent said that people are poor because they are lazy, and 29 percent said that poor people usually have lower moral values. In a Pew Research poll (2014), over 63 percent of respondents believed that African Americans who can't get ahead are mostly responsible for their failings.

5 Rose and Baumgartner (2013). For a discussion of how racial stereotypes play into these depictions, see Gilens (2003).

6 A recent article in the *New York Times* (Kirp, 2015) described what it called a radical move by a Houston organization that starts from the premise that a better way to help the poor is to first ask them what they think needs to be done rather than simply imposing policy from the outside. What is striking is that this is considered radical and not an obvious first step.

7 Eisenstein (1988) argued for new cinematic forms for "opposing the individualism of the west." He wrote: "Down with individual figures (heroes isolated from the mass) . . .; down with the individual chain of events (the plot intrigue)—let us have neither personal stories nor those of people 'personally' isolated from the mass" (79).

8 For example, Jill Godmilow (1999) writes that "though the liberal documentary takes the stance of a sober, non-fiction vehicle for edification about the real world, it is trapped in the same matrix of obligations as the fiction film—to entertain its audience; to produce fascination with its materials; to achieve closure; to satisfy. . . . It ends up confirming and making comfortable the class status of that middle class audience, by providing an opportunity for compassion, for up-lift, for hope, and finally, for self-satisfaction—and perhaps complacency." See also Allan Sekula (1978), Martha Rosler (1989), and Hito Steyerl (2006).

9 Ataman on http://www.kutlugataman.com/site/artworks/work/10/ (accessed February 24, 2016).

10 In a few instances where the sound or image quality was too low, a few videos were not included, but all subjects appear in the credit sequence at the end of the film, with, whenever possible, video portraits as well as names.

7

Skip Intro? Short Intro Videos as a Reflexive Threshold in the Interactive Documentary

Tina M. Bastajian

More than a boundary or a sealed border, the paratext is, rather, a threshold or—a word Borges used apropos of a preface—a "vestibule" that offers the world at large the possibility of either stepping inside or turning back.

(Genette 1997, 1–2)

Introduction

Database or algorithmic cinema, interactive and database narratives and, more recently, the emergence of the interactive or web documentary (i-Docs)[1] have increasingly become part of the cross/transmedia landscape. These works invariably exploit short filmic assets, nodes, units, and small numerical units (or SNUs).[2] These would include web-based works, media installations, location-based storytelling, and other tangential mobile viewing/listening modalities. Databased digital content becomes distributed and tagged, often migrating assets from one project to another platform. Or, in the case of participatory and crowd-sourced works, content can be continually added and refreshed within the various types of database environments.

Short and discrete video clips are in essence the building blocks of most web/interactive documentary works. However, what remains for many of these works is how they uniquely formulate and situate short stand-alone video segments that provide an introduction to the project and overall thematic. In further distinguishing the "short film experience," film theorist Pepita Hesselberth and philosopher/filmmaker Carlos M. Roos assert that "short films challenge the borders of the disciplines that study them, thus urging us to confront questions regarding the conditions of moving-image production (technological affordance, creative process), and the configurations of time, space, and the self (time/space formations, perceptible materiality) that lay at the heart of cinematic experience" (2015, 5).

Embarking from this reflexive possibility of short films, this chapter will look at three interactive documentaries' short intros: *Cue China* (2014), *Planet Galata* (2010), and lastly, my own interactive work in collaboration with Seda Manavoğlu, *Coffee Deposits:::Topologies of Chance* (2010). I will appraise these short intro audio/videos by underscoring how these short narrative units provide the interactant/user to enter a passage or threshold in unison with French literary critic Gerard Genette's concept from *Paratexts: Thresholds of Interpretation* (1997) in relation to the surrounding interactive narrative components. In turn, I will explore and discuss each project's distinct usage of reflexive tendencies found embedded within the narrative itself, through the navigational design, and their idiosyncratic cinematic *dispositifs*.

I argue that these short "intro" or threshold videos provide a unique, liminal, reflexive, and discursive space. By doing so, I draw upon aspects of reflexivity demarcated in linear documentary forms, suggesting film theorist Bill Nichols' "reflexive mode." In his seminal *Introduction to Documentary* (2011), Nichols maps out six documentary film modes:

> The processes of negotiation between filmmaker and viewer become the focus of attention for the reflexive mode. Rather than following the filmmaker in his or her engagement with other social actors, we now attend to the filmmaker's engagement with us, speaking not only about the historical world but about the problems and issues of representing it as well. This intensified level of reflection on what representing the world involves distinguishes the reflexive mode from the other modes. (194)

Thinking through the notion of the threshold or passage can potentially extend and resituate this "intensified level of reflection" to existing documentary theories on reflexive impulses. Perhaps it is in the traversal of these in-between spaces, both literally and metaphorically, that such reflexive impulses reveal and nuance the transitional nature of the personal and collective, often carefully positioned within a distinct set of subjectivities.

Prelude: An aural threshold to the in/visible

It's a small world after all. It's a small word after all. It's a small, small world.[3]

I would like to contextualize how I came upon this topic by discussing a work that was included in the 2015 International Documentary Film Festival Amsterdam (IDFA). It was part of the annual parallel program consisting of the interactive documentary (DocLab) themed program, *Seamless Reality*. The work *Cue China* (26 min) by the UK artist Ant Hampton straddles live performance, together with complex interactive installation components. Paradoxically, its intro is neither video nor web-based, but rather a short pretaped audio script that a prescheduled audience of two sit and listen to while strategically being placed for screening positions by a gallery attendant. This hybrid documentary is described as "a non-fictional portrait within a fantasy encounter" vis-à-vis a complex mirror, projection and screen construction enabling participants to gaze into this "uncanny territory, as the faces of audience / performer, consumer / maker, supply / demand are literally fused—and confused" (Hampton).

It was this threshold and its disciplining of the spectator that piqued my interest to explore interactive documentaries' intros.[4] The audio reminded me of what is known as a *cut-scene*. Originating as a term in game theory from the late 1980s, cut-scenes are short openings or interludes that "occur between periods of gameplay, giving a player a break between levels or narrative sequences" (Wolf 2012, 151). While not widely considered to be interactive, cut-scenes are generally thought to provide rest periods; however, elements such as expository dialogue, gameplay rewards, or other narrative devices are often employed to reveal certain backstories or additional illustrative information. Most interactive documentaries with stand-alone intros allow for navigating away and/or, at the very least, give agency to let (impatient) users move the video play head further along. *Cue China* amplified this cut-scene by proxy, and as an interactant, I was disciplined in a physical sense while snugly seated between orientating devices to keep me still. Such conditions made it difficult to "skip intro," navigate, or walk away. Nevertheless, I understood on a deeper level that entering and inhabiting this space was an extension of a "possibility," in which I made a contractual decision, and hence to use Gerard Genette's paratext axiom, "I stepped inside" (1997, 1–2).

To put the project into proper context, Hampton's work was motivated by the Apple scandal from 2009 that exposed workers to the highly toxic solvents n-hexane, used to clean the screens of iPhones and known for causing neurological and respiratory disorders, cancer, and paralysis. As Samuel Gibbs of *The Guardian* has noted, n-hexane "is used rather than conventional solvents such as isopropanol or other alcohols because it evaporates around three times faster: that means washed screens are dried more quickly, so workers can clean more of them in a given period" (March 12, 2014).

Entering the work, the interactant sits and listens to viewing instructions. A female voice fills the space: "In *Cue China*, there is no speaking to each other and there is almost no instruction to move in fact. Sitting very still for each other is almost all that is required. . . . Keeping still for hours on end is just one aspect to life for many factory workers in China." We continue to hear an overly detailed explanation of the inner workings of the projection apparatus and simulated cinematic *dispositif* (see Figure 7.1), "Because of the angle the glass is at, that reflected image is up over the other person's face. Also up there in the center to one side there are a couple of mirrors, . . . there are areas of light that bounce off the mirrors and light your [the users'] faces. So what you see can be one or the other or a combination. This is why you are being positioned precisely."

The work creates a reflective and reflexive space to expand varying levels of subjectivity that anticipate our staring into these projected, mirrored, reflected,

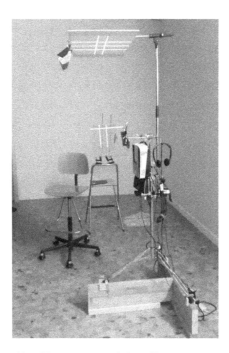

Figure 7.1 *Cue China* (Ant Hampton, 2014). Installation view IDFA 2015. Photo: Tina Bastajian.

and virtual laptop screens, which unfold the uncanny presences from short webcam interviews with factory workers Jia Jing-chuan and Guo Rui-qiang. The voice continues by referring to a set of editorial cinematic conventions that ask the participants to ponder the ramifications of workers' rights, implicating us as users and heightening the notion of the *glocal* and our collective and voracious thirst for faster, better, cheaper technology. "In the show you will be both the same person, when you see the person in front of you, you are looking at the version of yourself in the story. But you also see things from first-person perspective that is to say as usual like now from inside your own head with your own eyes. . . . In the cinema, switching from one to the other like this is apparently called shot counter shot. The footage has been edited and placed within a fiction; anything they say however is translated faithfully."

Hampton demonstrates what Nichols calls an "intensified level of reflection" as he directly confronts the viewer by revealing his working processes as armchair traveler/artist, and at the same time tacitly implicates us all within our shared globalized economy. This becomes particularly clear when he states: "I have been pondering about how we think about victims of globalization and what constitutes presence. . . . I did not travel to China. . . . I've *[sic]* still have never been, the whole process of research, interviews writing, recording and editing was done from my home using an Apple Mac with a shiny screen."[5]

The audio narrative and ludic disciplining found in Hampton's threshold provide more than a backstory or rest period similar to a cut-scene. Instead, we must first pass through a conceptual doorway at once actively and passively reflecting on the stasis and precariousness of workers in China. We enter and pass through a reflexive space that forms a contemplative yet highly compressed narrative.

Preamble: *Planet Galata*—a dramaturgy of units

Planet Galata (2010) is a web-based interactive documentary about the Galata Bridge in Istanbul directed by Berlin-based Florian Thalhofer and Istanbul-based Berke Baş. The project website states, "The Galata Bridge in Istanbul is a cosmos of its own. Between shops, restaurants and inrushes of tourists we meet people for who the bridge is home, hope and purpose in life." Like the crossing of a threshold, viewers enter into this cosmos from a low-angled perspective of a boat traversing under Istanbul's Galata Bridge. The image is split screen and is oriented on the left, while the right side remains black and idle until it becomes activated as the opening credits play out. Meanwhile, one may notice the embedded Korsakow video player has a very small moving play head that users can interact with.

The Korsakow open-source software serves as the basic architecture behind *Planet Galata*'s ecosystem. Such forms of databased narratives made with varying types of platforms utilize short clips, assets or units that "can shift, deviate and diversify as it goes on, according to the choices the audience makes at select points. The results of their choices can be predetermined or randomized, according to the filmmaker's design" (Crossover, 2015). Filmmaker/Korsakow software developer Florian Thalhofer (in co-development with Matt Soar and David Reisch) has implemented these Smallest Narrative Units as integral building blocks to the editing of assets together with their assigned keywords and set behaviors. In a review by Crossover Labs, they briefly describe the logic behind the SNU: "The in-keyword describes the SNU, and an out-keyword matches it to others in the project. Labeling the SNU in this way determines the behavior of the unit in relation to the whole film" (Crossover, 2015). They assist in creating an infinitely modular and random experience, which in some sense would make it difficult (or even impossible) to isolate a fixed and particular set of sequencing.[6]

Planet Galata employs a partially navigable introduction in distinction from other interactive documentary short intro sequences. This is important to note since quite often interactive documentaries utilize strategies similar to film trailer or teaser formats. The late scholar Lisa Kernan has referred to trailers as "both narrative and promotional texts . . . offer film viewers an italicized, alluringly reconfigured narrative space of ellipsis and enigma" (2004, 8). While the short paratextual subtype of the trailer is also extremely relevant, Kernan's definition foregrounds the double logic at work found within most trailers, which, in essence, diverges from my overall thesis and chosen objects of analysis.

Through a very close reading of *Planet Galata*'s introduction, that is to say when left unnavigated, what emerged was a predetermined design and narrative strategy that lie underneath this assembly of SNUs. This revealed a nuanced and reflexive voice on the editorial processes behind the databased structure in which it was created. Given the nature of the complexity of this work, it is necessary to first describe the basic flow of the opening.

Planet Galata's intro continues from the ship gliding under the bridge on the Golden Horn. This image is split screen and oriented on the left side, while the right remains black and idle. The interface of the embedded Korsakow video player, as already mentioned, allows the interactant to see a very small play head moving, and with some resolve, users can forward the video to the end in order to skip the intro altogether. Within the intro, at about the 45-second mark, the left side transitions to an idle black screen and an image of the bridge by day appears on the right, prompted by scrolling text. When the text is rolled over, it puts the still image into motion, and reads, "The Galata Bridge is the strangest bridge I have ever seen. Only few people find it beautiful, but without a doubt she has character." It is at this point that you can navigate away from the intro, as we are first presented with the first social subject, the technical director of the bridge, Ömer Yildiz. The text reads: "The King of the Bridge," as the right screen mirrors the left with the text or tag for this character.

If you were to let the sequence play out, without navigating away, the introduction would remain as a stand-alone sequence starting from the 45-second mark to two minutes. The interplay between the right and left split screens (with distinguishing rollover texts, ambient shots of the bridge, clips briefly identifying various characters, etc.) plays through to a specific end point without navigating away to an active clip. This way, through the diegesis of the threshold, the user/viewer encounters eight primary characters and their corresponding code names (e.g. Ömer/The King, Woman/Something Better, Kemal/Naive, etc.).

The introduction eventually leads the interactant to the culminating section entitled "HAIR" that gives the first appearance of an explicit interaction from the voice of the filmmaker (see Figure 7.2). Turkish turns to German as we hear Thalhofer repeat a conversation with his mother: "There are fabulous barbers in Istanbul, my mother told me on the phone." The right screen is locked, and the introduction that activated the HAIR sequence with the filmmaker and the other customers framed with scissors and razors in action is played out. The left half of the frame (figured below) splits into four sections, and the work continues from there to form varying arrangements of clips depending on the interactant's navigational choices. Through further navigation, the barbershop segment will ultimately be expanded upon as we meet the barbers and customers to hear about the Galata Bridge and other related anecdotes that rhizomatically branch

Figure 7.2 Screen shot interface/haircut *Planet Galata* (Florian Thalhofer and Berke Baş, 2010).

off via the Korsakow engine. The same short clips or SNUs of the intro can be accessed further along at other points of navigation (see Figure 7.3). However, it is through the notion of the intro passage, a crossing, or bridge, to which the threshold further demarcates and accents its assets and by extension, may also reflect upon on the project's reflexive attributes.

Such reflexive cataloging of cities is most notably found in Dziga Vertov's film *Man with a Movie Camera* (1929), which has been called the first film to demonstrate aspects of database logic. Manovich relates the importance of Vertov's work to the later tendency when stating that "Vertov's goal is to seduce us into his way of seeing and thinking, to make us share his excitement, his gradual process of discovery of film's new language. This process of discovery is film's main narrative and it is told through a catalog of discoveries being made" (12). Nichols reinforces Manovich's observation by stating that *Man with a Movie Camera*, as a reflexive documentary, "deconstructs the impression of unimpeded access to reality and invites us to reflect on the process by which this impression is itself constructed through editing" (2010, 196).

Shots similar to Vertov's opus and reflexive signifiers are absent from *Planet Galata*: images that capture the act of a cameraman filming or witnessing the montage process of celluloid running through an analog editing device. However, it is through the assigned behaviors and tagging of SNUs at work, specifically in tandem with the introductory threshold of the video assemblage, that *Planet Galata* offers an oblique angle from which to explore further reflexive impulses within the interactive documentary form.

Figure 7.3 Screen shot interface/alternate view *Planet Galata* (Florian Thalhofer and Berke Baş, 2010).

The introduction suggests a loose blueprint or map for the entire project that consists of these short units formulated through an amalgam of narrative, design, and navigation.

Planet Galata reflects the generative cosmos of the city, bridge, and inhabitants, and the inner cosmos determined by the assigned behaviors of the SNUs. The reflexive impulses found in the introduction drive the dramaturgical interplay, design, and montage creation in this opening catalog of units. That is to say, the varying behaviors attributed to the units; looping of SNUs; sound and textual prompts; active frames; varying interface and split screen configurations; idle black frames; and so forth.

The intro leaves the viewer at the locale of a barbershop in the presence of the cleanly shaven and waxed filmmaker along with the other barbershop customers. While somewhat abstruse, the cut locks of hair remain curiously out of frame, as we see an elliptical process of trimming, combing, grooming, and so on. I can't help be reminded of Vertov's wife Elizaveta Svilova in the editing room, preparing, trimming, and arranging the "cuts."

To a certain extent, the elliptical form of Thalhofer's haircut sequence calls attention to the invisibility of editorial choices, to which the interactant continues their journey with *Planet Galata*. It is within and beyond the intro and the threshold that these small numerical units underscore the city and project's underbelly, to heighten both the combinatorial exhaustion of editorial (algorithmic) choices as well as the vast and unknowable (virtual) database of Istanbul's denizens.

Coda: Traversing adventitious detours

In the concluding passages, I would like to address our working processes (in collaboration with artist Seda Manavoğlu) while developing the interactive documentary *Coffee Deposits:::Topologies of Chance* (2010) by drawing upon the two aforementioned works to reflect upon the intro as a reflexive threshold.

Coffee Deposits is shaped into a hybrid between documentary forms and the ludic, contoured into an interactive environment (i.e., DVD-ROM, web, and installation configurations). Our project's initial intent was to build upon our in situ and mobile Turkish coffee cup reading encounters as a storytelling and divinatory device. The work is set in the environs of public spaces in Istanbul that reflect a multiplicity of layers and movement via extended walks, GPS traces, and documentation—a slow mapping of unpredictable and rapidly shifting urban patterns and diverse stories and accounts by those who inhabit, walk, dwell, witness, work, and protest in the city. *Coffee Deposits* embarks from a short introduction passage to the main interface consisting of seven sections, each with its own distinctive navigational logic: *contours; palimpsest; mediums; pattern recognition; belly of Istanbul; traceuse; and mobile networks* (see Figure 7.4).

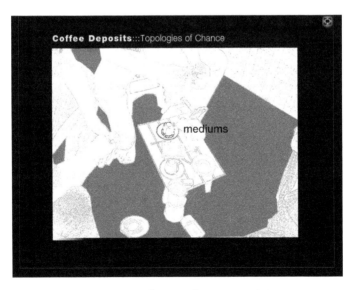

Figure 7.4 Screen shot main interface *Coffee Deposits* (Tina Bastajian and Seda Manavoğlu, 2010). Courtesy of the artists.

The video introduction we created is similar on some basic levels to *Cue China* and *Planet Galata* in that it posits our reflexive working process: contemplative interaction with social actors, modes, and formulations of applied technologies, as well as with cities or locales. *Coffee Deposits*' threshold space punctuates varying and recurring tropes from the larger archive that are distributed into the seven sections. These tropes or narrative units are compressed to convey the ambivalence from our street traversals that ensued to unravel various (cultural, religious, historical, legal, and gender-specific) concerns. It should be noted that we included the option to move the video play head forward and also to *skip intro*, which we rephrased instead as *go to* navigation, in order to collide and underscore both those we encountered and our own immobility in Istanbul, while perhaps foreshadowing the digital journey ahead for our own curious and responsive interactants.

Such decisions during the editing and design process manifested organically with an emphasis on process, and how the ambient mediums (coffee cup readings and GPS/mapping strategies) became a trope in which to negotiate, articulate, and speculate on the multiple viewpoints and disorientations that resonated with the urban flows and subjectivities we encountered.

This is echoed in our short intro triptych that triangulates snippets of a scene from Jean-Luc Godard's *Deux ou Trois Choses que je sais d'Elle [Two or Three Things I knos About Her]* (1967), which depicts in extreme close-up, a swirl of black coffee and bubbles while a philosophical voice-over contemplates the cosmos. This then blurs into the sediments left on a coffee saucer as a self-reflexive voice-over questions the GPS technologies' inability to capture the nuances of our movement and flow of a city, its inhabitants, and other related qualities. A shot of a coffee cup is then turned over until the end of the segment when it is interrupted by a reenacted 2:00 a.m. telephone call between Seda and a local fortune-teller. This threshold space frames, albeit in compression, the ambivalence and mixed messages with regard to exploring the local coffee-fortune trade and the speculative coffee codes and adventitious detours we encountered.

We attempted to create strategies within the interface and narratives to cast an ironic lens toward data visualization, to challenge geo-located vernacular, to problematize the compression of the groundwork in location-based media practices, and to suggest the limits of database documentaries. Our project's archive, similar to *Planet Galata*, consists of perhaps an unknowable and unnavigable terrain in terms of the limit of the database and the inhabitants of Istanbul. This introduction as threshold obliquely addresses and implicates the interactants through a more conceptual passageway similar to *Cue China*, but without the aspects of physicality.

These three distinct modes of interactive documentary introductions (*Cue China*, *Planet Galata*, *Coffee Deposits*) as recounted in the form of written threshold sequences can perhaps evoke and challenge media-makers and interface designers to approach this liminal space differently. I would imagine that future research into such video intros could greatly expand both my limited analysis, as well as survey diverging tendencies found in other intros given the ever-changing interactive documentary form. Nevertheless, using the literary concept of the paratext provided an entrance to explore this somewhat uncharted terrain, as well as to cultivate and refresh the i-Doc lexis. In tandem, by experimenting with innovative reflexive devices and formulations (narrative, navigational, cartographic, textual etc.), short intros to interactive documentaries can engage interactants to reconsider the option to "skip intro" and to step inside these transitory, yet poignant, openings.

Notes

1 See http://i-docs.org/ (accessed April 6, 2016).
2 The term 'SNU' was coined by Heinz Emigholz. More information on SNU's, or smallest numerical units can be found here: http://korsakow.org/learn/faq/#snu (accessed April 6, 2016).
3 *It's a Small World*. 1962. [song]. Lyrics Richard and Robert Sherman. Glendale: Walt Disney Publishers.
4 On the disciplining of the spectator, see Elsaesser (2006).
5 The above transcripts from Ant Hampton's *Cue China* were made from a recording taken with my Android phone during the International Film Festival Amsterdam (2015).
6 For more detailed information on the construction of the Korsakow software, see http://korsakow.org (accessed April 6, 2016) and Soar (2014).

8

The Viewser as Curator: The Online Film Festival Platform

Geli Mademli

Over the last decade there has been a major transformation in the film festival world with regard to the mechanism of the films' outreach. An increasing number of film festivals have decided to explore the potential of digital technologies and build customized video platforms where they upload smaller or larger parts of their annual selection. While the content of the festival can be archived, connected, or distributed, the overall ambience and constellation of an offline festival cannot easily be transposed to the standards of an online environment. Focusing on the time-condensing aspect of the film festivals in particular, this chapter addresses the changing role of the festival curator in the transition from offline to online film festival events, claiming that in the online festival viewer/ users (or viewsers) are more and more often interpellated to perform functions that in traditional film festivals define the curatorial role.

In her book *Film Festivals: From European Geopolitics to Global Cinephilia* (2007) media scholar Marijke de Valck describes the specific temporality of the festival as an "event of short duration, where films are shown in an atmosphere of heightened expectation and festivity" (22). Arguably, any film festival thus provides a condensed and compressed experience in terms of time, space, and content. It is an ephemeral event of limited duration, periodically programmed in a concrete time frame, with a dual scope: to showcase a distillation of recent film production and to bring together different agents involved in distinct stages of production during a short period of time in a local, site-specific environment. Every festival aspires to increase revenues, maximize the facilitation of professional networking, and intensify the overall feeling of exuberant ambience, while minimizing its assets, exhausting venue capacity and compressing more— often simultaneous—activities in the given period. The challenge of film festival curatorship, then, it can be argued, is perhaps primarily a matter of temporality: How does a curator handle a network of simultaneous interactions between viewing subjects and viewed objects in an ephemeral event?

It is a commonplace in film festival jargon to call festival curators programmers. Though the terms curator and programmer are often used interchangeably, especially among peers, the latter term is more often used and perhaps for a good reason. Just as a computer programmer develops the detailed instructions that allow devices to perform their functions, a film festival programmer develops modules that facilitate the operations of different interested parties in the film industry. The primary task of a curator in charge of (a particular subsection of) a film festival is to select, and then efficiently program, the autonomous units of cinematic time in a schedule that brings them together in a meaningful way, often resulting in a complex structure that can be reassembled in multiple ways. In addition, the curator is called upon to act as an intermediary agent, balancing the needs of different groups—from filmmakers and festival audiences, to distributors and benefactors—investing as much in the festival content as in the interpersonal relationships and role conventions that sustain it.

Although it may seem counterintuitive to envisage such a lively social event, like a film festival, migrated to the online realm, this move makes much more sense when taking into account the event's compact and modular nature. Film festivals entered a new era in 2005, when DivX Inc. announced the launch of the first online film festival under the name Green Cine.[1] The company, which at the time provided the most widely diffused video compression technologies, planned and promoted a festival whose program was linked to the extensive roster of an online DVD rental service of the same name that counted more than 35,000 titles and 9,000 titles of video-on-demand. The audiences were not only allowed, but even encouraged, to download the finalists' films in high fidelity through a secure channel, albeit within a limited time window. Each download from a different IP address was counted as a vote for the audience award. Now fully automated, the films could hence only reach competition standards after an act of data transfer from one computer system to another. It is no coincidence that compression was the main commercial service that DivX Inc. first introduced to this platform. Since then, compression has become a modality for online film festivals.

Green Cine Festival stopped operating in 2015 due to financial complications, but within the decade of its existence, it had already left an important legacy in the film festival world, as different agents (from directors and film buffs to producers and cultural institutions, from individual film professionals and independent companies to teachers and students) had become poised to fully deploy the potential of Web 2.0 to connect different remote users and provide access to undifferentiated content. Various individual viewers grew the habit of using online film festival platforms (such as Festival Scope) as tools to broaden their knowledge of emergent, state-of-the-art filmmaking worldwide, to spot new talents, and to exchange expertise and insights among peers. Green Cine's initiative was thus an important milestone in the online festival's development, but it can be argued that the ground was already fertile for change.

In the transition of film festivals to online platforms, the parties involved in festival networks were called to confront the cinematic's changing site, and to question whether they would interpret the traversal from online to offline (and back) as an undesirable dichotomy that would force them to make radical choices, or as a challenge that would enable new, hybrid media practice. Major institutions like the Sundance Institute and the Tribeca Film Festival made the deliberate choice to start exploring the possibilities of streaming and festival-on-demand at an early stage, with the "personal user" and his or her perspective in mind. In addition to content streaming, these festivals, and soon others also, began to add parallel features in their program, with the aim of building a model of remote participation of both filmmakers and audiences to be incorporated in the local festival event. The resulting Tribeca's Filmmaker Feed (a "button" designed to aggregate various social media of specific filmmakers) and Tribeca Q&A (an open online forum that enables remote audiences to pose questions that emulate the typical interview sessions following festival screenings) are features that enable direct communication between home viewers and filmmakers without the interference of a host, expert, or curator. As Chuck Tryon has noted, these developments, indeed, "reinforce the idea that the festival is no longer tied to a geographical space but is, instead, a global phenomenon, one that invites everyone with internet access to participate" (2013, 162).

How do these developments, then, affect the role of (and meaning given to the term) curator within this era of the film festival enriched, and at times even replaced with, online activity? In her comprehensive essay on the practice of film curatorship in the digital age, film scholar and programmer Roya Rastegar (2012) elaborates on the downside of accessibility and participation. The main challenge for the curator in film festivals, besides his or her own impending disposability, Rastegar argues, is the issue of abundance. As digital technologies have permitted greater access to the networks and means of film production, thus arguably democratizing the system, the ensuing rapid growth of filmmaking activity has resulted in a growing number of films created, disproportionate to the number of the films that can be catalogued and streamed, in both traditional analog and digital, online and offline channels.

In Rastegar's view, the result is what she calls a *curatorial crisis*, by which she refers, with some urgency, to the impossible task curators see themselves confronted with, of having to at once *filter* the enormous body of production, and account for increasingly more knowing and fragmented audiences with progressively more complex infrastructures of collection and exhibition, both online and offline.

The emergence and thriving of online film festival platforms today can be interpreted as a side-effect of, and possibly a solution to, this curatorial crisis, invoked by the abundance of moving image production, resulting from a plethora of available digital resources.

Where the curatorial practices of selection in film festivals are largely invested with (and subjected to) what de Valck calls a "dogma of discovery" (2007, 20), the view(s)er in the online environment of a festival platform is similarly invested with a discourse of navigation and exploration, in a network of interwoven peers that appears egalitarian and fluent.[2] As each view(s)er applies his or her own customized practices of outlining categories (using simple tools like bookmarks and folders), and documenting (using feed buttons and screenshots), now made possible on every desktop, a classification emerges that enables multiplicity and difference, thus lacking the strong sense of liability to which the traditional role of the film festival's curator subscribes.

Online festival platforms interpellate their users by prompting them to sign up, login, post, share, comment, in total compliance with the principles of media convergence.[3] Though their technology is often developed around user experience, the personalized tools provided by the online search engines do not primarily aim to present individual profiles, but, rather, strive to disseminate visual information among an abstract online community, thus moving data analytics and numerics a step forward. The modalities of interacting with these websites are based on the amplification of personal choices and voices by way of user-ratings and comments. By introducing these multiple channels for choosing, sorting out, uploading, downloading, evaluating, and analyzing video content, the user's engagement with these websites, I would like to argue, assimilates the status of curatorship, albeit of a different—more personalized, and yet still strongly interpellated—kind. Transposed into the fluid and hybrid environment of the online festival platform, moreover, the premediated circulation of film material seems to undergo a dynamical transformation when compared to the traditional film festival's programming schemes. Transformation now happens with each single "refresh" action, carried out by a multitude of individual users and facilitated by the technological apparatuses that are personalized-by-design.

Filmmakers seem to comprehend the potential of these platforms as regular exhibition spaces, allowing them to circumvent the established curatorial authority that pervades the process of collection and circulation in offline festival environments. Moreover, the network of professionals that mediate between the film and its audiences (or, if you will, between the various parties involved in the chain of production, distribution, and exhibition, itself undergoing a significant transformation) seems to be replaced in online festival platforms, at least in part, by network technology. Within this network structure, the exposure and potential distribution of a filmmaker's work no longer seems to be (solely) dependent on the expertise and filtering acts of an individual human being, that is, the festival curator, but is an outcome of a chain of computerized actions in which both humans and technology partake.

A case that helps exemplify these mechanisms internal to the mixed reality of the curatorial praxis in online film festivals is the well-known Canadian National Screen Institute (NSI)'s online Film Festival,[4] an event that no longer is defined by a limited calendar period, local venues, and the physical presence of both material infrastructures and people (filmmakers, curators, audiences, etc.). The festival was initiated in 2009 and is part of a vast array of cultural activities supported by the NSI, one of the largest cultural institutions in North America. It unfolds on a year-round basis and comprises a selection of Canadian films that can be submitted to compete for an award throughout the year. A different jury is appointed every three months. By expanding the duration of the festival indefinitely, and enabling a different structure of reward, the NSI Festival challenges the ephemeral aspect of the traditional festival event. It also undermines the customary programming scheme by enhancing its modularity, allowing films to be viewed as stand-alones to be watched singularly and not as part of a program slot that is redeemed in a ticket value (a permission, the critical reader might be inclined to add, clearly ingrained by the prospect of the user's unremitting impulse to click on). In a string of curatorial gestures afforded by the platform system, the user is invited to condense and systematize its otherwise dispersed content, in acts of clicking, posting, sharing, and so on.

Perhaps not coincidentally, from the point of view of the overall theme of this book, the submission guidelines of the NSI Film Festival (which is nowhere identified as a *short* film festival) reads: "We're not looking for any particular 'type' of film"; however, "the film must be less than 30 minutes (the shorter the better)," while it is "imperative" for the film to be available on YouTube or Vimeo. The implications of this statement are threefold. First, it positions the platform's filtering mechanism in relation to massive online video resources such as YouTube. Second, it exposes the "big data" logic behind these filtering mechanisms, where "the shorter the better" is first and foremost suggestive of a quantification of data that increases disposability (on/off), making the process of filtering easier and, certainly, less humane. Third, what is perhaps most interesting within the present context is that the website's precondition of brevity in place here, seems to be more important than the thematic clustering and contextualization of filmic content that demands the expertise of the curator's "handpicking."

The fact that online film festival platforms like the NSI on the one hand try to keep themselves distinct from massive video platforms like YouTube, but on the other hand derive from, share, and filter their content, highlights the ambiguous nature of their curatorial process. Like YouTube and other massive websites that feature an abundance of videos, the NSI site interpellates the view(s)er, not by framing the content of the visual material with semantics, but by building habits based on the quantification of data and calculative informatics. For example, the home page of YouTube is an apposition of "recommendations" that are based on numerical comparisons: What was mostly watched in the last couple of hours? What did people with similar viewing profiles to yours select to watch in the course of time? Thus, under the pretext of the personal user owning his own channel lies what Wendy Chun (2011) calls a "programmed vision," a vision that Chun writes "shamelessly use[s] shifters—pronouns like 'my' and 'you' that address you, and everyone else, as a subject" (67; italics in text).

In a wide spectrum of software-based online and offline activity, and of quotidian explorations of the web associated with data mining and commercial exploitation, the diagrammatic possibilities opening for curatorship in the fluid space of the online film festival—a hybrid reality of sorts—are yet to be studied. The question is, however, what kind of curatorship we are talking about: the curator as programmer or the program as curator?

Notes

1 For more information on DivX Inc. initiative, see their press release. Available at: http://files.shareholder.com/downloads/DIVX/0x0x51344/b6254f83-b495-4506-bb2f-009ec7f2c78f/DIVX_News_2005_6_1_General.pdf (accessed May 18, 2016).

2 For an elaborate analysis of the link between curatorial practices and larger discourses, see Rampley (2005).

3 A key term in Rastegar, interpellation (Althusser 1977) makes an indirect reference to Marxist (film) theory and its critique of institutions embodying ideologies, which she applies to the festival institutions. Film festivals, she argues, interpellate individual viewers to enter ready-made schemas and predetermined collective experiences. As mediator of (and subject to) this interpellation, the curator of film festivals, Rastegar attests, needs to acknowledge the importance of her mission and to justify her choices, "accounting for the specificity of these audiences [which] reveals the culturally defined categories driving film selection and production and, consequently, film culture" (2010, 310–11).

4 Available at: http://www.nsi-canada.ca/film-festival (accessed May 18, 2016).

Part Three

[Compressed]
Pleasure & Productivity

9

The Contingent Spectator

Francesco Casetti

In 1907, the Italian writer Giovanni Papini listed a series of key characteristics that identified cinema and that made it worthy of philosophical investigations. Among these characteristics, compactness is the first to be mentioned. He writes:

Compared to live theatre—which it partially intends to replace—motion pictures have the advantage of being a shorter event, less tiring and less expensive, and therefore they require less time, less effort and less money. (1907, 1)

This is particularly important because it illustrates cinema's strong links with its times. According to Papini:

One of the characteristics that is becoming increasingly central to modern life is a tendency to save money, not because of fatigue or miserliness—on the contrary, people today produce more and are wealthier—but rather because with the same amount of time, effort, and money, one can obtain more. The cinema satisfies all of these tendencies towards thrift at once. (ibid.)

Modern civilization is underpinned by calculations, and film provides excellent solutions. Papini also defined the links of cinema to its broader context in noting how it responded to new needs in the media landscape as well: its features, including compactness, make it more effective than not only theater but also daily newspapers or illustrated magazines.

Newspapers describe events shortly after they occur but without the images; magazines provide the images but they are motionless and fixed in space, while motion pictures show us the pictures captured on film while they are happening. (ibid.)

Finally, cinema permeates the new modes of urban life:

> [Film Theatres], with their invasive lighting, with their grandiose triple colour posters replaced every day, the raucous arias ringing out from their phonographs, the weary announcements by red-uniformed boys, are now invading the main streets, closing down the cafés, opening up to replace the halls of well-known restaurants or billiard rooms. (ibid.)

Papini's argument overturns the usual approach to cinema. While it is important to analyze the kind of world that film depicts on the screen, it is even more important to understand the kind of world in which film operates. Context—whether modern civilization, the media landscape, or urban space—reveals the reasons why the audience leans toward one product instead of another: it discloses the symbolic values that turn out to be most appealing and the type of experience that spectators are looking for. If we want to understand the nature of cinema, we must adopt an *environmental approach*.

It may be useful to recall Papini if we want to investigate the current forms of compactness—the ones that film is rediscovering after its long association with "theatrical" media. The relocation of cinema into new spaces and onto new platforms gives it new opportunities, and short forms flourish. In what sort of environments (cultural, technological, spatial) are these forms located? What kind of "economy"—if there is one—do they respond to? And what sort of values related to spectators' experience do they address and articulate?

I want to begin by turning to the internet, in order to enumerate some of the compact forms that we frequently find there. First of all, we find the prolongation of already well-established products. Vimeo is full of short films made by apprentice filmmakers, mostly students still attending film schools. Here we have the persistence of a tradition: the short film is the first step in a professional career leading toward feature films. Watching these products is a process of looking through a kind of archive or database in which we can discover potential talents.

More interesting is the reworking of traditional formats. Here we move toward less traditional domains. "Faked trailers" can help us in our exploration. Some years ago, *Brokeback to the Future* by Gillian Smith (a mash-up of *Back to the Future* and *Brokeback Mountain*, reworking in two minutes and twelve seconds the plot of the former as though it were the story told by the latter)[1] and *The Shining Recut* by Robert Ryang (a one minute and twenty-four second spoof of Kubrick's film, transforming it into a family comedy)[2] made this genre popular. By mocking "serious" movies, they elicited a playful form of viewing far removed from any "religious" relationship with cinema, indicating that spectators were interested in discovering new forms of enjoyment.[3]

Following the success of these early cases, today we can find on YouTube hundreds of these short films aimed at disrupting the meaning—and the reputation—of a movie through a reediting of its trailer. The kind of experience they offer is in line with their predecessors, but it is also demarcated by more specific elements. In particular, we find the presence of well-defined subgenres. One of them is the so-called "honest trailer," characterized by a voice-over that makes fun of the advertised movie, listing all of its defects. The "honest trailers" follow a very standardized format: all use the same type of voice and the same sequencing of images. Consequently, the viewing experience is expected to be strongly formulaic. The fact that "honest trailers" are generally hosted by a specialized YouTube channel, *Screen Junkies*, reinforces this character.[4] And yet there is a clear element of attraction: "honest trailers" are most appreciated when they are most verbally aggressive. What makes these films fun is the hyperbolic character of the commentary. The filmmaker's execution matters less.

Similarly, but marked by contrary qualities, there are the so-called "sweded trailers." This term describes "the summarized recreation of popular pop-culture films using limited budgets and a camcorder" and finds its origin in an episode in Michel Gondry's *Be Kind Rewind*.[5] Here the constraints are even stricter: the filmmaker must remake the original trailers shot by shot, using whatever actor, prop, or setting she wants, but meticulously reproducing the position of actors into the frame, the type of actions they perform, the shape of the landscape in which they move, etc. Every single frame is perfectly duplicated by different means, resulting in a product that is both like and unlike the original trailer. These constrictions, because they are so engaging and detailed, elicit a form of evaluation opposite to the one carried out in respect to the "honest trailers": what spectators appreciate here is precisely the filmmaker's performance, more than anything else. Not by chance, the "sweded trailers" usually end with a link to a "Behind the scenes" video with some information on the swede-making and to a "Side by Side Comparison" in which the original runs on a split screen in parallel with its remake. Something akin to the "bonus content" of the usual DVDs, these provide further evidence of the filmmakers' bravura and bravery. The "sweded trailers" too are generally hosted by a specialized YouTube channel, *Dumb Drum*, and some franchises, like *Star Wars*, are more popular than others.[6]

A third subgenre of faked trailers is composed of trailers for nonexistent movies. There is a wide range, but one website, *Trailer Wars*, offers a regularly updated collection of them, and at the same time promotes their production through an annual award, public debates, etc.[7] The quality of these products is quite low: they are openly amateurish works, based on a coarse irony, with poor images and a voice recounting implausible stories. Among others, we find *Ben-Her* ("Moses becomes romantically entangled with his artificially intelligent burning bush")[8] and *Apukalypse now* ("An entire city is food poisoned on Thanksgiving, forcing one brave doctor to battle his way through the sick to his loved ones").[9] And yet these faked trailers are highly representative of the grassroots production that feeds most of our social networks.

Beyond the faked trailer, another compact format worthy of interest is the film excerpt. Spectators make a selection of passages from one of their favorite movies and post it online. What results is both a personal scrapbook and a promo: not by chance, comments by viewers generally refer either to the beauty or appropriateness of the selection, or to a previous experience of the same film in a movie theater. The practice of extracting what is considered the best from a whole is closely tied with the modes of spectatorship facilitated by VHS or DVD, which allow a viewer to linger on some sequences and to skip others.[10] At the same time, this practice recalls the early "anthologies" of Greek and Latin cultures, with their Garlands and Florilegia aimed at establishing a "canon." This practice also endorses the idea that a narrative is always "elastic": it can be condensed or expanded according to the needs of the storyteller and her audience.[11] Consequently, the compiler here plays a threefold role: she is a contemporary spectator who ideally moves back and forth through a movie; she is a sort of critic who expresses an evaluation through her choices; and she is a magician who tries to preserve the pleasure of the entire film in five-to-ten minute shorts.

The last category I want to mention allows for what might be called a "voluntary compactness." Every video online has a bar below it where the user can check how far the movie has progressed; with the cursor, it is possible to move the arrow forward and to shorten the time of the presentation, while still being able to see the sequence of frames. The viewer is in the paradoxical situation of missing large portions of a movie, but at the same time still having an idea of its visual content. A movie "becomes" shorter in the act of viewing; it shrinks, without any cut (also see Neta Alexander's piece on "Speed Watching" in Chapter 10).

Of course, there are many other kinds of compactness; the ones I have focused on here help us to understand the "where" and the "why" of the current short films. The general context in which these examples exist is the contemporary audiovisual sphere, characterized by a multiplicity of platforms, an overlapping of genres and formats, multi- and trans-media production, a hypertrophy of products, and a global reach. Within this context, a particular kind of spectatorial attention develops. What matters is capturing the interest of an audience who surf on the net, giving them good reasons to slow down and focus on an object, while still remaining in motion.[12] The goal is to create an experience that we cannot obtain without a certain amount of attentiveness and awareness,[13] but also one that merges concentration and mobility,[14] and consequently preserves the pleasure of the never-ending deterritorialization and reterritorialization that marks a rhizomatic field.[15]

Compact forms offer a good response to this new "attention economy." First of all, they rearticulate the general context into more exclusive niches aimed at accommodating spectators' specific needs. For example, Vimeo—whose access often requires a password—works as a sort of portfolio in which a filmmaker can pile her work for a spectator eager to be informed and ready to render a verdict. "Honest trailers" create a more formulaic niche, in which spectators enjoy only exaggeration. "Sweded trailers" offer a wider space for critical appreciation and aesthetic pleasure, because spectators can retrace the productive process and can compare the remake with the original. Trailers of nonexistent movies create a sort of wild space, that, nevertheless—as the presentation of *Trailer Wars* website underlines[16]—brings together the pseudo-professional and the recreational, the local and the global, the virtual and the actual, as is typical of many environments created by the internet. Film excerpts offer a more personal space, in which personal taste, critical appreciation, and public advertisement merge. Finally, voluntary compactness represents a totally contingent space that is generated by the new practices of viewing.

Second, our examples display characteristics that help spectators incorporate a stop-and-go movement into their viewing. They possess a *lightness* that gives the spectator a sense of freedom: to linger does not imply an absorbing halt, and engagement does not imply a concerted effort.[17] The kind of enjoyment provided by faked trailers, with their desacralization of film spectatorship, is an example of such lightness. Their compact forms are also immediately *identifiable*: indeed, they inscribe within themselves all the signals that lead spectators to recognize their genre or subgenre, their scope, and their range. To identify here does not mean to appropriate; spectators are not requested to go in depth. What they do is not so much to "read" a movie as to "grasp" it. The formulaic mode of viewing triggered by "honest trailers" or by "sweded trailers" exemplifies this condition. Furthermore, the short films that we have encountered display a sort of *proximity*: if on the one hand they refer to cinema, on the other hand they belong more to the everyday, with its empty moments, sparks of curiosity, spaces of relaxation, and small pleasures. The way in which excerpts and voluntary compactness incorporate the current practices of film consumption outside the movie theater is a good example of this proximity. Finally, compact forms are characterized by a sort of *conversion*: spectators often are also producers. This is especially true for fan communities: here one role easily switches to another, hence the presence of a set of rules that everybody is aware of.

Third, our examples develop a particular form of intensification of experience. An experience emerges when a subject is taken by the events that she faces; unawareness is concurrent with a state of inexperience. The compact forms that I have briefly examined try not only to capture but also to enhance spectators' attention: brevity favors both the availability and the concentration of the viewers, and gives room for their awareness.[18] And yet this intensification of the experience never entails the immersion that we enjoy in a movie theater: we linger on a moving image, but we do not let it take possession of us. What we do is something else: we test ourselves, we develop some new skills, and we advance our adaptation to more sophisticated technological environments, expanding our field of action.[19] In this sense, the experiential intensification offered by these compact forms is a form of training: compressed forms are an exercise for our eyes.

Specialized niches, features that allow spectators to slow down without ceasing movement, and an experience that merges pleasure and training—compact cinematic forms respond to the current media landscape and fit the current "attention economy" in their own particular way. Far from being marginal entities, they contribute to the whole picture—and to our awareness of it.

Notes

1 *Brokeback to the Future.* Available at: https://www.youtube.com/watch?v=8uwuLxrv8jY. Uploaded on February 1, 2006 by Gillian Smith (accessed December 21, 2015).

2 *The Shining Recut, HD.* Available at: https://www.youtube.com/
watch?v=6s40Q6ODSI8. Uploaded on September 8, 2012 by
TheLateGrahamChapman (accessed December 21, 2015).

3 Jonathan Gray acutely states that the goal of this kind of products is to "intensify
certain textual experiences, less working against the industry's version of the text
than cutting a personalized path through it" (2010, 20).

4 *Screen Junkies.* Available at: https://www.youtube.com/user/screenjunkies
(accessed December 21, 2015).

5 "In the Michel Gondry film BE KIND REWIND, the character Jerry accidentally
erases the videotapes at Mos Def's rental store, and the pair remake all the movies
themselves. These versions become popular with customers, who are told they take
longer to arrive and cost more because they come from Sweden. Hence, the films
are referred to as 'Sweded'." *Urban Dictionary.* At http://www.urbandictionary.
com/define.php?term=Sweded. Entry by Annestacia on March 16, 2008
(accessed December 21, 2015).

6 See, for example, *Star Wars: The Force Awakens Trailer Sweded*, which reached
963,978 visits in less than a month. Available at: https://www.youtube.com/
watch?v=4fDlPI1vI2A. Uploaded on November 18, 2015 by Dumb Drum
(accessed December 21, 2015).

7 *Trailer Wars!*, URL: www.youtube.com/user/TrailerWars (accessed December
21, 2015).

8 *Ben-Her (Trailer Wars XLIV).* URL: https://www.youtube.com/watch?v=HKGO_
icIIiQ. Uploaded on May 27, 2015 by unravelingsyntax (accessed December 21, 2015).

9 *Apukalypse Now (Trailer Wars XLVI).* Available at: https://www.youtube.com/
watch?v=uubUE5ics14. Uploaded on September 30, 2015 by unravelingsyntax
(accessed December 21, 2015).

10 On this kind of vision and its theoretical implications, see Mulvey (2006).

11 The idea of an "elasticity" of discourse was largely explored in semiotics: see, in
particular the entry "Discours" in Greimas and Courtés (1982; or 1986).

12 On the tension between the need of slowing down and the persistence of what
Virilio calls a trajective, see Joselit (2007). I have discussed this and the following
issues especially in the chapter "Display" in my *The Lumière Galaxy* (2015).

13 On the lack of experience, see Benjamin (1999).

14 Tara McPherson has provided an excellent description of these two components in
her "Reload: Liveness, Mobility, and the Web" (2006).

15 On the process of deterritorialization and reterritorialization, see Deleuze and
Guattari (1977).

16 "*Trailer Wars* is a movie event based in Bellingham, WA, in which local creative
types shoot trailers for non-existent films based on a rotating theme. It's completely

OPEN to anyone." The history of *Trailer Wars* is available at: http://www.
trailerwarsbellingham.org/history/ (accessed December 21, 2015).

17 The idea of "lightness" has been explored by Paola Voci in her brilliant book *China on Video* (2010, 179–87).

18 Leon Gurevitch (2015) speaks of a "subject formation mediated specifically through an understanding of the self situated within a wider audiovisual network of promotional and consumer culture manifested in the screen as spectacle." We can apply his remark to compact forms.

19 On test, adaptation, innervation and field of action [*Spielraum*], see Benjamin (2008 [orig. 1936]).

10

Speed Watching, Efficiency, and the New Temporalities of Digital Spectatorship

Neta Alexander

To slow down is to die.
> —Tim Blackmore, "The Speed Death of the Eye" (2007, 371)

Controlling the projection speed of films was once a life-threatening profession: The highly inflammable nitrate film had to move slowly—but not too slowly—past the burning heat of the arc lamp, and projectionists who tried to meddle with this mechanical apparatus (or simply fell asleep while working) risked burning down both the projection booth and the movie theater. In the early days of cinema, silent films were projected at varying speeds regulated by the theater management, rather than by the filmmakers or production studios (see Brownlow 1980, 164). On May 9, 1908, the *Moving Picture World* warned: "There is no hard and fast rule that can be laid down governing speed. . . . It is as likely as not that the speed should be changed several times in different portions of the same film" (qtd. in Brownlow 1980, 167).

During the silent era, projecting a film at a speed slower than 40 feet per minute was deemed unsafe. This correlation between projection speed, potential danger, and possible death might seem a relic of the pre-digital days of yore. However, by closely studying a new spectatorial mode called "speed watching," this chapter will argue that the specters of the flammable celluloid strip surprisingly morphed into new—and often denied—correlations between the digital apparatus and the fear of dying (manifested and sublimated as a fear of boredom, inefficiency, or slowing down).

In the digital mediascape, the "viewser"—to borrow Dan Harries' amalgam of "viewer" and "user" (2002)—now occupies the place of the projectionist: internet

users can change the narrative tempo not only by using familiar functions like
fast-forward, rewind, or freeze frame (which have existed in different forms since
the 1970s) but also by compressing the cinematic work in unprecedented ways.
The emergence of compressed or compacted cinematic experience created by
"speed watching"—namely, the act of watching online videos at faster playback
speeds than normal—can serve to map the contours of consumption, efficiency,
and storytelling in a cultural and economic climate in which "to slow down is to
die," as Tim Blackmore demonstrates in his study of special effects in Hollywood
(2007, 371).

Streaming websites like YouTube or media players like VLC or Windows Media
Player now offer a feature that enables viewers to adjust the playback speed, from
a crawling 0.25x to a blistering 2x.[1] Assuming there are no connectivity issues, by
watching *Titanic* (1997) at 2x speed, the viewer can consume this 192-minute
epic tale of love and loss in a succinct 81 minutes, and move on to the next
deviant pleasure. This new cult of speed and "compactness" further denies the
reality of digital noise and disruptions—from buffering and limited bandwidth
to battery life and the digital divide[2]—by practicing new temporalities based
on sensory and cognitive endurance. It offers a compacted experience suited
to consumers who often watch films on devices with a battery life of several
hours or less.

The paradoxes of digital speed

Questions of cinematic speed and narrative tempo have been recently the focus
of numerous books, conferences, essays, and a seventy-page-long dossier of
Cinema Journal's Winter 2016 issue, which included various essays approaching
speed "as a property of the diegesis; as an element of film style; as an index of
specific technologies and modes of production; and as a facet of exhibition and
consumption" (Kendall, 116). While this chapter is very much in dialogue with
these essays and reviews, as well as with the works of Blackmore (2007), Timothy
Corrigan (2016), Steven Shaviro (2013), and Peter Wollen (2002), it will focus on
an undertheorized mode of consumption by moving away from the discussion
of "intensified continuity" (Bordwell 2002) or "accelerationist aesthetics"
(Shaviro 2013) as shooting and editing styles, and focusing instead on the gap
between production and consumption. How can we map the affective, ethical,
and libidinal economy that invites the viewer to compress a film in ways that

were never intended or imagined by its makers? And what are the paradoxes, motivations, and specters that inform the nascent mode of speed watching?

These questions can be answered by focusing on the tensions between productivity and procrastination, pleasure and guilt, and attention and distraction, as they manifest themselves in the viewer-generated compact cinematic work. To better understand how speed watching is different from pre-digital spectatorial modes, we should start with the first in a series of paradoxes on which it is based: *While speed watching is a technique supposedly meant to save time, it requires practice, training, and focused attention.*

This compact mode of spectatorship is based on a system of frame skipping, and it is therefore substantially different from earlier modes of time shifting such as the "fast-forward" function on VCR or "skip" function on DVR. In analogue systems, the fast-forward effect was generated by transmitting the frames at a faster rate. As a result, there was an inevitable loss of audio and frame synchronization, and the viewer's ability to follow the fast-forwarded sequence remained extremely limited. With a digital system, on the other hand, only a subset of frames can be included in the accelerated digital stream. An early study of digital video concluded that when playing digital video file in a 1:64 ratio (e.g., showing only one frame out of every 64), most viewers were able to perform adequately on a range of tasks related to narrative and visual understanding (Wildemuth et al. 2003, 221–30).

Aside from the technological differences, speed watching germinates a unique epistemological experience. The choice to fast-forward or skip to the next chapter is often a compromise between the viewer's schedule and the length of the cinematic work. When fast-forwarding a VHS cassette or skipping a segment on a DVD, the spectator is very much aware that he or she has missed something: the knowledge that the film was not viewed in its entirety cannot be ignored or denied. However, since fast-forwarding results in a blurry and imperceptible image, the viewer is not able to know what exactly he or she has missed. This knowledge gap might produce the disturbing Deleuzian notion of "unfinishness": it puts the viewer in a limbo of watching and un-watching.[3]

Speed watching, on the other hand, has a different affective and epistemological economy: it enables the viewer to consume the story and its dramatic events (action scenes, romantic encounters, surprising plot twists, etc.) while maintaining its unity, linear progression, and climax, resulting in the illusion that *nothing went missing*. It is therefore important to note that—due to nascent compression techniques and the fact that streaming software resample or simply skip every other frame—in most cases the dialogue and soundtrack can be easily understood and followed even when the playback speed is twice as fast, while the audio pitch remains very much the same.

This mode of media consumption, however, demands practice. Much like "speed-reading"—a variety of techniques and training programs used to improve one's ability to read as fast as 700 words per minute[4]—and other "time hacking" methods such as "speed running" (e.g., mastering a video game in order to complete all its stages in as little time as humanly possible), speed watching demands time, practice, and human labor. Avid speed watchers must train their eyes and minds to comprehend images and sounds that flash before them.

As Blackmore and various other film scholars have demonstrated, cinematic speed is a historical construct: "What passed for computer speed that made the eye winch in 1982 when Syd Mead's light cycles shot across *Tron*'s mainframe game board is now a laughable dribble of action seen retrospectively with affection by its creators and fans" (Blackmore 2007, 370). In his study of special effects and accelerated editing in Hollywood, Blackmore argues that contemporary blockbusters follow the logic of video games by intentionally creating visual overload resulting in "the speed death of the eye" (370). This "gamification" can also serve as a useful framework for the study of speed watching and the "visual acclimatization" (369) on which it is based. Building on Paul Virilio, Blackmore writes:

> Pushing processor and rendering speed, normalizing gaming vision, and settling the eye into the habit of seeing too much, all are useful in the world of combat where head-up, head-mounted, or helmet-mounted displays have been in use for more than three decades. Films that kill the eye, that possess it so completely, work to prepare the audience, apparently engaged in some form of relaxation or diversion, to look at and respond to yet more computer screens. The nongaming generation may be the last to feel ill when such images possess, rather than "catch," the eye. (371)

The emphasis on generational differences is telling since it touches upon the idea of the "super-user"—the digital native who can easily multitask, browse, text, produce content, and consume information at an unprecedented speed. While speed watching has only recently gained attention in tech blogs and trade press,[5] it is often described as a means for creating a digital *Übermensch*. In a short 2015 *Forbes* article titled "Why I Watch TV Shows and Video at Twice the Speed," for example, a contributor named Jan Rezab describes this spectatorial mode as a form of "time hacking" and explains that "for most of us, time—or lack thereof—seems to be an issue. As an entrepreneur, founder, CEO, and parent, I'm always on the lookout for great ways to squeeze more time out of the day."[6] After watching television shows and full-length features at twice the speed for two years, Rezab insists that his new habit has not reduced his ability to fully comprehend, remember, and enjoy digital content. In fact, he is now a more efficient entrepreneur-founder-parent-CEO.

Following Rezab's how-to piece, speed watching can be interpreted as an attempt to master time, instead of being its subjects. This phenomenon is not inherently digital: think, for example, of Walter Benjamin's beautiful description of Parisian dandies walking the arcades with turtles on a leash to show how rich they are in time, manifesting that they are in no hurry (quoted in Prouty 2009). The speed watcher, however, is the antithesis to the Benjaminian *flâneur*; instead of walking their turtles down the street as a creative manifestation of "conspicuous consumption" (Veblen 1899), speed watchers practice their mastery of time in the privacy of their domestic domain, where no one is looking (except, of course, the algorithm that tirelessly tracks every click of the mouse).

The fact Rezab opens a short essay on media consumption by confessing his need to "squeeze more time" unintentionally reveals the underlying logic of speed watching: it is not a mode of spectatorship and immersion, but rather a solution to the problem of "wasted time." It can therefore be described as a way to transcend the human sensorium by creating a cyborg-like mode of spectatorship: compact cinematics aimed at humans who—much like their machines—never stop, blink, or slow down, in a techno-religious process that is not devoid of mystical or spiritual connotations (Chun 2008, 299–324).

This, however, results in another paradox: *while speed watching endows the viewer with the notion of omnipotence and efficiency, it serves a neoliberal logic of productivity, prolongation of the workday, and the inability to distinguish between labor and leisure.* This might explain why Blackmore concludes his essay with a dystopian prophecy, warning us that there may come a day when the human eye will be deemed too slow, and "films will be downloaded directly to the visual cortex" (371).

A creative attempt to challenge the nascent digital logic of "time hacking" was made in 2003, when the experimental filmmaker Michael Snow reworked his seminal film *Wavelength* (1967) into the DVD WVLNT (*Wavelength for those who don't have the time*). In the updated director's cut, the 45-minute work is reedited as three superimposed 15-minute segments. As described by

Sven Lütticken, Snow's ironic gesture draws attention to the unwritten contract between the artist and the viewer, according to which the work of art should be experienced in a linear, continuous fashion in optimal viewing conditions (whether in the art gallery or the movie theater). Watching *Wavelength*—which consists of a painfully slow zoom movement taking place in an (mostly) empty room—in fifteen minutes foregrounds the trade-off between speed and comprehension. The joke is on us: while we supposedly saved thirty minutes, our ability to fully engage with the work's aesthetics, philosophy, and study of boredom and duration is highly limited due to the superimposed images and their blurry, intangible quality.

Furthermore, WVLNT invites us to form a hierarchy of value when it comes to speed watching: Is it ethical to alter the speed of an avant-garde work or an art-house film whose main subject matter is duration (as, for example, Chantal Akerman's *Jeanne Dielman or* Andy Warhol's *Blow Job*)? Should filmmakers be able to block the option of speed watching their works? And should the "purist" approach to cinema only apply to works elevated to the degree of art, while others—say, Hollywood blockbusters or action films—can give the viewser more freedom?

These distinctions are based on the assumption that digital spectatorship is often a distraction; it provides an on-demand, immediate, and superficial engagement after a long day of work. Despite the different historical, economic, and social contexts, this description is influenced by Benjamin's seminal distinction between the distracted masses and the art lover:

> Distraction and concentration form an antithesis, which may be formulated as follows. A person who concentrates before a work of art is absorbed by it; he enters into the work of art just as, according to legend, a Chinese painter entered his completed painting while beholding it. By contrast, the distracted masses absorb the work of art into themselves. Their waves lap around it; they encompass it with their tide. (2008 [orig. 1936], 39–40)

Following this distinction, it is tempting to criticize speed watchers as distracted, stressed-out masses drowning in the tide of information overload. However, a more productive approach would be to map the uniqueness of speed watching instead of positioning this technique in the lower end of the purist spectrum often implied by cinephiles and film scholars.

Unlike Benjamin's modern masses, viewers are part of an "attention ecology" in which "attention manifests itself as a softer form of power, one that shapes individuals as active participants" (Read 2014). Another paradox of speed watching—and a possible source of its attraction—is that it simultaneously functions as distraction and as a unique form of concentration. Applying Benjamin's definitions, it can be seen as an active form of spectatorship through which the viewer fully absorbs herself in the work of art, as well as a narcissist form of distraction enabling the viewer to absorb the work into herself. While streamed content often plays in the "background" and fulfills a role that is not substantially different from that of radio—namely, providing an audio track for a variety of activities, from texting to emailing, running, or cooking—speed watching demands the viewer's full and complete attention. It therefore holds the potential for a viewing experience that is much more focused and immersive than watching films at their intended speed.

This duality of attention and distraction can help us better understand the different motivations informing speed watching, especially in relation to earlier rituals of spectatorships. In practice, speed watching compresses the film by extending the logic of Hollywood continuity editing *ad absurdum*. It can therefore be understood not only as a means to master time, but also as a way of "hacking" the cinematic narrative. Instead of an imagined "distracted viewer" (or listener) on which the logic of digital compression is based (Sterne 2012), the speed watcher is free to make her own distinction between "signal" and "noise" in a way that turns her into an editor rather than a content consumer. She is therefore invited to cater the film to her own needs and desires. Take, for example, the star system. Within this mode of compact cinematics, the stars function as traffic lights: their appearances are signifiers that tell the viewer when to stop, slow down, or speed ahead. This, however, is not determined by the filmmaker or the studio; each viewer is free to choose his favorite stars and suspend the speed watching experience in order to earn more precious time with the subjects of her admiring gaze. While some actors will function as "noise," others will reclaim their status as the "signal."

At the same time, the source of the attraction is not the star system but rather the ability to transform the cinematic work into information—perhaps even "data"—waiting to be consumed. It is no longer a source of idle pleasure unfolding in a predetermined pace. The third paradox, then, is that—as opposed to early cinema—*the source of attraction is the complete lack of spectacle, and the elimination of the big screen.* Speed watching does not induce the dream-like state of consciousness associated with the darkened movie theater; instead, it is a technique that can only apply to small screens—either on personal computers, mobile devices, or "smart TVs." Much like speed-reading, it is focused on maintaining information rather than simply engulfing oneself in the pleasure of storytelling. Ironically, the attempt to skip frames without missing a thing can result in a new kind of hallucination, as if speed watchers are trying to maximize their efficiency by taking a sip from the psychedelic Kool-Aid Acid Test (a description which also perfectly fits the experience of watching Snow's DVD WVLNT).

Much like the intensified speed of films and video games, speed watching holds pedagogical, therapeutic, and even libidinal potentialities. In "Speed and The Cinema," Peter Wollen suggests that cinematic speed is a source of multiple forms of pleasure. Building on the work of psychoanalyst Michael Balint and his study of "philobats"—thrill-seekers—Wollen argues that chases, races, or other rapidly cut action scenes are "auto-erotic" since they provide the viewer with the thrill of excitement and danger and offer him "unfamiliar situations . . . far removed from the zones of safety and normality" (2002, 265). Following Wollen, Timothy Corrigan describes this encounter as an opportunity for viewers "to adjust to speed as a way to live with a modernist environment" (123).

In the neoliberal environment, however, the libidinal pleasure is less dependent on the eroticism of speed and danger. Instead, it is a result of the viewser's narcissistic illusion that positions him or her as a master of time; a viewser who is capable of "hacking" the system and compressing its products for his or her own needs and desires.

At the same time, speed watching serves to accustom oneself to "Network Time" (Hassan, 2007) and to a fragmented digital temporality based on "smashing the uniform and universal linearity of the clock into a billion different time contexts within the network" (51). According to Robert Hassan, once viewers use the internet, they lose connection to both the natural cyclical time of day and night, and to the industrial clock time. Instead, they immerse themselves in a subjective, fragmented, and liquid "cybertime."

This takes us back to the mechanical projection and its relation to death. What once was an immediate and real potential danger is now a much more subtle and repressed threat of slowness and inefficacy. The threatening aspect could be explained by a triad structure of guilt: we are not doing enough; we are doing too much—but not earning enough; or we are earning enough—but spending too much (or not spending enough). By "cramming" or "hacking" time, viewsers can try to save themselves from becoming irrelevant, unemployed, or extinct.

For a "too-perfect cinema"

Film and media scholars have much to gain from mapping these kinds of digital "imperfect cinemas" (Steyerl 2009) in order to distinguish them from previous techniques and rituals. In her study of the "poor image"—the misspelled or anonymous viral JPEG, video file, or GIF that "has been expelled from the sheltered paradise that cinema seems to have once been"—Hito Steyerl reminds us that these nascent media objects are here to stay:

> The poor image is no longer about the real thing—the originary original. Instead, it is about its own real conditions of existence: about swarm circulation, digital dispersion, fractured and flexible temporalities. It is about defiance and appropriation just as it is about conformism and exploitation. In short: it is about reality.

In a socioeconomic climate pushing for exponential acceleration, speed watching becomes increasingly tempting; its compact experience allures viewers with a seemingly "too-perfect cinema," the gist of the film's aesthetics and sounds combined with the visceral thrill of speed and the promise to eradicate boredom. Like the "poor image," it is not concerned with questions of fidelity, indexicality, or origins. Considering the ubiquity of video games and the intensified continuity offered by Hollywood, it was only a matter of time until speed watchers were born, eager to fit their mediascapes to their new reality.

Notes

1   The ability to change the playback speed and settings was first introduced in the early 2000s, although it initially required downloading video programming software like AviSynth, or using plug-ins like MySpeed™ for YouTube. These early techniques for manipulating the playback speed without changing the audio pitch or the ability to follow the images are described in various tech blogs from the late 2000s. See, for example, "How to Save Time by Watching Videos at Higher Playback Speeds," January 07, 2009. http://www.catonmat.net/BLOG/HOW-TO-SAVE-TIME-BY-WATCHING-VIDEOS-AT-HIGHER-PLAYBACK-SPEEDS/ (accessed February 12, 2016).

2   Due to the limited scope of this chapter, I will not discuss the influence of limited connectivity and "buffering anxiety" on the digital viewing experience. For a study of digital disruptions and what I call "perpetual anxiety," see Alexander (fc. 2017).

3   In his study of "Control Societies," Gilles Deleuze argues that "in disciplinary
     societies you were always starting all over again (as you went from school to
     barracks, from barracks to factory), while in control societies you never finish
     anything—business, training, and military service being coexisting metastable states
     of a single modulation, a sort of universal transmutation" (1990, 179).
4   For an overview of various speed-reading techniques, see, for example, James Camp,
     "Life is Short, Proust is Long," *The New Yorker*, April 1, 2014. http://www.newyorker.
     com/books/page-turner/life-is-short-proust-is-long (accessed February 12, 2016).
5   Many of these posts are short, technical, and anonymous—focusing on
     recommending the best software for speed watching and hailing it as a "time
     hacking" device. See, for example, a 2010 post on the tech blog *Digital Rune*: https://
     www.digitalrune.com/Blog/Post/1779/The-Speed-Watching-Technique (accessed
     February 12, 2016).
6   For the full text, see: http://www.forbes.com/sites/janrezab/2015/04/29/why-i-
     watch-tv-shows-and-movies-at-twice-the-speed/ (accessed February 12, 2016).

11

Visual Pleasure and GIFs[1]

Anna McCarthy

For Ken Sweeney

A GIF (Graphic Interchange Format) is a string of computer code with particular characteristics, although in everyday usage the term describes looped animations, usually samples, formatted to play on a variety of digital platforms. Considered solely as animations, GIFs are fairly rudimentary. Many exist simply to catch your attention, like spinning disks revolving in the wind outside a shop. Others are skillful visual one-liners: a loop of Oprah shaking her head with a caption saying *no, no, no*, or another of Benedict Cumberbatch frowning and saying, *what?*. Users insert these reaction GIFs into the social media stream the way players discard cards in a game of trumps, each time aiming for just the right spot.

And there are many other ways of using GIFs besides these. Some are more psychological than social. There are GIFs intended to bring about certain moods, offering atmospheric experiences of serenity in the form of a fireplace, say, or a waterfall.[2] There are GIFs that offer users guided visualization for slowing the breath. And there are the kinds of GIFs that I want to explore in this chapter. These are ones described, or "tagged," as hypnotic or satisfying, and which seem to identify themselves, in the system of networked objects that hashtagging materializes, as sources of intense visual pleasure.

This is not to say that all GIFs deliver pleasure. Within the realm of social media and online culture, what GIFs share with one another is not affect but rather a particular relationship to the media infrastructures through which they move, via endless small acts of reproduction. We might put it this way: GIFs are gluey.[3] Or, GIFs keep on GIFFing. These are pretty good ways of expressing the GIF aesthetic. Gluey, because GIFs create new meanings in the process of exchange. Their layers accrue, bearing traces of where they have been.

Therein lies the paradoxical temporality of GIFs as pieces of culture. On the one hand, we encounter them in the miniaturized durationality of the looped fragment. On the other, we encounter them unexpectedly, in the indeterminate *durée* that is the flow of social media. If a bound book or roll of printed film signifies some kind of cultural permanence, the mobile, mutable GIF embodies a fugitive temporality. You cannot predict *when* a GIF of a cat playing a musical instrument will appear at the top of your social media "feed," only to disappear once more. All you know is that the image, much like a comet with an erratic orbit, is sure to surface again.

But GIFs are also like zombies and pod people. They may come back, but they're never the same. Something has changed: resolution, aspect ratio, size. Or the image material has become encrusted with memes. The cat is now playing a set of drums as well as a piano. GIFs, you could say, are social from birth, and this is at least partly because they are constantly being reborn. Like reincarnated souls, they are destined for eternal circulation. Part of the enjoyment of GIFs in the context of social media involves observing their constant transformations.

The signature of the GIF format is the malleability of its contents, the GIF's easy transmigration from one platform to another, or from one user to another. The format was developed in the 1980s by CompuServe, an early computer networking service, as a set of standards for compressing image data in the form of a file and transferring it from one user to the other.[4] The ideological glueyness of GIFs lies in the format's modularity and interoperability. Designed to be shared, the GIF was an early, unwitting embodiment of the technocratic paradigm people would later, for a brief moment, call Web 2.0.[5]

Of the many critiques of the ideals that underlay such labels, let me focus on one, as it is small, concise, and repetitive; it's very *giffy*, we might say. It is simply that there is nothing 2.0 about Web 2.0. The history of modular and interoperable design is far older than the internet. It is central to the Industrial Revolution's principle of interchangeable parts. Known as the *American System* in manufacturing, interchangeability was an innovation of the American arms industry in the Colonial Period. The GIF's full name, Graphic Interchange Format, indicates digital industry's embrace of this principle, even if now it goes by other names.

The GIF, small and endlessly looping, a cinematic ubiquity on our daily screens, seems tailored for whatever we decide to call the present era of capital accumulation. If the newspaper and the novel are the key forms of the era Benedict Anderson called print capitalism (1983, 224), then the compact visual form of the

GIF might turn out to be the *locus classicus* of a new cultural economy, one in which value has transferred from the authority of the word to the modularity of content.

What would the implications of this be? Print culture sustained certain ethical principles, ones that at once endowed and acknowledged the power in words. In the profession of journalism, there were codified standards such as "objectivity" or "balance." In the profession of criticism, a robust scholarly print culture had, by the middle of the twentieth century, given the literary word a conceptual purity comparable to the truth that journalism aims to preserve in norms and practices defending against bias. This literary moment thrived on the axiomatic assertion of an indissoluble relation between something called form and something called content. To conceptualize the two as separate entities was a fallacy, even if the separation was only temporary, for the sake of argument or paraphrase.[6]

But those were the Before Times.[7] Such antiquated ways of thinking about content went up the chimney sometime around 1997.[8] GIFs belong to an age in which form and content have parted ways. There is no "form" versus "content" for undergraduates to debate any more, there is simply content—movies, TV, music, also known as the content industries—and the digital infrastructure that stores it, that shuttles it from one place to another, and endeavors to prevent people from accessing it for free.

I might suggest we call this the Content Age, only content is an entirely industrial category. We don't invite friends over to watch some content. There is no gesture for content in charades, no emoticon to signify it on the smartphone's keyboard. In the current moment, when we in the knowledge trade speak of content—and we speak of it freely, incessantly—what we are referring to is not something like "subject matter," welded to form and only perceptible through it. Instead, our usage seems to suggest that content is a substance that adheres to the skeletal information architecture designated by words such as *format*, or *platform*. Form is still in the language, although the concept has been re- or de-formed.

A molecular format, the GIF works in combination with coding language to integrate the content it carries into other formats. As a result, GIFs easily cross the (tenuous, barely visible) work-life boundary. This is especially the case if you work on a computer—if what you do, in other words, is knowledge work. GIFs are part of the infrastructure of web browser systems and instant messaging, they are the spinning disks we look at while we wait for the computer to perform a task. They are the elliptical dots that indicate someone is debating what to say in their text message replying to yours. GIFs are also a small but ubiquitous form of ambient imagery in social space. In NYU's department of Cinema Studies, for example, the staff who use the Keurig coffee maker are treated to a small GIF animation of coffee beans growing on the branch as they wait for their beverage to brew.

Every time I watch the content on the coffee machine, I am reminded that GIFs are part of the internet of things. They are one of the ways the electronic devices that supply our needs also solicit our attention, as audiences for advertising. And this, of course, is also what they do online. GIFs are part of the market research apparatus that monitors our attention as closely as possible. Email promotions rely on web beacons known as *clear GIFs* for user tracking. There are a lot of clear GIFs in your emails.

A clear GIF? The idea is perplexing, because GIFs are things to look *at*, not through. In many of their everyday uses, GIFs exude what Laura Mulvey (1975) once referred to, in relation to the female body in classical narrative cinema, as *to-be-looked-at-ness*. In part this is because, as loops, GIFs always start *in medias res*, so that a certain desire to understand what's going on keeps us looking. GIFs may be short loops, but sometimes it takes several viewings for the viewer to comprehend their subject matter.

This to-be-looked-at-ness of the GIF is comparable to, and continuous with, the to-be-looked-at-ness of the smartphone. Viewing a GIF on the phone can open up new bodily and ocular engagements—squinting, peering, double-taking—that wring indexical effects from the scale of the image itself and, in the case of the smartphone, the object.[9] But unlike Mulvey's narrativized female body, the to-be-looked-at-ness of the smartphone generates more anxiety than desire: in the self-improvement literature on productivity for knowledge workers, *avoid looking at your phone* is one of the first instructions for increasing concentration and focus.[10]

GIFs do not figure prominently in this literature of abstinence. Still, it is hard to imagine that the gurus and life coaches who produce it would approve of their self-managed reader aspirants taking time out from their productivity to watch some GIFs. Perversely, however, I want to suggest that certain kinds of GIFs— the ones that solicit our attention by promising a hypnotic and transformational experience—might have some use value in the toolkit of self-help that beleaguered mental laborers must assemble to make their jobs tolerable.[11]

This is not an idle speculation. Many of these fascinating, satisfied GIFs are scenes of work being performed. They sample and recycle industrial film footage, amassing an archive that includes not only scenes of cunning machines, but also bits from films about industrial crafts, such as glass blowing. To find these GIFs, simply search on the social media blogging website, Tumblr, under the hashtags #satisfying or #hypnotic; a host of writhing instances of perfection will appear on the results screen. Snips of people and machines at work, these hypnotic loops provide vicarious access to the linked sensations of precision, efficiency, and effortlessness associated with a job well done. We see drill bits go in, we see pencils sharpened, we see pineapples being cored and hay bales plopping from the backside of a combine. We see the skill and precision of a joiner, of a potter at the wheel. We see cakes on a conveyor belt sail through a waterfall of icing, again and again and again.

These visual pleasures originate in the spectacle of mass production, but the relationship they bear to our productive capacities is not immediately clear. A few years ago, there appeared in my inbox an email that promised in its subject line "The 100 Most Satisfying GIFs You'll Ever See." When I clicked on the link—how could I not?—I came to the website *College Humor*, which promoted its GIFs as a "brain massage."[12] A *brain massage*? It was interesting to see the language of wellness employed to describe images that were taken, in so many cases, from industrial films. Aggregated and repackaged, these GIFs were, most obviously, click bait; their primary purpose was to lure eyeballs to advertising. But the solicitation, with its promise of something that would alleviate tension, seemed to target me as one particular type of hypothetical user-viewer: the knowledge worker, semi-mobile, often based in the home, or the co-working space, or the café with free wireless. Why would I find such a thing appealing?

The answer may lie in the nature of knowledge work. It is a kind of labor carried out in places most would call safe, and which many make even safer and more private, by listening to audio on headphones. And yet some members of this workforce think of ourselves as personally vulnerable while we carry out our tasks. I'm referring not to physical vulnerability, but rather to a mental susceptibility, to the capacity to be overcome by the powers of chaos and distraction that screen-based work generates. It is a kind of work in which productivity is threatened by its own tools. In the case of mental labor, this means computers, routers, broadband, search engines, so-called social media.

These material things reify two seemingly conflicted paradigms for knowledge work: on the one hand, the computer as an industrial tool, on the other, the computer as an instrument for industrial sabotage.[13] Or, as knowledge workers are trained to think of it, the form of self-sabotage known as procrastination.[14] The friction between these two paradigms has generated countless press articles, books, DVDs, mp3 files, and YouTube videos. There are plug-ins, like Leechblock, that stop you from going online at certain times, or forbid you access to email and all the satisfying GIF invitations it might contain. There are iPhone apps that play binaural beats over new age music into the headphones of the mental laborer, with the idea of "entraining" the brain to generate particular kinds of brainwave frequencies associated with alertness and focus.[15]

All of these defenses against the knowledge worker's capacity to be distracted reflect ways of thinking about and cultivating productivity in the knowledge workplace that are not directly involved in the value-producing process, although they are necessary for its continued reproduction. They are homespun versions of the *wellness* programs corporate workplaces offer to soothe employees' souls and boost productivity simultaneously. Usually administered by human relations subcontractors, these programs showcase the corporation's efforts to recognize employees as persons. They might take the form of workshops on subjects such as elder care, mindfulness, or stress reduction, or simply offer perks like a free lunchtime yoga class or a fifteen-minute massage. Through symbolic gestures of noneconomic remuneration such as these, businesses create the impression that they are investing in the value of their human capital.

Home office denizens and mobile knowledge workers have no formal access to programs of work-life balance. Instead, they must download them. An app called *My Living Desktop*, for example, pushes contemplative imagery onto your computer screen every twenty minutes, imposing a mandatory "serenity break." *My Living Desktop* uses GIFs, but the close association between—let's be frank—GIFs and *free porn*, suggests that consumption of GIFs is more likely to threaten than enhance a worker's productive capacity.

Things could go either way in the case of GIFs that offer us, among other things, the experience of satisfaction.[16] "The 100 Most Satisfying GIFs," in their mesmerizing repetitions and beguiling shortness, present the viewer with moments of perfection. It is satisfying to sit at the screen watching "the beautiful labor of the machine," as James Nasmyth, inventor of the steam hammer, so evocatively put it (quoted in Marx 1976, 563). One GIF, showing a machine that twists pretzels, is particularly satisfying in this regard. Conceivably, these visual bites of things interlocking, twisting, and spinning together are therapeutic. They do for the brain what the nimble-fingered corporate masseuse does for the neck muscles. Although their origins lie in the domain of work, the promise of satisfaction has relocated them, so that now they occupy the therapeutic end of the continuum of sensory and bodily experiences at work. GIFs, such a hypothesis implies, are public material from which people in the knowledge trade create "work-life balance," training themselves to work better.

And that's only the content. There is training in the display format, too. The list of "The 100 Most Satisfying GIFs" distributes its pleasures over twenty pages, five GIFs per page. Like a box of sweets that has been subdivided into small, hundred calorie packets, this structure promotes rationing. And like those same little rationed packets, it challenges the will by demonstrating the availability of a good binge.

A person with disciplined habits might say: I won't have a biscuit with my cup of tea, I'll unwrap the package beforehand, while I wait for the kettle to boil, and I'll eat one, saving the other for later. Similarly, the productive knowledge worker says: *I'll just look at this one page. There are only five GIFs. Then I'll go back to writing my evaluation of someone else's ability to evaluate other people.*

The problem is that the unproductive worker says the same thing (and, indeed, that the disciplined person, before he knows it, has gobbled the whole box). In the unstructured contexts where knowledge work takes place, at any moment the productive worker could become unproductive, especially now that smartphones and other devices seem designed to exploit the distractability inherent in digital culture.[17] This distractability derives, often, from the ways that this culture propagates itself through a continual series of small, barely perceptible failures in connectivity.[18] Minuscule moments of waiting. All it takes is a slow connection: *Only five GIFs? I'll just click on the next page. And while that's loading, I'll look at my email.*

Therein lies the paradoxical temporality of the binge. Time is suspended in the moment of eating, or watching, an effect we seem to forget about when we start.[19] Perhaps this is because a binge usually starts as something else. It might be the need to fill in an odd piece of time, like the time it takes for the kettle to boil. Or it might be a rationed reward: I've marked five papers, so I'll just watch *one* episode of *Doctor Who*. In either case, the binge emerges from the feeling that time must be segmented, even if the experience itself feels like pure flow. Binge watching is the utopian version of Raymond Williams' concept of flow, in that it offers a televisual experience *without* the customary segmentation.

The perennial threat of the binge inhabits "The 100 Most Satisfying GIFs You'll Ever See," and with it, an ambient anxiety. The endless sequences of industrial imagery is a reminder that production—the generation of surplus—is a realm of human activity in which capitalism is never satisfied. What's more, the industrial film GIF taunts the hapless spectator, enmired in multiple tasks, by showing off what a process looks like when executed elegantly. Industrial film GIFs capture that moment in the visual culture of automation when a difficult task is made easy, and not just made to *look* easy. There are no failures, no abandoned first drafts, no embarrassing "reply all" accidents in this looping, exhibitionist domain, there is only visual satisfaction.

It's worth stopping for a moment and asking what, exactly, makes these images *satisfying*. I think it has something to do with the spectacle of immediate mastery, often, of mastery over physical materials with spectacular plastic properties, such as molten glass. But this is a property that is not limited to the industrial film GIF. And, indeed, the "The 100 Most Satisfying GIFs" site also features, albeit in smaller numbers, the enthralling display of craft, and nimble-fingered handiwork. Both are satisfying; the image is indifferent to any difference between human dexterity and the inhumanly accurate motions of full automation.

In this regard, the satisfaction promised by this web page is in line with all capitalist visual culture: it makes a story from the contradictions inherent in the system. The story it tells is, in the end, neither a tale of work, nor of procrastination. "The 100 Most Satisfying GIFs" is a story of reconciliation. Craft and automation can be shown to coexist. Any conflict between these distinct moments in the reification of labor under capital disappears in the solicitations of the image.

This is why "The 100 Most Satisfying GIFs" is such an appropriate form of worker self-care for the knowledge industry. Our "output" is no longer expected to consist of the pure, plastic products of a single mind. We are all supposed to collaborate, in teams, not only with each other, but also with machines—which can mean anything from pasting a link to some other person's work in our online publications, to asking machines to read thousands of novels for us while tracking the frequency of certain words.[20] The point is to override the opposition between automation and skill.

The fluid correspondence of industrial and industrious imagery in "The 100 Most Satisfying GIFs" makes it easy to overlook the secondary connotations of *satisfaction* at play in the giffy appropriation of the image of work. Craftsmanship is an image of satisfaction in the sense of job satisfaction. It is the image of a job well done. Automation renders satisfaction on a scale much larger than the individual task. Its mandate is consumer satisfaction, the maintenance of a supply adequate to demand. The craft image, one might say, is *satisfying*; the automation image, *satisfactory*. Yet, both document the process of transformation that commodities must undergo as part of capital's pursuit and expropriation of surplus, which is itself a process of transformation: unpaid labor transformed into value.

It seems hardly coincidental that these are the explicit conditions under which many in the "content creation" industries must work. Websites like *Medium.com* offer aspiring writers the chance to "grow" their careers by providing a platform in which they create content, for free, to be read largely by each other. If this has anything to do with craft, or apprenticeship, it is closer to the apprenticeship model espoused by reality television star and presidential candidate Donald Trump than to the subversive, crafty work-life of E. P. Thompson's drunken weavers. It's a good thing there are plenty of Donald Trump GIFs out there online to distract us. Until someone develops satisfying imagery to help us visualize what is happening to the labor process in the domain of mental labor, these, and the 100 most satisfying GIFs, will have to suffice.[21]

Notes

1   Some say "jiff," I say "giff," out of respect for the hard *G* in *Graphic*. However, in spoken English, this can cause confusion. People think you are saying the word *gift*. Why this footnote? Pronunciation is the least interesting thing about GIFs, but if you say you are studying them, it's the first thing people ask about.

2   See, for example, the Mac OS app *My Living Desktop* (Amuse, Inc.) For a full discussion of atmospheric GIFs, see Poulaki (2015).

3   Which is to say, GIFs, being gluey, occupy both sides of the distinction between "sticky" and "spreadable" media proposed by Jenkins, Ford, and Green (2013).

4   For an enjoyable and informative account of the GIF format's origins, see Eppink (2014).

5   Eppink (2014, 298). The most well-known critic of Web 2.0 is Jaron Lanier, who attacked the concept in 2006 and mounted an evolved and extended attack on its premises again in 2013.

6   See Jancovich (1993) and Brooks (1947). I am also extrapolating here from Moretti (1993), Krauss (1986), and Delaney (1999). For efforts to overcome the orthodoxy around form and content, see Barthes (1971) and Chatman (1971).

7   I borrow this phrase from Jon Nichols (via Nicholas Sammond, personal communication). I believe it is his original formulation.

8   This is when changes in AOL's pricing structure introduced the word "content provider" into the vocabulary of US business news reporting.

9   See Hesselberth (2014, 35) for a comparable discussion of the close-up.

10 See, for example, Perlow (2013). For an excellent study of the burden of maintaining a work-life balance, see Gregg (2011).

11 For a lovely and evocative description of the experience of durationality and loop spectatorship, see Poulaki (2015, 94).

12 "The ULTIMATE Braingasm Gallery: 100 of the Most Satisfying Gifs You'll Ever See." Posted on September 22, 2014 by Hannah Grant on *College Humor.* Available at: http://www.collegehumor.com/post/6991812/the-ultimate-braingasm-gallery-100-of-the-most-satisfying-gifs-youll-ever-see (accessed April 1, 2016).

13 See Gregg (2011). For an excellent discussion of these issues in relationship to cultural labor, see Lorey (2006).

14 The classic text on procrastination is *The Now Habit* by Neil Fiore (1989). A contemporary "classic" with a title symmetrical to Fiore's is *Do it Tomorrow* by Mark Forster (2007). On writers' use of self-control software, see Ackerman (2012).

15 Binaural Beats Apps are widely available on the Apple store. The authors of a 1998 article in the Elsevier journal *Physiology and Behavior* claim that certain frequencies stimulate attention (Lane et al. 1998). On the popular science end, see Woodward (2015).

16 Satisfaction is among the various positive affects, which, note two neuroscientists in a state of the field essay, are difficult to locate within the stimulus centers of the brain. (Morten and Berridge 2009) Perhaps this is because the experimental set-ups tend to conceptualize pleasure solely in terms of sweetness—the taste of sugar—and treat satisfaction primarily as an element in systems of reward.

17 See Schüll's account in *Addiction by Design* (2012, 13).

18 See Alexander's reflections on buffering (2017).

19 On the relationship between spectatorship, time, and eating, see Hastie (2007) and Holdsworth (2016).

20 This, of course, is the methodology of Moretti's *Distant Reading* (2013), the opposite of close reading.

21 For further discussion, see McCarthy (2016).

12

Solitary Screens: On the Recurrence and Consumption of Images

Pasi Väliaho

On the evening of September 22, 1907, during one of his regular trips to Italy, Sigmund Freud wrote a short letter to his family back in Vienna. The letter begins,

> On the Piazza Colonna behind which I am staying, as you know, several thousand people congregate every night. The evening air is really delicious; in Rome wind is hardly known. Behind the column is a stand for a military band which plays there every night, and on the roof of a house at the other end of the piazza there is a screen on which a *società Italiana* projects lantern slides. (Freud 1992, 261)

So Freud described an early version of modern media spectacles in the public space, which, combining with "awful" electronic advertisements that kept "flashing on and off" in one corner of the piazza, superimposed itself on the historical site. The lantern projections, Freud noted, were in fact mostly advertisements, interspersed, so as to "beguile the public," with "pictures of landscapes, Negroes of the Congo, glacier ascents, and so on." We are familiar with the composition of the audience of this spectacle: an idle crowd, in Freud's words "quiet and rather distinguished," had flocked together, not with the aim of exchanging thoughts, feelings, and opinions, but silently (as Freud repeatedly remarks), almost randomly, one can imagine, under the pull of music and the flashing of photographs of exotic locations, adventures, and commercial messages—indeed, capitalism's "phantasmagoria."

For Freud, the spectacle appeared, nonetheless, as nothing but "boring." The boredom, however, Freud wrote, was "interrupted by short cinematographic performances for the sake of which the old children (your father included) suffer quietly the advertisements and monotonous photographs." The sudden display

of moving images was able to break the monotonicity of the experience, and to
draw Freud, among thousands of other individuals, to its spectacle:

> They are stingy with these tidbits, however, so I have had to look at the same
> thing over and over again. When I turn to go I detect a certain tension in the
> crowd, which makes me look again, and sure enough a new performance has
> begun, and so I stay on. Until 9 p.m. I usually remain spellbound; then I begin to
> feel too lonely in the crowd. (Freud 1992, 261–62)

Here we encounter one of the key existential concerns of the past 150 years:
the tension between the individual (bourgeois) subject and the crowd, between
autonomy and deindividuation in a collective body (see Crary 1999, 367;
Väliaho 2013, 168–71). In Freud's account, cinema came across as a medium
of the masses and its nerves, able to bring about a sense of vitality (a "tension"),
a promise of life's fulfillment. What Freud articulated was the cinema screen's
power to capture our perceptual faculties; its power to keep us "spellbound"; to
affectively bind us to the screen and hence to one another.

Above all, one- or two-minute-long cinematographic performances took
hold of the viewer's attention as a prolonged state of expectation of ever new
stimuli. As the performances ended, one's perceptual focus was released to other
distractions—flickering electric advertisements, newspaper boys shouting—but
the images held the promise of their reappearance in a new guise. This promise,
we can surmise, obliged the spectator to stay put. Freud noted how cinematic
performances triggered a protracted mental state of anticipation, and how they
thus harnessed our mental capacities into capital accumulation through the
repetitive production and consumption of images (cf. Beller 2006).

What this capture of attention as a source of value and an object of discipline
undermined was empty, unproductive time—what Freud indeed characterized
as boredom. If Martin Heidegger (1995, 125–26) was right, boredom is the
experience of "time in its standing," that is to say, of duration as such, which
opens up the possibility of both concentrated reflection and random flights of
thought. In Freud's letter, cinematographic performances appeared as killers of
boredom. They demanded a mental disposition that combined immersion (in
the present moment of the spectacle) and anticipation (of future stimuli). Thus,
they eroded any experience of the presence of the present and empty moments
of reflection—even if only for a short period of time, before Freud in a sense
recovered himself, starting to feel too "lonely" in the crowd, and retreated into
the privacy of his hotel room.

We should note that Freud's letter is not only a testimony of bygone forms of image consumption and experience. Rather, with reference to cinematographic performances on the Roman piazza Freud also articulated one of the key aspects of our contemporary media environments: how media and, in particular, all sorts of screen apparatuses seek to intervene with and occupy the minutest intervals of our activities and existence. The cinema show at Piazza Colonna in 1907 was a step, even if a rather rudimentary one, in the long history of images and apparatuses that capture and organize the conditions and potentials of life, resulting in today's world of excessive, uncontemplative consumption, of public and private environments defined by the gleam of electronic screens, of denigrating social relationships and political cultures, of 24/7 stimulation by media, of short attention spans and their pathologies, and so on. Next, I would like to explore this world in a bit more detail, following the themes articulated by Freud, concerning the economy of attention and repetition of images, and focusing on a location vertically opposite to the piazza in Rome: the London Underground.

∗∗∗

Descending to the London Underground presents a treasure trove to any scholar of contemporary media, and of attention and screens, in particular. If not electronic billboards with moving image contents that greet the traveler on the sides of escalators at some stations, repeating their messages in synchrony with the speed of the escalators rolling up or down, one encounters large-scale advertisements, positioned on the sides of platforms as well as on the walls across the tracks to catch the eyes of people waiting, idle or hurried, for the arrival of the next train. While these advertisements have populated the walls of tube stations for decades—their contents changing in appearance, but not in essence—inside the carriages themselves, things have changed more rapidly. Even if my memory is still able to picture the day when people were able to plunge their heads into printed words only (a friend of mine even recalled the day when there were designated smoking carriages on the tube trains), free copies of *The Evening Standard* and *Metro* now vie with portable screens of various sorts, from mobile phones to "pads," which are operated by touching as much as they are to be gazed at. Surely, while some use these screens just to display digital copies of the old media of newspapers and books, even a series of cursory and discrete glances over fellow commuters' shoulders demonstrates that this is not most often the case. Some take their mobile devices to watch films and television programs, headphones dug deep into their ears (sometimes even laughing audibly, raising thus their fellow passengers' curiosity); others nervously tap their screens with their fingers, playing interactive video games. Some write their emails or text messages offline; others even use their phones to take so-called selfies, as unnoticeably as possible.

What does the Underground thus tell us of our contemporary culture of screens, and of the images that screens embody, display, and circulate? One observes that screen consumption in this location has its own particularities within the general economy of screen-based attention and anticipation—an economy the beginnings of which Freud's letter evidenced. Games, movies, and television episodes are watched in the tube in a periodic fashion with several interruptions: the program is paused when one arrives, say, at Tottenham Court Road and changes from the Northern to the Central line. The hectic pace in the station's crowded and stuffy tunnels doesn't allow walking half-heartedly, partly absorbed in the screen; but once back in a train carriage, the consumption can carry on. What one encounters in the Underground is thus not the mode of concentrated watching of a movie from the beginning to the end historically taught in the movie theater, not even the kind of "pensive spectators" who use the pause button to return to the same privileged moments of the film of their obsession (see Mulvey 2006, 191–92). Nor does the smartphone's or the pad's screen promote the kind of diffused attention that the television does (or used to do), stationed in the living room or the kitchen, often relegated to the background to keep watch of and give rhythm to the daily activities of cooking, eating, chatting, and so on.

The rhythm of screen consumption in the Underground is neither concentrated nor diffused. Instead, it is jerky (very much resembling the tube ride itself in this regard). One's immersion into the viewing or playing experience is repeatedly interrupted by external factors; by someone suddenly pushing you with their elbow; by announcements of stations or of generalized paranoia ("If you see anything suspicious . . ."); by the train suddenly stopping in the tunnel, causing worries about being delayed; by coming to the end point of the journey or having to change lines. But despite all this chopping of the contents by the rhythms of travel, one is compelled to continue watching or playing.

I would like to call this jerky (meaning both interrupted and compulsive) and repetitive, and thus always already prolonged, consumption of images, for want of a better word, "short viewing." By "short" I mean experiences of images that are momentary, abruptly stopping and starting again, as well as recurring. "Short viewing" is a symptom of our times; of technological conditions (the convergence of several media functions into one single portable device), to be sure, but more importantly, of the organization of existential rhythms of urban life. It does, however, have its genealogy—in the kinds of public screen spectacles described by Freud, among other things, and the patterns of repetition of images and protracted anticipation they established.

Like the modes of spectating in the Piazza Colonna in 1907, screen consumption in the Underground is above all a question of the production of subjectivity, of "refrains," to borrow a concept from Félix Guattari (1995, 15–17), that fix individuals to screens: "spellbinding" (to paraphrase Freud) forces that shape an individual existential territory within the tube carriage's physical as well as social space. What kind of an existential territory is screen viewing in the Underground capable of carving? Following the veteran anthropologist Marc Augé's observations about the Parisian Métro, and about the social changes related to the current state of multinational capitalism that Augé calls "supermodernity," one might describe it as a place of relentless solitude. "For such is, really, for those who take it every day, the prosaic definition of the metro: collectivity without festival and solitude without isolation," Augé (2002, 30) writes. In the utterly sanctioned and controlled space-time of rapid transit the traveler remains anonymous; one's eyes are only exceptionally meant to meet those of the fellow traveler; most often such indulgence is met with embarrassment. One is "alone together," caught in curious nodes of noncommittal being-together and sanctioned intimacy. This is a condition, according to Augé, that defines the existential space of (hopefully already quite) late capitalism generally, crystallized by locations such as the airport, the motorway, the refugee camp, which are defined by their transitory character and mediation by various kinds of "signs," from commands ("No smoking"; "No authorized access beyond this point") to advertisements. These, Augé argues, divest the individual from the social relations that previously would root her or him in one particular place and historical time: "The space of non-place creates neither singular identity nor relations; only solitude, and similitude" (Augé 1995, 103).

The purpose of what I have described as short viewing is not to alleviate this solitude, but exactly the opposite: to allow and augment it. While audio devices like Apple iPods and, before them, Sony Walkmen have been affording "accompanied solitude" (Bull 2005) in the public for some time now, this has been recently taken up by all sorts of mobile screens and the eyewash they emit.

Today's screen consumer is a solitary spectator. Short viewing in the tube is not to create a shared social space, but rather to permit the observer to cast her eyes away from the scrutiny of others, and so "hide" herself. It is to *envelop* the individual into a shielded space of interiority and intimacy, which is open to the curiosity of fellow passengers (What is this person watching? Why is she smiling?), but which is essentially impenetrable. Indeed, the primary social function of screen gadgets in the Underground is to block out any chance encounters of eyes, smiles, and gestures of "Hello." Screens are thus meant to afford mastery over the contingency of others—mastery that is epitomized by control over the interactive "touchpad."

It is astonishing how a screen as small as four inches wide can indeed have such a powerful mental effect in creating an invisible psychic "blanket" in which one can wrap oneself up so as to be cut off from the external world. Psychoanalyst François Roustang writes of how our bodies are distinguished by their "personal envelopes." According to Roustang (2000, xiii), the body "would not have any personal envelope if the people around it and the environment had not constantly provided something in which it could wrap itself." Ordinarily, the envelopes that constitute personality are inherently social and "relational": we in principle cannot do without encounters with others, and without fundamental openness to other people's gestures, smiles, and looks. But now it looks like this function of wrapping our personality has, in the context of the Underground at least, been taken up by screens rather than people of real flesh and blood. Hence, the power of screens to cut deep into the intimate core of individuation, and to perform isolation by substituting (at least momentarily) for the relations of dependency that constitute our subjectivity.

***

The solitary spectators of today's mobile screens appear to be diagonally opposed to the kind of affective members of the crowd described in Freud's letter. The constitution of both spectators, to be sure, hinges on abstracted streams of audiovisual material that recur, and by recurring, capture our attentive capacities and create long-lasting states of anticipation. But the key differences between the two modes of spectatorship are existential and political. On one side, we have the momentary loss of oneself in the crowd, an experience of the self becoming extinguished by the flicker of images that gives rise to a collective body; whereas the self can be recuperated in the experience of solitude when retreating into a private (mental) space. On the other side, we have a group of commuters in the tube carriage but no collectivity; the function of screens here is to disconnect people into separate units, or "monads," of consumption. We could describe the social operation of screens in the latter case as paranoid, in the sense of estranging the individual from (contingent) relations and establishing a sense of mastery and control.

The politics of the spectator of mass spectacles is familiar to us, oscillating between communism and fascism, as Walter Benjamin (2008 [orig. 1936]) famously observed. The politics of the solitary spectator may be less familiar. This is not the occasion to expand on this matter, but let me note that the individual who—instead of speaking, laughing, or touching—rather seeks to avoid the other, is an individual welcomed by current militarist, neoliberal regimes of the West. This is the comfortable and indeed acceptable madness of the solitary spectator: to conform to the primary mode of being of our "post-democratic" societies where any promise of being-together has been overcome by fearful individuals suspicious of contact, and where human eyes and touch have been replaced by "touchpads" and "likes."

Part Four

[Miniature]
Mobile Cinematics

13

Archaeology of Mobile Film: Blink, Bluevend, and the Pocket Shorts

Kim Louise Walden

Introduction

Watching film on tablets and mobile phones is now commonplace but just over a decade ago, such experiences were still just an aspiration. In 2002, Nokia ran a "Future Applications" advertisement featuring a woman sitting on a bus, watching a horror film on her phone. As she watches, she gets more and more agitated, until in the end she lets out a scream and the ad ends with the tag line "One day you'll be able to watch videos on your mobiles."

Following its predecessors—cinema, television, and computers—what became known as the "fourth screen" is now an established feature of the contemporary media ecology (Miller 2014, 210). But the earliest mobile media services took the form of TV show extracts, UK Premiere League football match highlights, and film featurettes. Among them was Fox TV's *24: Conspiracy* in 2005, which was a spin-off from the successful TV series consisting of 24-minute-long "mobisodes™"—a term trademarked by News Corporation to describe a serial mode of programming designed specifically for the mobile phone (Clarke 2013, 116). Mobile film festivals began to emerge such as Pocket Cinema at the San Francisco International Film Festival, Pixelache in Helsinki, and the Mobifest in Toronto, while notable filmmakers such as Shane Meadows and Sally Potter experimented with making films for viewing on phones. Looking back, much of this early mobile media looks rather rudimentary, but I suggest that these prototypes should not be just consigned to a footnote in the history of moving image culture as they are incunabula of prevailing cinematic formats today, and reflecting on them may throw light on the genealogy of contemporary digital film culture.

To investigate the first generation of mobile films made for the "fourth screen," this chapter proposes to take a media-archaeological approach. Building on the work of Friedrich Kittler (1999) and Michel Foucault (1989 [orig. 1969]) in recent years, archaeological ways of thinking about media have gained traction with those interested in how the past informs the present and, depending on who you read, vice versa. Jussi Parikka has argued that although the discipline of archaeology emerged out of a nineteenth-century interest in antiquarianism, its focus on materiality provides a promising way for contemporary media culture to come to understand itself at a time when technologies are developing at such pace (2015, 8). Moreover, as the media archaeologist Wolfgang Ernst observed, while media are often used to access historical evidence and think about the past, media technologies themselves may well be overlooked as material evidence of the past (2013, 6). As a method of enquiry into the past, Ernst proposes an examination of mechanisms to gain a clearer sense of how media aesthetics are shaped technologies (2013, 17). In the light of this, the chapter will begin by examining the affordances of third generation phones, which became available around 2005, with the promise of providing a platform for not only viewing audiovisual media, but for making films as well.

Third generation mobile phones

Following government auctions across Europe of third generation spectrum licenses in 2000, a new standard known as the Universal Mobile Telecommunications Service (UMTS) came into operation, which expanded bandwidth and improved network operation. UMTS would enable mobile telephony to deliver the kinds of services that hitherto had been restricted to landlines. With the aim of recouping investment in licenses and upgrading the network infrastructure, telecoms companies "rolled out" 3G services and set out to market a new generation of mobile handsets that would provide high-speed internet connection, email access, and most importantly, on-demand media entertainment by 2005 (Ofcom 2004, 22).

Of all the mobile phone manufacturers competing for their share of the market, Nokia was notable for the promotional strategy of its "N" mobile phone series. It sponsored an award at the British Independent Film awards for the "Best British Short Film" (Lights, Camera, Action 2003). It set up the Nokia Shorts competition in collaboration with the Raindance Film Festival in London accompanied by an online "Mobifilm Academy" providing advice on how to make films on mobile phones. Entries were limited to fifteen seconds duration and a shortlist of the best, chosen by a panel comprising industry experts, were screened at the Raindance Film Festival and on the Nokia website (Mobile Film Makers 2006). Clearly, Nokia saw commercial potential in promoting links between mobile phones and film (Lights, Camera, Action 2003).

Launched in 2005, the Nokia N70 was one of a series of 3G multimedia phones. Its screen was approximately 5 cm by 5 cm and it shared the phone's Interface with a number keypad. Screen size determines the way any display material may be seen. In the theatrical setting of a cinema, audiences look up at vast images projected onto a screen. By contrast, to view a film on a mobile phone, they must "peer" down into the device and look away from their immediate surroundings in order to focus on the small screen (Richardson 2005).[1] In this regard the mobile screen does not command the audience's attention in the way that a cinema screen does. Rather than a physical act of concentration, first and foremost, the mobile phone seems to demand a cognitive act of concentration.

Since then, mobile phones have become smaller and their screens have become larger. This is indicative of the shift from "traditional voice services" to visually based modes of communication and entertainment (Ofcom 2004, 9). This shift is evident in a number of defining changes in the design of screen technologies. The first generation of mobile telephone screens had favored a vertical aspect ratio, more commonly known as "portrait" mode, whereas on 3G phones, a "full screen viewing mode" with wide screen aspect ratio, known as "landscape" mode, became possible, reminiscent of the conventional letterbox ratio of cinema screens. The change of screen size and aspect ratio invited a move away from solitary modes of viewing (for a reflection on the "solitary screen," see Chapter 12). 3G phones like the Nokia N70 incorporated the same liquid crystal display (LCD) screen technology used in televisions. This made possible wide angle viewing with no distortion, enabling phone-based entertainments to become shared experiences.

The auditory features of the phone invited new forms of attention, too. At this time, mobile phone audio features worked in three different ways: through the phone's speakers; through ear plugs; and through loudspeaker mode for different situations. While the speakers and ear plugs are standard phone features, the introduction of the "loudspeaker" mode would seem to indicate again that mobile phone activity increasingly takes place *in front of* the phone rather than *through it,* confirming the development of the phone as a tool not only for communication but for audiovisual entertainment too (Repo et al. 2004, 6).

In "The Stories Tools Tell," Tarleton Gillespie suggests that in order to understand a digital artifact, not only should its technical affordances be taken into consideration, but also the materials that circulate around it such as advertising campaigns, press releases, instruction manuals, websites, tutorials, and other textual supplements. Gillespie's argument is that an understanding of an artifact is articulated through such materials by its own manufacturers in a process of "self-interpretation"—identifying what it does (and, implicitly, cannot do), how it can be used and be made sense of. Taken together, such materials create a "discursive formation" around the mobile phone that determines the meaning of the technology at a given time (Gillespie 2003, 112).

For example, the Nokia 70 model came loaded with what was described as "Movie Director" software. The phone's instruction booklet explained that this software could not actually make "movies" as such, but made "muvees™"—a trademarked algorithm that combined video and images from the phone's photo gallery with music to make short sequences, adorned with animations to send as multimedia messages (known as MMS). In the words of the Nokia 70's website FAQs, "It's like playing dress-up with your video!" (muveeMobile, 2006). Clearly, this "Movie Director" software redefines filmmaking. While the word "Director" suggests a goal-directed and visionary potential to *create* films, "muvees" can only *combine* images, sound, and text in a mechanical fashion, and personalize the results with opening and closing text to make video messages.

Yet, in spite of these limitations, the Nokia Shorts 2005 competition was championed by filmmaker Shane Meadows who sang the praises of the medium, pointing out how "it lets you get shots which might not be possible using larger camera equipment" (Mobile Film Makers 2006). Furthermore, the Nokia website was full of enthusiastic comments from Nokia Shorts competition winners. Taken together, these discursive "narratives" circulating around a 3G phone are indicative of the distance between aspiration and actuality for the "fourth screen" at the time. Quoting Philip Agre, Gillespie suggests that a reflection on the metaphors used in such discursive materials can provide insight into a medium as these discursive materials operate as "mediums of exchange" between different semantic fields and point to aspirations for the media they refer to (2003, 115).

Blink and Pocket Shorts

As the telecom industry was promoting 3G mobile telephony, a small independent creative technology organization called Blink in Huddersfield, United Kingdom, set up a project to explore the potential of the new handsets that were coming onto the market. With support from NESTA (National Endowment for Science Technology and the Arts), Blink invited filmmakers to try their hand with this new medium and eight films were commissioned. At the outset, Blink's directors Lisa Roberts and Andrew Wilson admitted to having very few preconceptions of what a mobile film might look like. The project placed few restrictions on these pioneering mobile film makers. The films were to be given a cinematic mode of presentation with title and credit sequences, but the filmmakers were advised to make films for the medium and "not try to create miniature versions of *Schindler's List*" (Roberts 2006).

Among the commissions were a series of four films lasting just over thirty seconds each, under the title *While you are Waiting* by Andrew Quinn and Gary McKeown (2005).[2] Contemporaneous research on uses of the mobile phone was indicating that mobile phones were already embedded into our everyday lives (Moore and Rutter 2004, 51), so the filmmakers took this as their starting premise. Each film took an everyday scenario: waiting outside a telephone box, waiting for a kettle to boil, waiting for the automated setting on the camera to take a photograph, or waiting for a friend. The films overlaid these familiar activities with rhythmic live-action collage to reveal what can be done with idle moments, to entertain the "waiters" while they wait (see Figure 13.1 below). In this way Pocket Shorts adroitly incorporated themselves into the gaps around humdrum everyday activities (Roberts, 2006).

Figure 13.1 *While You Are Waiting* (Andrew Quinn and Gary McKeown 2005). Courtesy Lisa Roberts.

With the widespread adoption of sms (short message service), now more commonly known as text messaging, the second group of Pocket Shorts capitalized on 3G phone capabilities to send video messages. A series of four 15-second films by Matthew Austin titled *My Inner Shorts* (2005) were based on the four most popular text messages, "Imissyou," "Congrats," "Goodluck" and "Where r u?" (see Figure 13.2 below). By adopting the conventions of texting in the film's titles, the filmmaker's rotoscoped animations aimed to reclaim ownership of vernacular interactions from the standard auto-answers and emoticons. Of all the commissions, this group of ultra-short films highlighted how integrated into social relationships mobile phones were becoming and how these films could provide the materials for the practices of friendship resembling little "gifts" or souvenirs passed between friends (*A Film in your Pocket?* 2005[3]). This is a practice that finds a contemporary parallel in instant photo and video messaging applications like Snapchat, which have become a popular way of sharing a moment, mood, or experience. Even though messages are time-limited to no more than a few seconds, these micromovies generate a powerful sense of what has been described by Ekman as "a surprisingly effective illusion of living continuously with one another" across different spatial locations (2015, 100).

The Pocket Short that proved most popular at film festivals and went on to be aired on broadcast television was *Evil Fun with Zimmy* by Andy Sykes (2005), a minute-long animated monologue about a childhood encounter with a novelty toy (see Figure 13.3 below). Not content with exploring the potential of the medium for communication, Sykes reconceived mobile film for storytelling as a stripped-down sequence of events in the shape of the message, joke, aphorism, or quip—in short, compact forms of communication.

Figure 13.2 *My Inner Short: Where r u?* (Matthew Austin, 2005). Courtesy Matthew Austin.

While 3G phones were superseded by even smart(er) phones, with the benefit of hindsight, it is clear that these commissions were not just one-off experiments but actually prefigured a move toward compact media formats in entertainment. In response to new circumstances, films have been fashioned into clips, compilations, and mash-ups, as well as serialized, becoming "mobisodes," "webisodes," and "vlogs." These media formats share in common their increasing brevity, as can be seen in the development of shorter and shorter forms of video on platforms like Vine, Instagram, and Snapchat, with film length limited to a matter of seconds. What the Pocket Shorts lacked in length, however, they made up for in duration. All the films commissioned by Blink were presented in a format whereby once they came to an end, they would replay automatically: a circular form of presentation known as "looping." From GIF-based photographic loops to the built-in replay feature of QuickTime and VLC video players, and now software applications on Vine and other sites, looping has become an established feature of "post-cinematic" film (Poulaki 2015, 95).

Journalists, media analysts, and academics have all observed the growing significance of short form content in the online environment over the last decade (Miller 2007; Grainge 2011; Deloitte 2015). In *Beyond the Multiplex: Cinema, New Technologies, and the Home*, Barbara Klinger has argued that the proliferation of short forms needs to be understood as a response to changes in the "attention economies" driven by contemporary media ecologies, in which

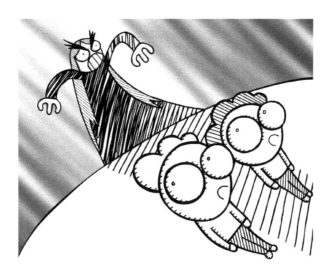

Figure 13.3 *Evil Fun with Zimmy* (Andy Sykes, 2005). Courtesy Andy Sykes.

short forms fit "seamlessly into both the surfing mentality that defines media experience and the multitasking sensibility that pervades computer culture" (2006, 199–200). Moreover, as Poulaki suggests, the looping structure used in the presentation of the Pocket Shorts has become a feature of compact forms as it enables them to expand in a "self-reproducing" duration to flexibly fill the time available (2015, 94).

Bluevend

Having explored the affordances of the format, the next challenge facing Blink Media was to find an audience for these films. While the first mobile media services tended to favor a "shrink-to-fit" approach repurposing material designed for showing on TV and cinema screens, Blink Media wanted to remain independent of the telecom companies, and their solution was to design a bespoke distribution system called Bluevend—a name created from a splice of Bluetooth technology and a vending machine (Roberts 2006).[4]

Bluevend was developed to enable the Pocket Shorts to be viewed on the platform for which they were designed and showcase these mobile films at film festivals. A personal computer was encased in a sealed acrylic box with a touchscreen interface (see Figure 13.4). Using Bluetooth technology, the

Figure 13.4 Bluevend: a Bluetooth-enabled film vending machine. Courtesy Lisa Roberts.

Bluevend transformed a personal computer into a small broadcast unit that could communicate with other Bluetooth-enabled devices within a defined radius (Roberts 2006). To access the Pocket Shorts, all that was required was a curious owner of a Bluetooth-enabled mobile phone, and films were selected from a menu and delivered on request for free. Bluevend made its first public appearance at the Edinburgh International Film Festival in 2005 before touring to festivals in Helsinki, San Francisco, and Rotterdam.

So, contrary to the promise that mobiles could lead to a "cinema without walls," the implication of using Bluetooth was that "placedness" actually became critical to the reception of these films. By situating the Bluevend in film festival venues, these prototypes retained a specificity to the cinematic experience. Roberts' observations of audiences' engagements with the Bluevend suggested that people tended to collect the films and then go on to share them with friends, transmitting them by Bluetooth from phone to phone (2006). So, the Pocket Shorts were distributed along the contours of friendship in a similar way to social media platforms such as Facebook with its "like" recommendations today. In this way, this mobile form of cinema both aligned itself with conventional cinema and exploited social media and digital technology in their projection and distribution. By so doing, these films enter into a dialogue with the classic cinematic *dispositif* claiming the place of their compact cinematics in cinematic tradition.

Conclusion

Media archaeologist Wolfgang Ernst has argued that technical media should be regarded as "active agents" conditioning what is possible at any given time (2013, 15). Through an exploration of the affordances of 3G mobile telephony, as well as the discursive materials surrounding the mobile phone in print and online, both the potential and limitations of 3G phones for filmmaking and film viewing have been brought into focus. Working with the specificities of the medium, pioneering filmmakers took up the challenge of creating films for viewing on mobile phones. The resulting films prototyped short form visual and textual practices and played a part in shaping the prevailing trend of compact cinematics. Furthermore, the bespoke distribution system, Bluevend, turned film spectatorship into a social experience, presaging the engagement of social media with the cinematic today.

Notes

1   Characterizing the act of looking into a mobile phone as "peering" can be understood in contrast to the "glance" associated with the other small domestic screen of the television, and the "gaze" at the cinema screen (Ellis 1982, 24). Moreover, "peering" into a mobile phone is suggestive of the prevailing mode of attention today—connectivity.

2   Andrew Quinn and Gary McKeown. 2005. *While you are Waiting* (Series of 4). Available at: https://www.youtube.com/watch?v=zWSb5FRlF0&index=8&list=PL 36F45C87E8FA3D7F (Box), https://www.youtube.com/watch?v=6P66eX2unYg& list=PL36F45C87E8FA3D7F&index=7 (Feet), https://www.youtube.com/watch?v =CatJD7iFj3g&index=5&list=PL36F45C87E8FA3D7F (Photo), and https://www. youtube.com/watch?v=GoXbiM7cQ70&list=PL36F45C87E8FA3D7F&index=6 (Tea) (accessed February 26, 2016).

3   "A Film in your Pocket?" 2005. *BBC* [Online]. Available at: http://www.bbc.co.uk/ bradford/content/articles/2005/11/24/pocket_shorts_huddersfield_feature.shtml (accessed March 8, 2006).

4   Bluevend was invented by Blink's co-directors Lisa Roberts and Andrew Wilson in association with Daniel Blackburn.

14

Children's Little Thumb Films
or "Films-Poucets"

Alexandra Schneider and Wanda Strauven

"Once upon a time, in the countryside, the sun was shining. Look! Everywhere! The sun is shining." These are the lyrics of an improvised song by a five-year-old girl, who on a sunny Sunday morning made a short video with a digital point-and-shoot camera in her room while lying down on the bottom of her bunk bed. Right after pushing the recording button, she started singing and moving the camera fluidly along, from a dried rose on the top of a book shelf to a plastic pink flower-lamp hanging on the opposite wall. While mostly capturing the upper bunk's bed frame and mattress, the girl also filmed glimpses of her knee (Figure 14.1), of the bed's ladder, and of the open door, on which her name figures in colorful wooden letters. It almost seems as if she wanted to add end credits to this little film, but then the camera lens is turned back to the dried rose of the opening frame. Total length: twenty-two seconds.

On another Sunday, in a city hundreds of miles away, another girl aged six made a little humoristic "home movie" with a smartphone. Holding the device upright according to the vertical format, she filmed from the dining room into the living room where her family was trying to get ready to leave the house for a walk. When hearing in the background her mother's request to her brother to put on his shoes, the girl decided to comment in voice-over: "And here he goes, he puts on his shoes. Daddy is putting them on as well. And Mommy is standing there, bossing everyone around." Then she continued in a singing voice: "Dum tadi tadim tadam dim tada. And here is my pancake." At this point, the camera is panned to the foreground of the not-yet-cleaned-up lunch at the dining table where a pancake comes into the picture (Figure 14.2). Total length: thirty-one seconds.

On yet another Sunday, in yet another city, a little two-year-old girl started to make moving images with her mother's iPhone. She shot about ten extremely short videos, all in the vertical format and all but one lasting only one second, while looking down either to some toys lying on the couch or to the tiled floor. In the video that lasts a bit longer, she managed to capture her feet in blue socks making little steps (Figure 14.3), while moving forward and crying out "Ayoh!," accidently also recording her mother's voice in the background. Total length: eight seconds.

Figure 14.1

Figure 14.2

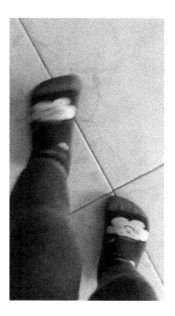

Figure 14.3

Today's children make their own little films. Most of the so-called digital natives discover and explore the recording option of all sorts of mobile devices quite intuitively, without explanation from their parents, at a preschool age. This new phenomenon of spontaneous (and experimental) filmmaking is compact in at least three ways: First of all, because of the size of the filmmaker, who is very young and who, in fact, becomes always younger and younger. Whereas today's first graders started filming at the age of four or five, the youngest generation make their first little films already at the age of two or earlier. But elementary school kids can still be considered "compact" filmmakers, so the age range is rather large.[1] Second, the practice is compact in terms of the size of the recording devices, which literally fit into the hand of the little filmmaker. The most common recording device today is without doubt the smartphone, but kids also film with electronic tablets, special toy cameras, and digital point-and-shoot cameras, also called compact cameras—here compactness clearly combines two aspects, which are miniaturization and mobility, or to put it differently: it is not only about size but also about portability.[2] Third, the output of the children's filming practice is compact, since their films consist, in general, of one single take. Most of them are very short, sometimes no longer than a couple of seconds. But they might also run for two or three minutes, depending on the subject and/or the available memory of the device.

We propose to refer to these short digital videos made by today's children as "films-poucets." Coined by Alexandra Schneider (2014), the term is inspired by Michel Serres's *Petite Poucette* (2012), a personal essay on knowledge and pedagogy—eclectic, euphoric, and often naïve—as many critics have pointed out (see for instance Olma 2014). Instead of reading it as an academic text, we suggest understanding Serres's little book both as a thought-provoking intervention and as a (very literal) fairy tale told by a grandfather. Indeed, Serres writes about the generation of his grandchildren, who live and think differently from previous generations. Because, according to the French philosopher, they write differently, they write very rapidly, with two thumbs:

> He or she writes differently. After watching them, with admiration, send an SMS more quickly than I could ever do with my clumsy fingers, I have named them, with as much tenderness as a grandfather can express, Thumbelina (Petite Poucette) and Tom Thumb (Petit Poucet). (Serres 2015, 7)[3]

As the above quote already shows, a first question arises when trying to identify the exact fairy tale we (Serres and ourselves) are alluding to: Thumbelina or Tom Thumb? The title of Serres's book, at least in its original French version, is a direct reference to the fairy tale *Tommelise* by Danish author Hans Christian Andersen (first published in 1835), known in English as *Thumbelina*.[4] Andersen's tale is about a girl who grew out of a barleycorn to a size no bigger than a thumb. More than an adventure tale with a clear plot, the story evolves as a succession of tableaux (or "takes") in which Thumbelina meets with different types of insects and animals (a toad, a butterfly, a beetle, a mouse, and a mole) until she finds, with the help of a swallow, a fairy boy of her own size.

However, Serres also mentions "Petit Poucet," which in English translates to Little Thumb, Little Thumbling, or Tom Thumb—all alternative names for Hop-o'-My-Thumb, the hero of an old French fairy tale, published in 1697 by Charles Perrault as *Le petit Poucet*. Hop-o'-My-Thumb is the youngest of seven brothers who live in poverty. When abandoned by their parents in the woods, the boys find the way back home thanks to the little pebbles dropped along the way by Hop-o'-My-Thumb. He also saves them from the hands (and mouth) of an ogre, whose seven-league boots he steals. In spite of his small stature, the huge boots fit him like a glove. They somehow magically adapt to his small feet—just as today's smartphones, designed by the industry for adults, fit perfectly in the child's hand.[5]

In his essay, Serres explicitly refers to the altered body of the new generation, more particularly to the fact that they no longer have the same heads as their parents, because they no longer live in a "metric space, coordinated by distances" but instead in a "topological space of neighborhoods" (Serres 2015, 6). For the compact filmmaking of our "petites poucettes," the situation is the other way around: the kids are exploring a different space because of their different body (size). Good examples are the typical low-angle shot, the lowered horizon or the absence of a horizon, as is for instance the case in foot shots. In fact, our tiny filmmakers are much younger (and therefore physically smaller) than Serres's "petites poucettes" who have reached the age of majority (Serres 2015, 15). Another important difference to point out is that, while Serres reinvents Petite Poucette and Petit Poucet as generic persons, our "petites poucettes" are concrete children in concrete family situations.[6]

Even if Serres, throughout his little book, remains vague not only on the exact source of inspiration for the name of his female protagonist but also on the fairy tale(s)'s relevance for his general argument, we like to embrace the meta-level dimension of his writing. In our view, this is the most productive connection with Perrault's *Le petit Poucet*, a tale with a clear meta-fictional quality—thanks to its alternative ending ("There are many people who do not agree with this last detail. They claim that Little Thumb . . .") (Perrault 1889)[7] and its rhyming moral, to which we will come back at the very end of this short chapter.

As much as Serres is philologically confusing in his reference to the fairy tales, the same could be said about his media-ethnographic observation: the thumb is not the only or main finger that the new generation of Petit(e)s Poucet(te)s are using for texting, posting, calling, and snap-chatting. For their digital practices, they rely on all fingers, even if it is true—as also pointed out by Lorenz Engell (2012)—that the thumb has not only developed dexterity but also adopted some important functions of the index finger, such as pointing and selecting, through our daily use of (digital) media devices. Whereas Serres is referring to the smartphone mainly as a device of spoken or written language, that is, a tool for communication and information, we are calling attention to children's use of the smartphone as a tool for filming.

As Till A. Heilmann has argued, there is an intrinsic connection between the digital and the finger as such. He writes:

> What is "digital" about digital media? Every answer seems to point, like an index, at our fingers—the fingers that taught us to count and to devise of number as an abstract concept (cf. Dantzig 1940); the fingers that, since the beginning of graphism, have guided our instruments in writing and drawing (cf. Leroi-Gourhan 1964) and thus made possible mathematics (cf. Mersch 2005); the fingers that implemented mathematics in ever more technologically advanced machines and media, up to and including the computers of our day (cf. Kittler 1993); the fingers we use constantly to press the keys, buttons, and switches on almost any electric, electronic, or digital device from an alarm clock to an automated teller; the fingers that let us control the various interfaces of digital media, from the keyboard of our desktop computer to the touchscreen of our mobile phone. (Heilmann 2014, 42)

This is also true for our compact filmmakers: they are using their fingers to count, to paint, to put on (finger) puppet shows, and, in addition to all this, to shoot little films. While filming, children use their thumb and index finger interchangeably to push the icon buttons on the smartphone's touchscreen.

So far we have tried to argue for the productivity of the notion "film-poucet" (little thumb films in English, Däumlingsfilm in German) for a media practice we vaguely sketched as (very short) digital films made by (young) children on (small) mobile devices. Besides their compactness, what else typifies the "films-poucets"? As illustrated by the three examples that have been "retold" in the introduction, most often they come with sound (direct ambient sound, sync singing, humming, voice-overs, or dialogues), but there are also silent examples. The act of filming often evolves as an inventive form of playing, of exploring the world, of inscribing oneself into the world. But at the same time, children also use their compact camera in order to document something—their room, toys, or something they have built or crafted with Lego, Kapla, or other building blocks, or a dish they prepared, a flower or a vegetable they picked. Here it remains unclear why the filmmaker has chosen the moving image mode instead of the photographic mode, as both the captured object and the camera are not moving. It seems as if there is something about the duration of the image the filmmaking child is interested in; as if, during the shooting, she is putting her gaze into the recording; as if, in order to look attentively, it is more adequate to film instead of taking a picture.

In terms of their aesthetics, the films-poucets oscillate between movement and stillness, between photography and cinema. Still pictures taken by young children often come in a series, a series that bears some proto-cinematic quality because of the inscription of time and movement between the single images.[8] It is not the unique image that counts but the repetition, the series of images. Obviously, the little filmmakers do not stick to the opposition between still and moving image practices, but rather blur this distinction. This is as much the case for a statically recorded tomato, for a still image taken while deliberately moving or rotating the camera, or an excessive series of snapshots, all of them somehow transgressing our supposedly clear distinction between a photo and a film. One could argue that they just do not know better—but then aren't they surrounded by image practices that are in-between? As much as pictures nowadays can be thumbed through on a touchscreen like the pages of a book, they can be set in motion, animated by the single touch of a finger. It is therefore not so surprising that today's children are exploring various techniques of putting motionless objects into motion, of animating their "dead" toys with their shooting—for instance, by slightly dancing with the camera and adding rhythm via a song or humming.

A last important aspect to mention here is that most little thumb films are rarely watched, shown, or shared, so the quality of a shot—its uniqueness or seriality, its stillness or movement—is not conceived from the perspective of a future audience, as there is often no audience at all; the compact filmmaker herself rarely revisits her films. Most parents find the little thumb films by coincidence on memory cards or via back-ups. But then the "never-looked-at-ness" could also be a hint that this child practice is less a documentation via images than a kind of archival practice that relates to the mundane practice of children collecting things (in order to store experience in material objects). Like the little thumb films, collected stones, sticks, leaves, etc. are often kept but hardly ever reused. Yet, again quite similar to the films, these collected objects are not supposed to be thrown away. They are collected/made, kept/stored, but not revisited/watched.

This brief description of some selected characteristics and peculiarities of the compact cinematic practice of the "films-poucets" is not meant to be exhaustive. There is much more to be said and differentiated about them. And even the term might need some adaptation, as it was no coincidence that we selected as our opening examples three films made by little girls, or "petites poucettes." This is not because boys don't make "films-poucets" but because female filmmakers are "marginal" figures in history; and, like Serres, we want to turn the girls into the protagonists of the twenty-first century. Let us briefly reconsider the case of the six-year-old girl who points the camera of the smartphone to her parents and her brother on a Sunday afternoon and makes a reportage or "home movie" of a typical family scene. Whereas most home movies have been made by fathers (to make a long story short and a bit stereotypical),[9] this one is shot by the young daughter who makes the familial roles (and tensions) quite explicit with her "live" voice-over. The little thumb film opens up a new perspective for the future of home video, made no longer by fathers but by "petites poucettes."

So why not call their compact film productions "films-poucettes" instead? Let us go back to the different fairy tales: we would like to borrow from Andersen's *Thumbelina* the succession (and seriality) of takes, its nonnarrative (or not plot-driven) structure as well as the name of its protagonist. But maybe like in Serres's tale our "Petite Poucette" is rather to be considered the female version of Perrault's tale: she is the smallest or weakest one of a huge family, a new generation of internauts, whose little hand perfectly adapts to the new recording devices. Finally, Petite Poucette's smallness is connected to the smallness and apparent futility of the films.

One of the many practical problems of researching the little thumb films is, indeed, their ephemerality and precariousness. Most of them are easily forgotten or simply deleted; only the ones considered worthwhile by the parents are being kept and stored for the future. And here the moral of Perrault's "original" *Le petit poucet* comes into the picture again:

> It is no affliction to have many children,
> if they all are good looking, courteous, and strong,
> but if one is sickly or slow-witted,
> he will be scorned, ridiculed, and despised.
> However, it is often the little urchin
> who brings good fortune to the entire family. (Perrault 1889)[10]

Expanding on the topic of hidden skills and the sudden benefits that might accrue from the youngest, shortest, and most unnoticed, this moral also applies, as we would like to claim as conclusion, to the film-poucet(te) and other forms of compact cinematics.

Notes

1   This chapter is based on an ongoing joint research project on children and media. Over the last three years, we have been collecting data (videos, still images, self-made toys, and drawings as well as field observations) from around fifteen families across Europe. The social background of the children's families is rather homogenously middle class.

2   For a genealogy of compact media, one could start with the compact as a cosmetic product, originally developed for concealing and transporting face powder in the late nineteenth to early twentieth century, and then jump to the compact camera, which was advertised not only for its size but also for its simplicity in use. Both the powder box and the compact camera perfectly fit into a handbag. Swiss artist Pipilotti Rist once called the medium of video a "compact handbag" (*kompakte Handtasche*) in which everything fits: "painting, technology, language, music, lousy flowing pictures, poetry, commotion, premonitions of death, sex and friendliness" (Hauser and Wirth 2009). The story could then touch upon the compact car, developed after the Second World War, and go on to the compact disc, aka CD. On compactness in respect to the still image and sound, see for instance Goggin and Hjorth (2014), Stingelin and Thiele (2010), and Fickers (1998).

3   The original reads: "Il ou elle écrit autrement. Pour l'observer, avec admiration, envoyer, plus rapidement que je ne saurai jamais le faire de mes doigts gourds, envoyer, dis-je, des SMS avec les deux pouces, je les ai baptisés, avec la plus grande tendresse que puisse exprimer un grand-père, Petite Poucette et Petit Poucet" (Serres 2012, 14).

4   While Serres's essay was, indeed, published in English as *Thumbelina: The Culture and Technology of Millennials*, the German translation, which appeared in 2013, opted for a different title: *Erfindet euch neu!: Eine Liebeserklärung an die vernetzte Generation* (Re-invent yourself! An ode to the connected generation). The German publisher probably realized that Serres's intertext was more complex and that he was not only alluding to Andersen's fairy tale.

5   On the design aspect of today's mobile devices, see Cooley (2004).

6   Nevertheless, the children whose material we are collecting remain "without names" for privacy and child protection reasons. On the issue of namelessness, see Strauven (2016).

7   The original reads: "Il y a bien des gens qui ne demeurent pas d'accord de cette dernière circonstance, et qui prétendent que le petit Poucet . . ." (Perrault 1842, 177).

8   On the notion of inscription and its connection to media archaeology, see Schneider and Strauven (2016). Here we also point out the dimension of play and the exploration of different temporalities in the child filming practice.

9   On home movies, see Schneider (2004).

10   The original reads: "On ne s'afflige point d'avoir beaucoup d'enfants, / Quand ils sont tous beaux, bien faits et bien grands, / Et d'un extérieur qui brille; / Mais si l'un d'eux est faible, ou ne dit mot, / On le méprise, on le raille, on le pille: / Quelquefois cependant c'est ce petit marmot / Qui fera le bonheur de toute la famille" (Perrault 1842, 178).

15

Of Flipbooks and Funny Animals: Chris Ware's *Quimby the Mouse*

Yasco Horsman

Drawing extends the act of the hand, and with it the wrist, the forearm,
the gaze, and finally the whole body. Against the intellectualizing to which
we have wanted to reduce it sometimes, drawing produces a rhythmic
configuration of the real born from the very rhythm of the body.

Daniel Arasse, "The Memory of Drawing" (cited in Nancy 2013, 43)

In an interview given in 2005, the Japanese artist and occasional game designer Iwai Toshio recalled how his first encounter with small-screen handheld electronic toys, such as Nintendo's Game Boy, reminded him of the pleasures and fascinations that he had first experienced as a schoolboy, when he had created small flipbooks. He says:

> For me, the existential meaning of the flip book and the digital game are directly connected, bypassing the history of film and television. For example, I thought that the Game Boy was an electronic flip book when it was released. It could be carried around easily and played anywhere. The touch of one's fingers was directly registered via moving images and sound. I think the Game Boy restored the value of the flip book, which had been dormant for more than a century, by returning it to our hands in electronic form. (Iwai Toshio, cited in Moseley and Saiki 2014, 69 n. 14)

For Iwai, the miniature screen of the Game Boy, which can be held, touched, manipulated, and kept in one's pocket, evokes the history of optical toys that predates cinema's large-screen, projected images. The Game Boy *bypasses* this history, and awakens the pleasures that belonged to what film historian André Gaudreault has called the pre-cinematic continuum of "animated pictures": those optical toys and technologies that arose in the mid-nineteenth century—the zoetrope, praxinoscope, and, indeed, the flipbook—which film historians have long seen as mere forerunners of cinema, as not-yet-fully-formed film (see Dulac and Gaudreault 2006; Gaudreault and Gauthier 2011). Yet as Dulac and Gaudreault (2006) hold—and their views are echoed by Iwai—these technologies offer attractions markedly distinct from those of projected film. The flipbook, for example, as Iwai spells out, evokes feelings of intimacy, ownership, and manipulability, and promises experiences that are first and foremost not optical but *tactile*, as it relies on one's fingers flipping through the pages, magically producing moments of animation. As Mary Ann Doane puts it, the flipbook's attraction depends on the prospect of enjoying a moment when its user "seem[s] to hold movement in his or her hands," an occasion of intimacy not found in the spectacle of projected cinema, which emphasizes the distance between spectator and images (cited in Gunning 2013, 65). This intimacy relies on a *miniaturization* rather than an enlargement of the image. Doane (2009) writes:

> Unlike projection techniques . . . [the flip book] produced an apparent immediacy and intimacy in the relation between the viewer, the apparatus and the image. . . . Unprojected and generally opaque, the image of movement could more readily be seen as both an ocular and a tactile possession. The reduced form of seriality of the loop constituted a type of miniaturization of time and movement. (153)

In this chapter I will reflect on these miniature "tactile" pleasures of "animated pictures" that were lost when cinema "made it big." I will do so by turning to the work of comic book artist Chris Ware. Ware is known for his ambitious graphic novels such as *Jimmy Corrigan, the Smartest Kid on Earth* (2000) and, more recently, *Building Stories* (2012), but in his earlier work, published in his series *The Acme Novelty Library* (1993–present), he shares with Aiwa a media-archaeological preoccupation with nineteenth-century optical toys such as the zoetrope and the magic lantern slide show, as well as the chronophotography of Eadweard Muybridge, all of which are frequently invoked.[1] Ware combines these fascinations with a formal investigation of the techniques, styles, and figures developed in early comics and animation. In particular, his series *Quimby the Mouse*, first published as a newspaper strip in *The Daily Texan* (in 1990–91) and later collected in two volumes of *The Acme Novelty Library*, reads as an investigation into the nature of small-scale "moving pictures." In what follows I will study Ware's use of flipbook conventions in *Quimby the Mouse* in relation to a stylistic feature and an iconographic figure that are each central to both early animation and comic books: the technique of line drawing, and the figure of the "funny animal," with its plastic and flexible body. Both are, I propose, linked to what Doane calls the "miniaturization of time and movement" that is typical of the flipbook, considered as a form of compact cinematics, which Ware seeks to revive in his work.

Flipping images

The *Quimby* comics narrate the stories of an anthropomorphized mouse called Quimby (named after Fred Quimby [1886–1965], producer of the Tom & Jerry cartoons), who lives through a series of surreal adventures (a second head pops out of his body, which ages and dies) and engages in everyday activities (he rides in a car that gets stuck in traffic, visits an old house, and opens an unsuccessful luncheonette), all rendered in one-page stories that lack clear punchlines. Gradually the series matures into a complex psychodrama involving Quimby and his pet (or lover), the cat Sparky, whose name recalls the nickname of the author of *Peanuts*, Charles Schulz (1922–2000). Sparky has no body but only a head, which Quimby carries around, sometimes stores in cupboards or on shelves, or puts next to a tree in his garden. The pair come to have an abusive relationship that recalls those of other famous cat-and-mouse couples such as Tom & Jerry or Krazy & Ignatz. Sparky is kicked around, shot, punished, scolded, and ignored by Quimby, only to be picked up again and caressed in scenes of remorse, in stories that each time start from scratch, with both figures completely intact, as if the mayhem that had come before had never happened. The couple always reverts to being ready to inaugurate a new cycle of violence and regret.

The antics of Quimby are all presented on large-scale pages, whose size, lavishly decorated margins, and typography, evoke the full newspaper-page-sized Sunday comics of the 1910s and 1920s by artists such as Winsor McCay, Lyonel Feininger, and Fred King. Central to each *Quimby* page are a series of equally sized, minuscule, mostly wordless images, often as many as a few dozen per page, each one not bigger than two square centimeters, drawn in a style that recalls the animated "funny animal" cartoons of the 1910s and 1920s. Like Felix, Mickey, or Oswald the Lucky Rabbit, Quimby is drawn in a few lines, with heavy contours (see Figure 15.1 below). He has a black body with a white snout, rounded features, and wears nothing but white gloves and

Figure 15.1 Chris Ware's *Quimby the Mouse*. Courtesy of the artist.

shoes. The tiny panels in which Quimby moves differ only minimally from one another (a body part moves, a head turns or is picked up) while the sparsely drawn background, framing, and "camera angle" remain the same. As one's eyes glide along the strip's images, going from panel to panel in a steady but fast movement, a slight, wavering effect of near-animation is produced that suggests the flickering images of a flipbook, which also, as Doane puts it, offers us not *movement* as such but a passage from "static immobility" *to* movement (2002, 199).

A link with the flipbook is explicitly established in the comics themselves. An early episode depicting Quimby driving a car is called a "kine-comic" and a "cut out movie," and the reader is invited, in a detailed set of ironic instructions, to cut out the pictures, staple them together, and hold the resulting stack of pages in one's "left hand with thumb and first finger and flip pages between thumb and first finger of right hand" (14) (see Figure 15.2 below). Other *Quimby* strips evoke the conventions of silent animation: Ware has tears, stars, and drops of sweat spring out of Quimby's and Sparky's heads, inserts intertitles and onomatopoeic sound effects, and has one page even suggest the scratches and lines of damaged celluloid. But since *Quimby* remains, after all, a comic, a sequence of images placed one next to the other, the effect of animation as one's eyes glide over the images is continually undone at the very moment of its emergence. Unlike with

Figure 15.2 Quimby's *Kine-Comic*. Courtesy of the artist.

a flipbook, where one image is overlaid on the previous one, thereby erasing it, Quimby's antics are never rendered as a *single* moving picture. The images are always visible as a sequence of *separate* moments. The result is that as one "reads" Quimby, one experiences both stasis *and* animation. Or, rather, one is reminded that movement is not "there" *on* the page, but is present only as a mental image that accompanies one's reading, and vanishes if one stares at any one panel for too long.

In the two *Quimby* volumes of *The Acme Novelty Library*, as well as in the *Quimby* book that was published in 2003, these quirky "kine-comics" are accompanied by several pages of ironic "paratexts," which evoke the typography, graphic style, and language of American magazines and newspapers during the turn of the twentieth century. We encounter as announcements, advice columns, jokes, and quasi-legal patents for Acme's "comic-toon" process, as well as a series of kits to create optical toys such as the aforementioned flipbook, a cut-out theater, and a set of instructions to create a Sparky automaton. *Quimby the Mouse*, then, presents us with a self-conscious investigation of both the technology and the aesthetics of the animated cartoon—its language, codes, styles, and conventions, as well as the *figure* that dominated animated pictures: the anthropomorphized animal, with its indestructible body that, like those of Quimby and Sparky, can be endlessly stretched and bounced, which can fall apart and be reassembled, and which provides its audience with what animation theorist Norman Klein (1993, 2000) has called the spectacle of "ani-morphosis": the magic of animated figures that morph into others, and shape-shift before the viewer's eyes.

As Klein (2000) explains in a carefully argued essay, silent animation's "spectacle of ani-morphosis" offers, as the flipbook does, a pleasure of a particularly *tactile* nature. Animated cartoons, he recalls, first sprang out of a stock vaudeville routine: the "lightning hand" sketch, in which a caricaturist performed for his audience by conjuring figures out of a few lines of chalk on a blackboard, which he then transformed by adding a few extra lines and erasing others. The early animated films of J. Stuart Blackton, Emile Cohl, and Winsor McCay were animated versions of these lightning-hand routines, but now the audience could be delighted with images that "magically" drew themselves on the silver screen while still evoking the gestures of an invisible drawing hand. As the animated trick film morphed into the animated cartoon, a link to the hand of the animator remained present in animation's reliance on line drawings, which, as Klein suggests, are never merely representations *of* something but must also always be indices of the body that made them.

As animation historians such as Jay P. Telotte (2008) and Donald Crafton (1982) have pointed out, in the mid-1930s, the aesthetics of the animated cartoon underwent a gradual shift. The genre lost some of its tactile quality when the slightly anarchic, ani-morphing energies of the silent cartoon were replaced by a more realistic aesthetic that aimed at creating an "illusion of life." As Sean Cubitt (2009, 2014) explains, this shift coincided with the adoption of several standardized drawing techniques that sought to "tame the line" and give substance, volume, and stability to animated bodies. Chris Ware's pseudo-animated *Quimby*, then, marks a self-conscious return to an earlier period of animation, to the shape-shifting antics of a figure that is not yet a full character, to the tactile aesthetics of line drawings, and to the intimate pocket-sized pleasures of the thumb-operated flipbook. At the heart of this return is a re-miniaturization of the image, which becomes more intense as the series progresses. In the early comics Quimby's body is drawn in a style that suggests "volume," but later on he shrinks in size until he is almost a stick figure, having thin lines for arms, legs, fingers, and tail, each rendered in one pen-stroke. In addition, the panels, which themselves decrease in size until the last page of the book, contain a dazzling series of 325 tiny pictures that are decipherable only when one holds the page close to one's eyes (see Figure 15.3 below).

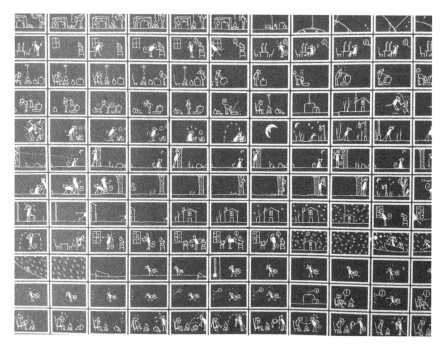

Figure 15.3 325 Tiny Quimbys (fragment). Courtesy of the artist.

A pocket-sized memory palace

However, if Ware's re-miniaturization of animation offers a return to what Eisenstein (1986) calls the "protoplasmatic" universe of early animation—that is, the unstable world occupied by not-yet-fully-formed creatures who can morph into all sorts of shapes—it does so with a difference. The earlier funny animals, such as Felix or Krazy & Ignatz, seemed to live in an Edenic universe where actions have no consequences, and everything can always start anew.[2] As Slavoj Žižek puts it, the cartoon world of the 1920s and early 1930s knows neither moral laws nor superego commandments. Its characters inhabit bodies that are "polymorphously perverse" and not yet libidinally "mapped." They give in, without restraint, to sadistic and oral impulses (2001, 1 ff.; see also Žižek 2000, 389 ff.). Quimby's stories, in contrast, are strangely haunted by feelings of guilt and remorse. Every story in which Sparky is chastised, scolded, hit, and mutilated is inevitably followed by a series of panels that show Quimby overcome with shame and self-reproach: he cries a fountain of cartoon-like

Figure 15.4a–c Quimby & Sparky. Courtesy of the artist.

tears, or creates a snow sculpture of the cat so as to beg it for forgiveness; or, more frequently, he is depicted as paralyzed, staring into space, wearing a blank expression. These latter moments are typically depicted in unframed panels, or ones that are somewhat larger in size or are placed slightly tilted on the page (see Figure 15.4a–c). They interrupt the steady movement of the eye, freezing the animation of the pictures that had come before, allowing them to be contemplated in an arrested moment that seems to correspond to the second thoughts of Quimby himself.

The feeling of regret that permeates the Quimby pages is heightened by the elaborate images on the page margins, depicting nocturnal landscapes, deserted houses, and falling leaves in a style that recalls nineteenth-century engravings. The melancholia connoted by these drawings is made explicit in a separate series of ten Quimby stories that can be cut out and folded together to form a "souvenir" booklet. Whereas most previous Quimbys had been silent, these introduce a "voice-over," first rendered within the panels themselves, then imparted by large calligraphic letters that meander across the page, with words invoking fragmentary conversations of a relationship in the midst of falling apart, resonating ironically with the pictures. "You must not think that I love immersing myself in self-pity," for example, hovers over a series of panels in which the tears of a crying Quimby and then of a weeping Sparky gradually overflow the panels. "I'm feeling much better, thanks," and "Well, personally I don't see any reason for you to be so upset," cover, like a banner, sequences of Sparky being shot at point-blank range, kicked up a hill like a football, hammered down, and left outside a door.

These sentences, always in the first person, seem to be uttered at a moment removed from those of the pictures. A page directly following the "souvenir booklet," for example, states, in bold letters substantially larger than the figures of Quimby and Sparky, "I hate you. And I am sure of it this time even though I have nothing to say to you and I don't care if I ever see you again. . . . [But] if I ever *do* happen to see you again, I know exactly what to say." This line, which both confirms *and* denies the interruption of a conversation that has been broken off, accompanies, again, a succession of images in which Quimby, drawn even sparser than before, commits a new string of violent acts against his cat companion.

Unlike the preceding pages with the mute Quimbys, these pages rely for their overall effect on an intricate combination of words and images, and the two different types of temporality implied by both mediums: the flickering present of the semi-animation, brought to life by the eye that glides along the page, and the engraved temporality of the heavy words, which seem to have been added to the images as an afterthought that retroactively colors them. The process of reading the text and watching the pictures, furthermore, appears to play out against each other. Whereas the images need to be processed linearly, as one has to move from left to right in one steady tempo in order for them to move, the words often zigzag across the page, moving from left to right, then from right to left and vice versa, forcing the reader to slow down as she tries to discover the right order of reading. While deciphering the words, the images are always visible in the periphery of one's gaze. But their animation is now suspended. They have become frozen in time, and are there to be contemplated in thoughts that are pervaded by the feelings of guilt or spite and resentment evoked by the text.

When he collected his *Quimby* comics in one volume in 2003, Ware wrote a long introduction to the book, rendered in tiny, nearly illegible print. Perhaps easy to skip at first, this essay has him looking back at his comics from a distance of ten years, understanding now that the feelings of loss and remorse of the later Quimbys was an inextricable but unplanned part of the Quimby project itself. The comics, in particular the later ones, he explains, were all drawn during the period when he was coping with the loss of his grandmother, first while she was slowly deteriorating during a prolonged period in hospital, and then, after she died, when he found himself obsessively visiting her deserted home, a house where he had spent large parts of his childhood and was now hoping to revive memories of a past that were rapidly withering away, all the while, as he puts it, drawing strips of an "increasingly littler mouse" wandering through large, empty spaces.

The Quimby project, then, with its pictures that flicker in and out of animation, whose "aliveness" is continually conjured up only to be interrupted by second thoughts of regret and remorse, was produced, Ware realizes in hindsight, during a period when its author was possessed by a yearning to gain access to the past, to discover in the empty backdrop of his former life an entryway through which memories would start to flow. "I've never been able to shake the feeling that somehow somewhere all of my memories and experiences, though "in the past," are all still really *there* somehow," Ware writes in the introduction. By returning to the places of his past he hoped to find a way of "reconnecting the right cables," so that the past would come to life again, "like some sort of abandoned amusement park."

Ware's *formal* experimentations, then, his use of the flipbook's aesthetics to create pages that hover between animation and rumination, and that combine the retroactive temporality of writing with the flickering present of animated pictures, unconsciously testify to a desire to "reconnect the cables" to his past, and turn a deserted house into a "memory palace," a space where images of the past light up as one moves from room to room.[3] With its strange combination of the liveliness of flipbook animation and the stagnation of second thoughts, the Quimby project reads as an embodiment of that which Ware fantasized about, as he sought to plug in the right cables to transform the old, static space of his grandmother's house into a functioning "amusement park," from which revived impressions of the past would flow. The *Quimby* book, Ware implies, should be understood as a metaphorical depiction of precisely such a "memory palace," if not of a series of rooms, then a series of pages that allows the reader to conjure up images, moving from panel to panel.

Yet as a metaphorical depiction of a memory palace—or a mnemotechnic amusement park—the *Quimby* book remains ostensibly pocket-sized, despite the actual size of its pages. Its tiny panels never offer the full cinematic illusion of a past that unrolls as a film before one's eyes. Instead, it presents us with minuscule, hesitating images of a past that is only temporarily reanimated: glimmers of movement, and fleeting apparitions of a moment in time that slips through one's fingers as soon as it is conjured up, freezing again into a sequence of static panels, contemplated in thoughts saturated by feelings of loss.

Conclusion

Quimby the Mouse, then, marks a self-conscious return to the magic of the flipbook. Like the handheld Game Boy, which was brought on the market shortly before Ware's comics were drawn, it bypasses the history of cinema as a series of enlarged, projected images to remind us of the device's proto-cinematic pleasures and attractions, which combine the tactile and the optical and offer a sense of intimacy that "real" cinema cannot provide. Central to Ware's return to the flipbook is a process of miniaturization—of the images, but also of "time and movement" itself, as Doane puts it in her gloss on the flipbook. Whereas animation in the cinema, from the mid-1930s on, gives its audience optical illusions—bodies with volume, spaces with depth—Ware's tiny figures, in their minuscule panels, give us the tactile intimacy of line drawings, and invite the spectator to breathe life into them by moving her eyes from panel to panel. Like the images of a flipbook, the stuttering panels of *Quimby* give us not the overwhelming liveliness of the spectacles of the silver screen, but rather a series of flickering time- and movement-images whose animation is never fully present. Yet, it is precisely the primitive, hesitating quasi-animation of the flipbook-like images that gives Ware the chance to reflect on the convoluted nature of memories as images that are, for a moment, truly "there," only to waver and fade, and to be soaked up by second thoughts, ruminations, and regrets.

Notes

1 For an analysis of Ware's references to optical toys in *Jimmy Corrigan*, see Bredehoft (2006).

2 Adam Gopnik (1986) uses the word "Edenic" to describe the world of Krazy Kat.

3 The metaphor of a "memory palace" is used by Frances Yates (2009 [orig. 1966]) to describe a mnemonic trick that allows one to remember things by relating them to specific spaces. For a discussion of *Jimmy Corrigan* and *Building Stories* that employ this notion, see Sattler (2009).

16

Mobile Cinematics

Maria Engberg and Jay David Bolter

When Walter Benjamin (1968) argued that film represented the decline of aura, his argument was medium-specific. As a technology of mechanical reproduction, film eliminated the distance between the viewer and the object of viewing. Aura was defined as "the unique phenomenon of a distance, however close it may be" (222). It is natural to ask whether and how Benjamin's characterization of film might apply to various digital media forms (see Bolter et al. 2006 for more on Benjamin's importance for studies of digital media). The question appears particularly appropriate at a time when various cinematic forms and genres are being refashioned for delivery on mobile devices.

In only a few decades since its commercial start in the 1980s, the cell phone or mobile phone has become a global cultural phenomenon. No longer only a device for voice calls, today mobile phones are regularly used for a wide range of communications and activities in many people's everyday lives.[1] As Gerard Goggin (2006) has shown, mobile phones are brought into situations that foreground their mobility, ubiquity, and versatility. What interests us are the ways in which mobile phones and other mobile devices engage the viewer. In comparison with the traditional, predominant viewing practices for film and television, mobile viewing is a more individual and potentially isolated experience. In part because of the smaller screen, the handheld nature of the device, and the common use of headphones, mobile cinematics belong to what Michael Bull has called our "iPod culture" (2007)—a culture in which, as Bull has pointed out elsewhere, we relish the ability to be able to "create [our] own urban aesthetic experience of the city through privatizing strategies of iPod use" (Bull 2013, 495). Mobile devices offer verbal-visual experiences that can be and are used in complex patterns and strategies by users who are "managing" their lives through and with the help of these versatile mobile devices.

When film and videos originally conceived for presentation on larger screens are consumed on handheld tablets or mobile phones, we have a compact cinematics in the literal sense. This drastic change of scale already constitutes a changed relationship between the viewer and the cinematic object and suggests a new aesthetic in which the viewer's experience is more tactile.[2] In addition to watching conventional films and videos on these small handheld screens, mobile users are being offered a number of born-digital forms, including videogames, Augmented Reality (AR) and Virtual Reality (VR). In some of these forms (AR), video or animated 3D graphics are blended into the user's visual and aural surroundings. In other forms (VR), the user's current visual world is replaced with a 360-degree static or moving image, that is, a panorama. Both user-contributed and professionally produced "VR films" are appearing in increasing numbers for download from YouTube and for consumption through various handheld or head-worn devices.

These born-digital forms of mobile cinematics are compact in terms of their playing time, and gesture toward genres that are amenable to shorter narrative forms. In viewing these mobile forms, the user's comprehension of space and scale is intimately connected to immediate proprioception and interaction.

Mobile cinematics constitutes an important contemporary addition to the viewing practices of traditional cinema and television screens. Although a traditional viewer seated in a darkened theater or on a sofa at home is not necessarily passive or immobile, she nevertheless maintains a certain distance from the moving image. In the theater the viewer cannot affect the stream of sounds and images at all; at home she does so with a "remote" control. With mobile applications, the viewer controls the stream by directly touching the screen. In the case of panoramic VR films, for example, she can change the orientation of her point of view either with a sweeping motion on the screen, by moving the device itself in her hands, or (in the case of a head-worn device) with a turn of her head. The sense of touch or proprioception becomes a more important, if not equal, element along with vision and hearing in the aesthetics of the experience. In the case of mobile VR films, the viewer is often asked to wear headphones in order to make the experience more immersive. At the same time, for many of these mobile applications, the experience becomes less unified when the senses are brought into play serially as well as simultaneously and because the viewer-as-user is often made aware of the physical and digital environments in which the experience is embedded. Immersion is not what these applications strive for.

For these reasons, mobile cinematics may be characterized as polyaesthetic, in contrast to the relatively unified viewing habits of traditional cinema.³ This mobile and compact form of cinema engages the viewer's touch and proprioception as important elements of the experience along with sight and hearing. Of course, one can identify similar moments of change throughout the history of cinema—for instance when handheld cameras became widely available during the Second World War, liberating filmmakers from the constraint of heavy cameras. As Hesselberth (2014) has pointed out, this newfound mobility encouraged new cinematic sensibilities in avant-garde and documentary films in the postwar period.

VR films

When on November 8, 2015 the *New York Times* distributed a cardboard VR viewer to over a million subscribers, the American newspaper of record raised significantly the profile of digital panoramas in general and VR films in particular. *Wired* magazine claimed that this was to be VR's "mainstream moment" (Moynihan 2015). In addition to distributing the viewing device, the Times partnered with VRSE (vrse.com) to produce a 360-degree documentary film entitled *The Displaced* (Ismail and Solomon 2015). Although the film can be viewed in a web browser on a laptop, the viewer gets the full VR effect by downloading an app to her phone and inserting the phone into the cardboard viewer that she holds up to her face. The result is a seamless (although not truly stereoscopic) moving panoramic image.

The Displaced is in some ways a conventional documentary, in which three children describe in a *cinema verité* documentary style how various political conflicts have disrupted their lives. A defining formal difference between VR film and the conventional documentary, however, is that here the filmmaker cannot control point of view. Within each relatively long take, the filmmaker simply sets up the 360-degree camera and then allows the actors to move around it—a technique reminiscent of very early cinematography. In some shots we are allowed to see the camera being operated by those who are being filmed—for example, by a small boy who carries the camera on a stick through the streets of a village in Lebanon. Within these shots, the viewer's attention can be directed by techniques similar to those used in dramaturgy. Motion (e.g., a plane flying overhead) attracts our eye, as does sound (e.g., a conversation between actor/participants), creating expectations of where the action is likely to be. The VR platform seems ideally suited for panoramic views of the countryside, here reminiscent of the travelogue and nature photography favored by Cinerama and early IMAX films. These panoramas lend grandeur even to the bleak environments of war-torn Ukraine, the refugee camp in Lebanon, and the camps in the swamps of South Sudan, which are the documentary's main locations.

The VRSE site (vrse.com) features other examples of VR films, many created by its CEO, filmmaker Chris Milk. In describing this work, Milk makes a classic claim of remediation—that VR constitutes a new medium whose particular qualities allow it to achieve greater authenticity than conventional film:

> We talk about virtual reality as "the last medium." It's the first medium that has actually interfaced on a truly human level with our human senses—two of them right now, eyes and ears. Ultimately, what we're talking about is a medium that disappears, because there is no rectangle on the wall, and there is no page you're holding in your hand. It feels like real life. (cited in Johnson 2015)

Yet when Milk suggests that the medium interfaces with two of our senses, sight and hearing, he is in fact omitting the most innovative part of the interface offered by VR in general and VR films in particular, which is the proprioceptive. Proprioception contributes strongly to the sense of immersion and presence.

In one sense Milk's rhetoric echoes what digital media enthusiasts have been saying for years: that VR is the ideal immersive media. Indeed, Oliver Grau (2003) and others have argued that VR is the technological culmination of the centuries-old desire to reproduce and inhabit a perfect transparent medium. It is true that panoramic VR belongs to a tradition of viewing techniques and practices that dates from the late eighteenth century, when Robert Barker introduced the panoramic exhibition in Scotland and England and initiated a vogue that continued throughout much of the nineteenth century (Oettermann 1997). In the later nineteenth century, when large-scale painted panoramas were giving way to other forms of spectacle (eventually including the cinema), panoramic photography became a special genre with its own apparatus and aesthetics. The genre of analogue panoramic photography continued throughout the twentieth century, until the 1980s and 1990s when the advent of 3D computer graphics and videogames provided new ways both to generate and to view panoramas. Panoramic "skyboxes" became a common method for depicting the background in first-person shooters and other action videogames. VR films differ from these immersive videogames in that the emphasis is not on interactive gameplay, but rather on viewing what is essentially still an artifice in the tradition of cinema. Static panorama apps such as Sphere have been available for years; they are now joined by filmic panoramic viewers such as the Google Cardboard. Today we are on the verge of a marketing wave of inexpensive portable cameras and software for user-generated static and moving panoramas.

The claim of transparency for VR has been based primarily on sensual immediacy or the "lack of mediation" (Lombard and Ditton 1997). Chris Milk, however, comes to VR as a filmmaker, not as a computer scientist, and he regards VR films as remediating not only the sensory authenticity, but also the emotional engagement that has been the hallmark of "serious" mainstream cinema. Milk wants "to engage an audience on a deeper human level than any other medium that has reached them" (Johnson 2015). Milk makes this connection between medium-specific technique and emotional engagement explicit in his March 2015 TED talk entitled: "How virtual reality can create the ultimate empathy machine" (Milk 2015a). Here he equates technical point of view with emotional engagement: because the viewer sees the camp in Jordan all around, she can feel more deeply the plight of the refugees. Immersion is what makes VR "the ultimate empathy machine"—a machine that "feels like truth." Milk's anecdotal proof is that he took his film *Clouds over Sidra* (Milk 2015b) to the economic summit at Davos and was able to engage economists more deeply in the refugees' plight. The argument that VR can "connect humans to other humans in a profound way that I've never seen before in any other form of media" (Milk 2015a) is one that is often repeated in connection to immersive media, such as VR, which are viewed to be more authentic. Milk's claim seems specifically addressed to the media form that his film both belongs to and refashions, the documentary.

The figural and the panoramic

Scale has long been one of the ways in which our two major visual media were distinguished: cinema has been the large screen and television the small screen.[4] While that distinction has become less clear-cut in recent decades, as home monitors have grown in size, the mobile phone and tablet now have a definitive claim to being our media culture's small screens. The mobile cardboard viewing device further complicates the question of scale, as it offers a visual immersion that seems to surpass IMAX. Proprioceptively, however, mobile VR remains intimate, close to the body, in a way that IMAX, or even conventional film or television viewing, clearly are not. Drawing on the work of the cognitive scientist Daniel Montello (1993), computer scientists Evan Barba and Blair MacIntyre have analyzed how AR and VR applications are "correlated to specific positions, movements, and actions of the human body" (2011, 121). These positions and movements can be translated into spatial scales or segments of perception of the world around us. Building on the definitions of scale by Montello, Barba and MacIntyre suggest that the scale closest to the user or viewer is labeled the *figural* scale. At this level, the depicted objects are in front of the user and can be experienced through manipulation. The next two levels are the *vista* and the *panorama*. A vista includes everything a user can see at one glance, including objects beyond reach. The panoramic scale, the full 360-degree surround, cannot be taken in in one glance: to apprehend a full panorama, users must either manipulate the visual material that they are viewing or turn their own bodies.[5]

This taxonomy of spatial scales helps us to appreciate what is innovative about VR films as a media form, particularly when they are viewed with devices such as Google Cardboard, Microsoft Hololens, or Oculus Rift that separate the viewer completely from her surroundings. Conventional film and television viewing is at the scale of the vista: the viewer is too far from the screen to manipulate it, but at the same time she can take in the whole moving image in one glance. But watching a VR film is a hybrid experience—both figural and panoramic. The viewer has immediate tactile and proprioceptive control of the image-making apparatus, but she also knows that there is always a part of the panoramic image that is beyond her view. There is always a surplus, and in order to inspect that surplus, the viewer must engage with the apparatus. Watching a VR film is an experience not of distance but of proximity, no matter how vast the panoramic sweep of the photography may be. The most distant panorama is always near at hand.

The peculiar form of sensory engagement with a 360-degree moving image shown on a handheld device may be what allows Milk to claim that VR films inherently have an empathetic character. But at the same time it complicates his claim of immediacy. The tension between the figural, the vista, and the panoramic scales constantly reminds the viewer of the complex mediation that constitutes this new media form. The polyaesthetics of VR film reminds us of the polyaesthetic experience of mobile technology in general. The user is seldom entirely alone with one experience or one sensory channel. The sense of immersion with any mobile form is at best temporary and mitigated. This is also true of watching traditional films and videos in the mobile format, because the very design of the smartphone constantly exposes the viewer to interruptions (text messages, phone calls, notifications) and to the lure of multitasking.

The VR cinema of attractions

The Displaced and *Clouds of Sidra* are for the moment among the most prominent VR films, but they do not by themselves completely characterize this nascent media form. The practice of VR filmmaking is already so sufficiently widespread and diverse that recognized categories, if not genres, have begun to emerge. Production companies (such as vrse.com and dimensiongate.com) have been formed to offer a range of such videos: from artistic to commercial. YouTube has established an upload format for panoramic videos, and the YouTube channel #360video already has over 750,000 subscribers. Most of the video uploads do not aim for the narrative coherence and empathetic catharsis that Milk emphasizes in his TED talk. Their subject matter is simply the occasion for the spectacle of 360-degree presentation: for example, flights as seen from the cockpit of an aircraft or nature panoramas. Other videos are harder to classify, such as the rather baffling New York Times' *Take Flight*, which depicts ten well-known film actors floating in a starry sky, accompanied by the playing of string music (Askill 2015).

The variety and genre fluidity of VR films suggest a comparison to the first years of film around 1900, and specifically to Gunning's analysis of the period as the "cinema of attractions" (1986, 1995), when the audience was amazed by the uncanny ability of the camera to reproduce reality, although not necessarily fooled into mistaking the image for reality. Today's VR films share some of the qualities of the cinema of attractions. There is the expression of amazement and the pleasure of the spectacle. There is also the direct address of the audience by the film. In the case of silent early films, direct address was accomplished by various techniques of camera placement or by having the actors acknowledge the camera (Gunning 1995, 825). In VR films, instead, the narrator often speaks directly to the viewer, praising the immersive technique and explaining how it works. Finally, we can see an analogy in the context of presentation. The early cinema was associated with vaudeville entertainments; short films were even sometimes in a "variety format" with vaudeville acts (Gunning 1986, 68).

YouTube could be called the internet's vaudeville with its enormous variety of subject matter and quality. Although full-length films are now available on YouTube, most of its videos are short and make a single spectacular point, and its interface with its suggested links is designed to seduce the user into watching video after video.

There are, however, two important differences between the early cinema of attractions and VR films. Gunning was describing a period prior to the dominance of narrative in cinema, whereas VR films are appearing now after a century, in which the mainstream has been defined by cathartic narrative. Hence, some VR filmmakers (e.g., Chris Milk) are consciously trying to assimilate VR films to the narrative tradition, while the bulk of production seems to focus on pure spectacle. The other key difference lies in the nature of the remediating claim. The ghostly, black-and-white moving images described by Gorky (Gunning 1995, 821–22) had a peculiar evocative effect as shadows of reality, but the experience of viewing them was not polyaesthetic. Today's VR filmmakers, often in their direct narrative address of the viewer, emphasize the proprioceptive qualities of mobile viewing. VR film perfectly illustrates the new paradigm of mobile cinematics.

Aura and mobile cinematics

We return to the question with which we began: does mobile cinematics contribute further to the decay of aura that Benjamin ascribed to screened films? Benjamin defined aura as "a sense of distance no matter how near" (1968). We can think of Benjamin's definition in tactile and proprioceptive terms—a work of auratic art can never be touched by the viewer; it is always out of reach, like Benjamin's mountains on a summer's day. The apparatus and technique of cinema in Benjamin's time were supposed to destroy aura in part because the camera could dissect the scene, entering the space occupied by the film actors. But this claim of destroying the distance was metaphorical. Even if the camera could penetrate the space of the scene, the viewing audience remained physically distant from the screen itself and the images that played on it. Mobile cinematics, particularly as illustrated by these manipulative VR films, brings the farthest panoramic landscape so near that it is literally at the viewer's fingertips. As we noted above, however, with VR films, there remains a surplus and inaccessible distance, which suggests that even direct manipulation cannot completely eradicate aura. If photography and film created a crisis of aura, the polyaesthetics of mobile cinematics both intensifies and complicates that crisis while rendering literal Benjamin's metaphor of distance.

Notes

1 Although these cultural shifts express themselves differently in various parts of the world (see Agar 2013), the dominance of mobile phones over other forms of communication is quite clear today with 4.4 billion fee-based cell phone users globally. http://www.statista.com/statistics/274774/forecast-of-mobile-phone-users-worldwide/ (accessed December 28, 2015).

2 Here we refer to the perceptual sense of touch and proprioception, not a metaphorical response to the visual, as in Laura Marks' notion of haptic visuality (2002).

3 By *polyaesthetic*, we mean the ways in which media objects evoke a sensory experience that requires multilayered perceptive engagement. Inherent in the affordances of the media chosen, touch, sight, and sound can be called upon in the meaning-making process. Obviously, the physiological processes behind our sensory experiences are complex and move beyond the scope of this chapter; however, by polyaesthetic, we wish to foreground that this condition is not only a material choice but an aesthetic and media strategy as well. For a discussion on polyaesthetics and media studies, see Engberg (2014).

4 See, for example, Creeber's *Small Screen Aesthetics* (2013), which examines the aesthetics of television as a medium on traditional television screens as well as computer screens, though not mobile devices.

5 Other scales, such as the environmental and the geographic can only be experienced by locomotion and, therefore, require other types of temporally sustained, locative media such as Alternate Reality Games. Those go beyond the scales that are relevant for mobile cinematics.

Part Five

[Compacted]
Urban Ecologies

17

Screening Smart Cities: Managing Data, Views, and Vertigo

Gillian Rose

There is a long history of imagining how the cities of the future might improve on those of the present. The past fifty years have seen two periods in particular when many architects, planners, designers, and visionaries were imagining new urban futures. The first was between 1960 and 1974, and the second began a decade ago and is still underway (Dunn et al. 2014). Both can be seen as responses to periods of structural crisis and transformation that were expressed especially clearly in urban social relations, city governance, and built environments. In the 1960s and 1970s, physical blight and social unrest seemed to point to the failure of modern architecture and postwar planning; more recent visualizations have responded to the urban consequences of irreversible climate change and the need for cities to become more sustainable.

In response to the current urban situation (which is of course immensely complex and diverse), many city governments, corporations, start-ups, and think tanks are advocating the "smart city." According to recent research by Rand Europe, over half of the cities in Europe are hosting two or more "smart" initiatives.[1] The term "smart" refers to the use of various kinds of digital technologies to achieve environmental sustainability by encouraging and enabling the more efficient use of resources, especially energy and water. Other goals include increasing economic growth by developing new products and markets, ensuring urban security by surveilling populations, and increasing democratic participation in city governance (Crang and Graham 2007; Hollands 2008; Rossi 2015). As such a list might suggest, "smart cities" are complicated assemblages of various things—technologies, policies, data, products, and discourse—with a wide range of aims and effects. Among all the hype, experimentation, idealism, policymaking, research, play, and commercialization, several large corporations are making an extended effort to visualize smart cities. Indeed, the term "smarter city" was trademarked by IBM in 2011. It matters a great deal to these corporations that not only are certain stories told about smart cities (Söderström et al. 2014), but also that they are visualized in particular ways. This chapter focuses on just one example of this corporate urban vision: a short film made in 2012 for the engineering company Siemens.

The film can be seen in a building funded by Siemens called The Crystal. The Crystal is described on its website as "the world's largest exhibition on the future of cities" and "one of the world's most sustainable buildings."[2] Designed by architects Wilkinson Eyre and exhibition designers Event Communications, it cost around £30 million and opened in 2012 in London's Docklands. The exhibition's focus is urban sustainability, and the emphasis is on mostly digital solutions to the problems faced by cities now: population growth, climate change, building design, energy, water supply, planning, security, transport, and health. At the center of The Crystal building and the culmination of its vision is a film called, modestly enough, *Future Life*. Designed and produced by digital media studio ISO,[3] *Future Life* lasts four minutes and twenty-five seconds. It runs on a continuous loop, projected onto a very wide, curved screen in a darkened space in the middle of The Crystal's ground floor. The film is also available on Siemens's YouTube channel, of course, where as of late January 2016 it had received 31,355 views, 143 likes, 5 dislikes, and 9 comments; the channel hosts an eight-minute version of the film too.[4] It can be seen as well on Informa's Internet of Things World website,[5] and a screenshot appears in a report entitled *Smarter London* by the think tank New London Architecture (NLA 2014, 5). Yet another version is hosted on ISO's website, where a one minute and 42-second Vimeo video of the film being watched by a variety of visitors to The Crystal is embedded.[6]

Future Life seems a paradigmatic piece of compact cinematics. It is short, shown on a variety of small screens and thus in various sites, and designed for viewing in situations that are not necessarily about "watching a film" (cf. Casetti 2015). It is also typical of much compact cinematics in that it is difficult to categorize using conventional definitions of media and genre. Its funding by Siemens would suggest that it is an advertisement—but there are no Siemens products, brands, or logos to be seen in the film, only three cities that run smoothly because they are "smart." Indeed, Siemens branding is very low-key throughout The Crystal. *Future Life* isn't quite cinema either. It is much smaller than an IMAX screen and its viewers can come and go as they please. Indeed, its physical layout is strongly reminiscent, not of a theatrical cinema screen, but of a panorama: the side edges of the screen are not visible to viewers sitting on the viewing bench provided. Nor are its creators filmmakers in the conventional sense. The film was part of a package of visual and interactive materials designed for The Crystal by ISO who describe themselves as a "content design and development studio." ISO are not unusual among such companies in employing live-action directors, 2D and 3D animators, graphic and interface designers, scriptwriters, software developers, social media managers, and producers. Specializing in "cultural projects for public, private and commercial clients," they produce "digital media, interactive software and immersive installations." In other words, to use the more succinct phrasing of their Twitter page, they are "digital experience designers." To create *Future Life*, they shot film and "added CGI modeled buildings [designed in collaboration with the architectural practice NORD] and live action composited sequences."[7] *Future Life*, then, exemplifies the sort of product created more and more often by digital visualization studios who use a variety of graphic design, filming, animation, editing, and modeling software to create content that crosses both media and genre.

Future Life looks at 24 hours in London, New York, and Copenhagen in the year 2050 (see Figure 17.1). Drawing on a long history of visualizing cities from the air, it opens with a photo-realist, oblique aerial view of Central Park in New York, albeit Central Park with four geodesic domes glittering in the early morning sunshine: the voice-over says that it's 7:03 a.m. We then fly slowly across the city, other recognizable landmarks now surrounded by huge white buildings. The facades of rectangular office blocks are display screens, there are trees on roofs and inside the glass-clad buildings, and twirly wind turbines are everywhere. The flight path is a little bumpy and the faint sound of rotors suggests we're in a helicopter. But we can't "really" be in a helicopter because, almost immediately, blue text boxes appear on the screen, pointing out for example "high rise capsule apartments" and "community agricultural farming." The film then cuts to a series of interior scenes with individuals (old, young, and ethnically diverse) who are interacting with similar floating screens, making menu selections and video calls. The next scene is another aerial view, this time of Copenhagen, again digitally modified with new buildings. Both cities are pictured in the familiar colors of a thousand commercial architectural visualizations: white, grays, pale blue, pale greens, a color spectrum of corporate bland or "developer slick" (May 2012, 21), where pale sunshine illuminates clean buildings, calm people, and lots of trees.

Figure 17.1 New York in 2050, as pictured in *Future Life*. © The ISO Organization 2012.

From corporate bland, the film cuts to its other color palette: neon data-glow (Degen et al. 2015). The screen now shows an animated digital map of Copenhagen. Waterways are dark blue, there are areas of dark gray land, and against these and a black background are built-up areas glowing pink and violet, blue wind turbine icons, and luminous pulsating yellow lines of electricity transmission. We then zoom down and across the map, which morphs into a white three-dimensional model of buildings, onto which a photo-realist skin is then layered. The film has thus shifted from map, to planning model, to oblique photographic aerial view in a couple of seconds. No time to pause, though: once again we are wobbly and flying, across Copenhagen with more blue text boxes hovering in the sky, and we then sink down to ground level. There is a brief photo-realist panorama of buildings across open water; the view rotates across the panorama before cutting to another domestic interior with another screen-swiping inhabitant. Since the nineteenth century, the difference between the aerial view of the map, plan, and model, and representations of people in streets and public spaces "suggest that the individual's lived experience of places and the planner's oversight of the whole socio-economic system that a city is, are points within a rotation from vertical to horizontal" (Macarthur 2013, 190). In this sequence, however, *Future Life* enacts a continuous flow through all heights and angles, blending one into the next and citing four of the most important modes of designing and planning cities—maps, models, panoramas, and aerial photographs—before peering into a domestic interior. They are all assimilated in one easy transition via the digitality of the film's production; all are now simply visual options to be turned on and off at the behest of the visualization software package, it seems.

The short film then takes us back to New York, once more to an aerial photo-realist view of the city (see Figure 17.2). This time, the photo-realist skin is not peeled away. Instead, the surface textures and sunlight of the city dissolve as neon data seeps from facades and beams between buildings. The entire "city" (as over

Figure 17.2 New York again, as pictured in *Future Life*. © The ISO Organization 2012.

Figure 17.3 New York's City Cockpit in 2050, as pictured in *Future Life*. © The ISO Organization 2012.

a century of realist representational forms have encouraged us to understand it) fades into a luminous, semitransparent, three-dimensional model, described by ISO on their website as a "holographic visualization."[8] Buildings become opaque glowing cuboids, with rays of colored light beaming between and beyond them. For a moment the background is entirely black, just like the earlier neon glow map of Copenhagen and the black space in which the film is screened in *The Crystal*. But the holograph then emerges as a digital model sitting on a table (see Figure 17.3). Human figures appear around it, in suits, their eye-level at ours, once again tapping and swiping floating interfaces, this time to resolve urban challenges like traffic jams by turning stationary glowing red dots into mobile green ones with a single gesture.

The dissolve from a photo-realistic oblique aerial view of New York to a holographic model is striking. It has been suggested that smart initiatives are layering a "digital skin" over the physical bodies of existing cities (Rabari and Storper 2014), but *Future Life* has suggested the reverse twice now: that the city as we have come to know it, as it has been shown ever since the invention of film and photography (which themselves remediated older traditions of drawing and painting urban spaces), is just an optional surface—a Photoshop layer perhaps—just one of a series of technical choices available for representing the city, each as usable as the other and all equally available. Casetti (2015, 131) suggests that the "hypertopia" of contemporary cinematics "fills our 'here' with all possible 'elsewheres.'" Perhaps *Future Life* should then be described as hyper-hypertopic, since it shows not only three different cities in the future, but also, in its visual profligacy, fills its viewers' "heres" with all possible ways of showing those elsewheres.

Mark Dorrian has suggested that such explicit visualizations of the construction of urban images may induce a kind of vertigo because their constantly "transcoded indexicality" generates "a condition of constant deferral within the image" (2005, 10, 96). This is a particular risk in *Future Life* because the film has taken some care to show its viewers future urban life using the same visuality that it imagines such life to require. The holograph of New York—which places the film's viewers as yet more bodies around the city-as-model—shows Siemens's "integrated management information and decision support system" called "City Cockpits." The name was registered as a trademark in 2010 and harks back to the airplane as the source of its aerial view. As we have seen, the short film makes its viewers feel as if their photo-realist aerial views in the film were indeed from a cockpit as we judder gently over cities in *Future Life*'s helicopter. Moreover, those floating blue text boxes that annotate our oblique fly-throughs are repeated as the means by which both the inhabitants and the managers of these future cities interact with it.

One means to allay such nausea, Dorrian suggests, are the conventions of engaging with three-dimensional urban planning models. Dorrian describes the comfort they offer as their edges clearly delimit the city, giving attention a spatial limit and halting its vertiginous fall. Perhaps this explains why the City Cockpit in *Future Life* is so quickly placed on a table: to render it bounded and thus legible. Dorrian also notes the comfort of the oblique aerial view, generating as it does the pleasure of seeing things together, pictorially composed (2015, 104). (Hence aerial views have also "always represented *strategic* vision" [Dorrian 2015, 152].) The figures pictured manipulating the City Cockpit model have this calming overview, and it is offered to *Future Life*'s viewers throughout the film. And there is also, without doubt, the pleasure generated by the technical virtuosity and beauty of the short film's flights, swoops, zooms, dissolves, and emergences, which Buchan and Janser (2015) point to as a defining feature of animations.

Indeed, this spatial affect may well be the most important feature of *Future Life* because it is an affect generated by so many forms of contemporary digital visualizations. As Manovich (2013) has pointed out, while many images continue to remediate older visual forms (maps, models, oblique aerial photographs, and urban panoramas, in the case of *Future Life*), the software through which such forms of compact cinematics are made is also inflecting their visual and spatial forms. Visual "digital experience" is now designed by creating and manipulating objects in three-dimensional space, and Manovich (2013) suggests that this software is enabling the emergence of a widespread "new design language" of mobile, high-definition, fast-moving animations (179, 260). Such an aesthetic may not be global, but it is certainly pervasive in commercial digital visualizations and, as such, it seems to be shifting what the aerial view does. Although that view is still important to the "strategic vision" of urban managers and planners (and *Future Life* suggests it will still be so in 2050), it no longer offers "a global view of particulars" (Bann 2013, 89). Its "heuristic potency" (Robic 2013, 174) seems to have faded somewhat, in an age when Google Earth, Hollywood superhero movies, computer games, and Google Streetview have made aerial views and panoramas everyday occurrences, popular desktop distractions, and estate agents' aids (Gilbert 2010). Such views are now so familiar that, in order to convey specific informational content, they have to be annotated, for example, with floating blue boxes; for *Future Life* to succeed in explaining the "smart city," explicit commentary is required (and *Future Life* also has a calm, explanatory voice-over throughout).

What is left, then, of the aerial view is not its synthesizing insight, but its sensation (Castro 2013) and, in particular, its spatiality. In her discussion of animation, Buchan suggests that "many non-conventional, hyperrealist animation films create visual neologisms in the particular animated space-time that are the true "characters" of the film" (2013, 8). The spatiality through which *Future Life* envisions "smart cities" in 2050 is perhaps its most striking feature. Its movement and angles that wobble, the zooming in and out, the shift from aerial view from above to ground-level view, its virtuoso display of multiple forms of representation, its smooth transitions between these, its pulsing networks—this is an affective spatiality that enrolls viewers of the film in pleasurably enacting the mobile untethered spatiality of digital visuality, in which we "locate ourselves in simultaneous spaces, multiple temporalities, and data-rich, simulated environments," anywhere with a smart screen and internet connection (Elsaesser 2013, 228). In that sense, *Future Life* does indeed design an embodied "digital experience" for its viewers, and one that is emerging, not in 2050, but right now.

Notes

1 http://www.rand.org/randeurope/research/projects/eu-smart-cities.html (accessed January 14, 2016).

2 https://www.thecrystal.org/ (accessed January 14, 2016).

3 http://isodesign.co.uk (accessed January 14, 2016).

4 https://www.youtube.com/watch?v=zuPIyqUc9oA and https://www.youtube.com/watch?v=xK9TP_B95nQ (accessed January 14, 2016).

5 http://iotworldevent.com/iot-channel/siemens-the-crystal-future-life-video/# (accessed January 17, 2016).

6 http://isodesign.co.uk/projects/the-crystal-av-installations-interactives (accessed January 17, 2016).

7 All information from http://isodesign.co.uk/profile and http://isodesign.co.uk/projects/the-crystal-av-installations-interactives (accessed January 20, 2016).

8 http://isodesign.co.uk/projects/the-crystal-av-installations-interactives (accessed January 20, 2016).

18

Of Compactness: Life with Media Façade Screens

Ulrik Ekman

This chapter engages with the issue of compact cinematics by analyzing Niejo Sobejano's Contemporary Art Centre, the C4 building in Córdoba, Spain (see Figure 18.1 below). This building and its creative invention of a media façade by the Edler brothers are here considered as a thought-provoking example of the contemporary development of urban media architectures, which change our notions of cinematics. My analysis demonstrates that a mixed-reality cinematics is at stake in which both analog and digital films are undergoing material, energetic, scalar, and temporal transformations. I show that this development grants the individual pixel new kinds of autonomy and compository potential, presenting the urbanite with multitudes of small, microtemporal components for moving image atmospheres whose expressions range from the invisible through vaguely ambient and middle-ground clarity to bursts of light demanding focal attention. Such architectural and environmental dynamics push cinematics toward a disorganized and molecular complexity of multiple temporal and relational pixellation processes. An individually, socially, and technically interactive mixed-reality cinematics concerned with the potentials for actualizing new compositions of compact pixel molecules begins to break with notions of passive and sedentary film reception, representational images, the tradition of the orthogonal 2D screen in a theater with four walls, and the focal cinematic apparatus. It is the complex variability of new pixels, algorithms for their composition, and (in)visibility that contribute emergent cinematic urban infrastructures whose image atmospheres increasingly shape, code, decode, recode, and overcode urban affectivity.

A screen transcoding milieux

Perhaps everything is moving in complexity, no one is there, and no thing is visible—a pre-cinematic condition. But even disorganized complexity has directions, relative orderings of fluctuations, and perceptible concretizations. It is true, however, that a dephasing of being, a disindividuation, always poses a problem of the oscillations of the environment and a cut into these by an ecotechnics to actualize parts of a technical tendency, perhaps permit a mode of perception. This is the case with the arrival of C4 in Córdoba and its media façade. From out of the outside it leaps to a set of urban milieux across which it goes on to actualize a diagrammatic architectural formation that may stay fragile or break down, but tends toward some relatively stable ordering and slowing down. It constitutes itself in an exterior milieu and time of the city, basing itself on an empty ground and the necessary materials of earth, water, sand, stone, glass, and metals. It sustains itself on an energetic associated milieu of climate, sunlight, and electricity; it affords both modes of perception (via holes, windows, sensors) and modes of action (via changes of the landscape, exhibitions, banners, and a dynamic urban recontextualization via façade images).

Figure 18.1 Dawn, Contemporary Art Center, Córdoba. Architect Nieto Sobejano. Photograph, copyright Roland Halbe, 2012. Image courtesy of the photographer.

It approaches an interior milieu via an intermediary screen milieu. It inserts a complex three-dimensional architectural topography of walls mostly of glass fiber, reinforced concrete panels, fluorescent light tubes, and thousands of bowl-shaped indentations and holes. This sketches an actual limit around that fragile diagrammatic formation; it organizes a delimited space. Multiple environmental pressures on urbanization are mostly kept at bay outside, for a while. Inside, walls, floors, ceilings, doors, pipes, wires, and openings help secure the operation of an art museum and exhibitions. These delimitations, especially the intermediate milieu of walls and the associated milieu of perception and action, reinvent cinematics while recalling screen apparatuses *qua* dividers, shelters, concealments, and sieves for ongoing selectivity (extraction of resources, maintenance of boundaries, elimination of threats).

An invention of compact cinematics today must involve a screen apparatus qua a shielding membrane. It must have some self-maintenance of topological conditions, here the conditions for an urban spacing that continuously relates milieux of interiority to milieux of exteriority. C4 maintains as screen technics a membrane that is polarized and asymmetrical. It will let pass some kinds of bodies in centripetal or centrifugal directions, but it will oppose other kinds of bodies, always repolarizing itself asymmetrically via selectivity. It keeps an interior in relation to an exterior by operating at and on its own limit of self-maintenance. It prolongs itself and Córdoba as a complex urban "organism" forming diverse dimensions of interiority and exteriority. The screen wall facing the old city of Córdoba is an ongoing architectural structuration, which differentiates itself from the milieu in the environment and integrates certain differences. Prior to this it is a continuous transduction, a generative relational transport between numerous interiorities and exteriorities. This process of mediation remains exposed to the danger of a collapse, which could be brought on by the wrong speed, direction, or pattern of organizational movement.

C4 also opens onto and passes into the future, disastrous or not, while drawing upon and unfolding further what is created by Sobejano and realities:united. While the C4 building surely deteriorates, it is also in-formatively inventive. While a building, it also decodes the intervals of iteration characteristic of the formation of materials in the exterior milieu. Organizing an art center, it also decodes the intervals of iteration operative in the gathering of elements in the interior milieu. These decodings demonstrate that both exterior and interior milieux are unceasingly in transcoding, passing between the more or less heterogeneous spacing and temporalization of each of various milieux.

Moreover, this transcoding at the edge of the city invents a pattern for generative relations between the environment and urbanization. This transduction complexifies the delimitation of both Córdoba and C4 and their surroundings. The complexification notably plays itself out with the intermediate milieu and the associated milieu. C4 opens itself inside out and infolds outside elements via its intermediate milieu. It informs itself perceptually and expresses itself actively via its associated milieu. This includes communications among the intermediate and the associated milieu, which have them pass into each other but also suggest a unique new pattern of relational urban movement. One might say that a transcoding of milieux is sought that may admit the direction, organization, and future potential of buildings for an actively and perceptually context-aware sustainable city, one that increasingly composes itself as a glocalized world via an informational network of intermediate screen milieux.

Such an urban transcoding has only been concretized piecemeal; it demands the development of urban and architectural territories. Perhaps C4 presents concrete inklings of such a pattern of developmental trajectories in the urban disparate. In terms of cinematics, this unfolds on and as the outside screen of the building, and the inside screen. Especially in its complex wall tissues, the C4 building risks pursuing an improvisatory opening toward a future mesh of architectural buildings and other urban milieux. The inner and outer skin layers of C4 participate in a drifting movement toward a future informational screen. It is uncertain how such mediational architectural projects are to be conceived and engaged.

A screen patterning across territories and individual perceptive worlds

The transcoding of milieux performed by C4 and its screens, and by Córdoba, solves the problem of distinguishing an environment and a human urban culture. It moves beyond the lack of ground and foundation, beyond seeing to a minimum material form and a definite temporal coding of milieux that function. The reinforced concrete panelizations, the glass fiber texturings of the façade, and the flexible lightings of its media affirm an ongoing variation of material composition and a development of forms. Affecting milieux by establishing a rather certain spatial range, affecting temporal patterns by giving them a rather certain durability, the C4 project generates an urban territory and a house in an expressive act. C4 and its site constitute the styling of an urban place, the assembly of a signature building.

C4 sets an urban territorial stage, freeing various materials for expression. Territorially, it makes for an aesthetics of behaviors by inscribing a mark and drawing up a diagram, an expression that patterns productive repetition. It provides an expressive figure for an urban territory that operates with a contrastive background (an external milieu of varying nonlocalized conditions) and a foreground (an interior milieu of varying predispositions). This project provides an external urban pattern that sometimes makes this the recognizable landscape of Córdoba. It provides an internal urban pattern that sometimes makes these the recurring roles for a building and the perceptual and active impulses for urban citizens. However, these patterns are rarely constant, localized, or regularly periodized, but rather vary (growing in predominance or dwindling away) as irregularly temporal and nonlocalized. They do often tend toward territorializing a domain, giving it dimensions, sometimes a measurable Euclidean metrics. Hence they change the functions of the environment to ones associated with this city, this building, these individuals. They set up the functions of this building as an art center. They ensure and regulate the coexistence of citizens while differentiating them, professionally, as visitors, or otherwise. This territorial figuration (these external and internal urban patterns) proposes styles for ways in which architecture and urban individuals are to act and perceive. How are landscapes and abodes to be related? How is traffic to move? How are individual citizens to walk, gesture, see worlds?

All this requires that an internal organization of C4 holds up, not just in the sense of bringing into a fuzzy set the energy, materials, and individuals, but rather in the sense of creating relatively solid coalescences of the heterogeneous. The aesthetics of behaviors for this territory has to disjunctively compose in complex networks different localized and individualized components (some coexistences, others successions). Glass fibers and reinforced concrete materials compose with inserted iron beams, lighting fixtures, wires, and holes (see Figure 18.2 below).

Along its outside walls and in the intricate maze of corridors, doors, and rooms in C4, a great variety of individuals must be able to pass sequentially and coexist while affirming their ongoing differentiation. Such an aggregate internally holds together consistently enough disparate external and internal urban patterns (based on various insertions now and then, intervals here and there, as well as superimpositions of this and that thing, this individual and that group).

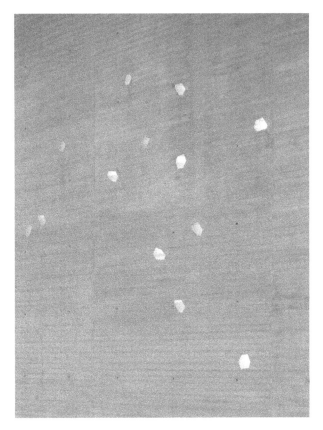

Figure 18.2 Foyer detail, Contemporary Art Center, Córdoba. Architect Nieto Sobejano. Photograph, copyright Roland Halbe, 2012. Image courtesy of the photographer.

The screenings proper to the internal and the associated milieux constitute especially creative expressions whose improvised solution to the problem of enacting and perceiving worlds signals a co-individuation of cinematic apparatus and individuals. The dynamic permeability in both directions of the superimposed external and interior screens is a hint that cinematics and individualization with twenty-first century architecture and urban territorialization have begun to depart from paradigms of the fourth wall, a static square movie theater, and sedentary individual perception of imaged worlds. C4 is a concretized, compact case of cinematics that are outside *and* inside, but primarily in a constitutive relational in-between of the territorially disparate. Individuations of inhabitants and visitors are visually and perceptually ongoing while on the move inside *and* outside an assembled building, but primarily in the disparate

Figure 18.3 Offices hallway, Contemporary Art Center, Córdoba. Architect Nieto Sobejano. Photograph, copyright Roland Halbe, 2012. Image courtesy of the photographer.

migratory relationality generating an urban territory and passages among many other territories.

Light waves, electrical light, and electronic light stream through multitudes of holes into the building to generate many continuously varying and complex, vague analogico-digital images of the world (see Figure 18.3 above).

Images are projected on the façade, to be perceived by passers-by, sometimes permitting a sense of events and situations inside the art center. Sometimes images of how the building perceives its more immediate outside are projected, permitting individuals a sense of what happens in the local territory. All this outlines a co-development: simultaneously the individuation with C4 of a technical screen apparatus and the individuation of individuals moving in Córdoba. It also organizes a dimensional local territory with some consistency, just as a person there tends toward maintaining herself or himself along with the pattern of perception laid out with the screening. However, this is not just development of local territory, a native abode, and the personal. It may be tempting to see it as part of the development from the radar screen surveying the environment through the 1980s command line screen monitor for personal computing to the still predominant and increasingly privatized graphical user interface variants of new media since the mid-1990s.

Certainly, this remains traceable in C4, whose screenings are also constitutively informational and reticular. Nonetheless, these screenings go inside out of this paradigm since in their interior organization, a much older set of patterns is reactualized with a difference, going back across the modern analog/digital divide so as to re-mark various screen materials and texture, solar and electrical energy streaming in, and a continuous variation of screen scales as well as different temporal flows of imagings according to daylight and artificial light. This paradigm is cracked open onto new outsides: the media façade relates interactively to networks of sensors and actuators in associated and external milieux; it relates to many other mobile and ad hoc networked screens in a new generation of cameras, tablets, and smartphones. The media façade depicts the local, but does this alongside many other places in the world. It contributes to increasingly intense migratory individuations through the local, enacted and perceived as mixed realities relating back and forth across local and distant activities. Individuals become such by insisting on their native place and its potentials for action and perception, but also by insisting on their more or less unique transversal moves to integrate a heterogeneity of other territories in an age of globalized networks. C4 as a cinematic territorialization operates with cross-cutting analogico-digital screenings of glocalizations.

A screen texturing transindividual and transterritorial affectivity

Groups of visitors perceiving with the interior screen and throngs of urbanites perceiving with the media façade make it obvious that individuation was never just personal but always already collective. Local citizens can be recognized in the social context lit by the screen inside the art center. An inhabitant of Córdoba can fall in love when seeing an image of a desirable partner from the neighborhood. The complex screening through the inner and outer media facades of C4 does not just concern an individual analogico-digital enactment and perception of a local world and its inhabitants. Both inside and outside the screens partake in generation of public urban spaces that concern socialities in (de)formation, offering ways to screen the collective individuation of networks of distributed subjectivities living through urban glocalities with mixed time images (see Figure 18.4 below). Such

Figure 18.4 Evening, Contemporary Art Center, Córdoba. Architect Nieto Sobejano. Screenshot, *Architectural Review*.

screens, increasing in number across the world, vary uncertainly in scale, content, dynamic context-awareness, and ad hoc viewer gathering.

This is unlike the more stable movie theaters, home theaters, and personalized computational cinematics. Taking off from the local and the native, passing among other localities and norms, these screens offer creative cinematic windows of the emergent world and sociality. One key problem concerns the construction of an affectivity woven consistently enough that passage across heterogeneous localities can form a relatively durable transterritorial glocal mesh, so that a highly differentiated transindividuality may gather for a while some glocal social body at the limit of Córdoba and C4. The screenings are not least concerned with delimiting affectively a set of behaviors and trajectories for bodies. Screenings order these enough that components of this building and those of other places in the world may do new things with each other. Then, collectives of people momentarily in Córdoba may actualize some of their potential for doing something else with many others in the world.

The screening process unfolding with C4 is a remarkable attempt at achieving and maintaining a relatively consistent affective texturing for an urban glocality and its emergent groups of individuals. It experiments creatively with what networked architectural and social bodies in mixed realities can do when gathering and departing. This affective texturing forms the urban background or contextual existential urban condition. It is from such ordering of how the sensible is to move that individuals and groups may distill an urban emotion, a feeling of existing in this unfolding urbanization. It does not just repel and distantiate other cities and people. It forms an attractor, invites proximity, helps generate a slow series of enjoyable movements in and around the art center for a great many groups from various places in the world. Such affective consistency is very fragile. It most often fails to hold in most cities on Earth. It will eventually dwindle away in Córdoba and C4. This self-organizational texturing of a transindividual, transterritorial affectivity is a marvelous process, albeit brief.

The screening process at play appears more physically, locally bound than most of what is known as early twenty-first century social and mobile media screens. Its development in certain respects passes beyond their capacity for actualization of a more non-territorial mixed urban reality and mode of sociality. As the glocal character of the screens and social formations bespeaks, the affective texture at stake does not stay with the building, Córdoba, and the local, the groups there and then. It also undergoes internal, immanent complexification of its organization, something that takes it elsewhere. C4 distinguishes itself from the milieux to become an individual building, then from the territory linked to the edge of Córdoba so as to become a signature building recognized in other local territories across the world. There is even a way in which it and its screens compose with a multitude of others. It concerns the recognition of an urbanism and an architecture that has freed itself from the locally territorial. It affects by calling for a recognition independent of place. Gathering with others in relation to C4 and its networked media façade cinematics goes beyond being a group more or less indistinguishable from others in the milieux of Córdoba. It goes beyond being recognized as an individual collectivity according to the local criteria. Immanent to this, an emergent social formation traverses a host of other localities and their affective registers for social behaviors. At the limit, this formation touches on the issue of what a social body can be and do with others once it takes off from native placements.

Living with C4, couples, groups, social chains develop by freeing up the native territory so as to seek in it openings and passages across others. In the superimposition of the interior and the exterior urban textures that make up the screen of C4, an arrow cuts across numerous mixed territories and many collective individuations. This screening displays an ad hoc process that attempts textured conversions of territories and urban populations into each other, barred only by urban and social disparation (what remains strongly asymmetrical and unequal). Often, if not malfunctioning, this process leads back to the texture of the local and the neighborhood. Or it leads to a slightly modified repetition of this texture where some other concrete places and social groups intersect. Even this, however, leaves a remainder of a non-territorial operator, an arrow that can be drawn out later by others.

The affective texture can be quite consistent and still indicate that being most intensely at home in Córdoba is a rather ambiguous matter. Both C4 screenings and the social formations relating to it may go deeply inside or migrate extremely far outside. Coming home can simultaneously be a matter of hearing the deeply interior heartbeat of Cordobean territory *and* a matter of having to arrive at the right intersection of yet unknown territories at the other end of the world. Both imply an opening of the limit of urbanized territorial consistency. They risk all sensible ordering of affectivity, re-posing as a challenge how to begin gathering other forces of the environment that will affect urban individuals and groups. Although a highly uncertain move, it could be that—somehow, at some speed of movement for bodies, with some people—the texture proposed by the C4 screenings just opens onto jumps in other directions, away from the urban territorial, the architectural abode, the glocal personal and social individuations.

A pixellated environmental screen

The screens of C4, the media façade, the networked relations of screens and of people are part of a globally evolving third wave of information technology and network societies. Large square screens and images as well as the dynamical relations with these formed by social groups could let on that a late modern cinematic screen apparatus and social individuation are quite undisturbed. Perhaps all remains with the mode of operation of the computer screen, digital film, and the viewer roles sketched for new media, social and mobile media, their small tech devices. While there is no denying the key role of this heritage, the screenings, cinematics, and social developments in Córdoba and many other places in the world also concern something else.

Computation moves out of the box in innumerable smart, context-aware ways to exist with new information-intensive mixed-reality environments and their human inhabitants. Socialities intensify the hyperdifferentiating and connective logics of network societies to exist in new ways with the technoaesthetic environments of ubiquitous computing and finely grained, momentary social meshes running through places across the world. But first and foremost, networked glocal screen cinematics and reticular urban socialities are developments that open up experiments with matters and life forms in the environment, attempting new ways to grasp the material, energetic, and social forces of life on the move there. They are to generate an ecology of

Figure 18.5 Early dawn, Contemporary Art Center, Córdoba. Architect Nieto Sobejano. Photograph, copyright Roland Halbe, 2012. Image courtesy of the photographer.

image atmospheres co-developing with an ecology of social envelopes. In both cases, the key moves are molecularization, a directional grasp of forces, and a procedure that may (or may not) lead to consistency of the technologically and socially disparate.

The C4 building and the socialities forming with it do seem to endure with consistency and live intensely with the environment. They seem quite well directed. However, their apparently large-scale and visible organization are somewhat misleading. They are continuously trying to collect and synthesize billions of molecules in passage: material components, light waves, energy resources, and not least endless bits and bytes of social and environmental information from a network of sensors, cameras, and ever so many human interactants feeding relational databases. Just when this media façade appears a consistent, orthogonal screen directed by human producers at a nearby audience, it will look at you with a quasi-human gaze and reveal its smart computational awareness of contextually relevant molecular information, knowing what you are about to do in the situation just before you do it (see Figure 18.5 above).

It hints at a machinic vision capable of seeing what you will see before you see it. Just when it seems to work in a most benign late modern way, it may display and demonstrate that finely divided, discrete, atomized populations and big data participate in a surveillance of the environment. It is not immediately possible to decide whether such screenings open up to new kinds of biopolitical training and control of a molecularized population, or whether and how such a molecularized population is what affords a new, non-territorialized social form of life for this young second millennium.

Not all concerns a minimal consistency, a minimal delimitation of the variability of molecular social network relations, although it matters greatly to be able to coordinate environmentally across the world, affording a new heterogeneously consistent form of life for some population. Not all concerns a minimal technical consistency, the arrival of a not-too-variable technical aggregate of molecularly networked forces that form a curtain of objects (screens, buildings, and cities), although it is important to grasp internal forces from masses of indirect, coexisting technical environmental relations. Rather, a key effort in the C4 building, the screenings, and the socialities forming with these concerns the achievement of *organized* complexity.

Ubiquitous computing microcomponents, screens, cinematics, mediations, architectures, urbanizations are all going environmental. Internal to what appears as recognizable forms and layers that vary at most in a couple of ways, it is a question of organizing inorganic molecular entities. This is accompanied by the organization of the social into populations starting from minor networked groupings of finely divided individuals. This is heterogeneous and variable, but it is a problem of complexity that can be solved consistently via technical interrelations and interdisciplinary social efforts. The organizational variability of a transindividual population passing through the art center in Córdoba and other places very often tends toward becoming more homogeneous, staying for some time with more probable states of a layered distributed network with clearly weighted relations among layers. Very often, the transversal set of numerous molecular technical components and relations at play (when the screens of C4 intersect with many other screens and media architectures across the world) stabilizes variability, moving toward a homogenization.

But the currently emergent screenings and social multitudes remain open to disorganized and even to irreducible complexity. Media architectural facades and their screens are still light years from standardization and remain in considerable flux (kinetically, energetically, scale-wise, event-wise, technically, aesthetically, socially, interaction-wise, content-wise). Likewise, there is not yet any obvious homogeneity over time to any organizational states of dynamically ad hoc networked molecular multitudes of the social living with screens (flash mobs, viral social media movements, Chinese shopping crazes, the Saffron Revolution, the Arab Spring). Perhaps this considerable divergence toward the more complex and toward less probable states is the reason why the social groupings and the complexly organized screen cinematics relating to C4 really deserve to be gestured toward as developments in which the problem of the compact inheres, the problem of how another cinematic and social crystallization happens, affects us, and moves on.

C4 screening is of the compact insofar as it inherently crystallizes an organized media façade screen, a myriad of moving cinema pixels bundling and coming to cohere compositionally in and as an environmental image atmosphere for and with humans. Life with media facades is of the compact insofar as immanent to multitudes of micro parts of individuals and groups, a flash social envelope gathers in an environment of urbanization. The question of compact cinematics is one raised by the autonomous movements and constitutive relationalities of a host of new kinds of screen pixels. It is a question raised by the movements and relationalities of a host of microcomponents for new social forms of life, by the disorganized complexity of all the little relations and particles of life forms in a global social, technical, and material environment.

Sobejano and the Edler brothers' creativity presents us with a question of compact cinematics and life with such. At heart this is the formulation of the question whether autonomous pixels in statistical accumulations will move toward the rather unlikely event of organizing a new screen apparatus for twenty-first century image atmospheres vacillating from the environmentally invisible through the vaguely ambient and middle-ground clarity to the bursts of light demanding focal attention to center foreground. It is the articulation of the question concerning compact socialization, a problem of an unlikely probabilistic organization of new social forms of human life from discrete environmental atoms and sub- and pre-individual resources. The current development of technosocial compactness may vary so as to remain with a disorganized complexity that permits organizational reductions to concrete individual screen technics going transversal and concrete individual social groupings interlinking transindividualities of different kinds. Or this development may disappear inside the compact without crystallization: it may vary in unsustainable ways, effacing individuality of technics and sociality in the irreducible complexity of the environment.

19

Codified Space: Cinematic Recodings
of Urban Reality

Justin Ascott

*When the world has been fully codified and collated and . . . we know
exactly and objectively where everything is and what it is called, a sense
of loss arises. . . . In a fully discovered world exploration does not stop;
it just has to be reinvented.*

(Bonnett 2015, 4–5)

Introduction

Codified Space is a short experimental film I produced in 2011, which won the
Tenderflix international film competition, and was screened at the London
Short Film Festival, and Stuttgarter Filmwinter. As an independent filmmaker
I typically work alone like a photographer, using lightweight, compact digital
equipment. I make short films of under ten minutes that explore issues relating
to urban spaces and places. Short form filmmaking appeals to me because the
temporal duration favors narratives that focus on single, defined themes and
settings rather than the complexities of feature-length temporal structures,
with the associated extensive planning and significant financial resources
required. In the timescale needed to complete a single feature film, I am able to
produce several short films—which greatly appeals because it allows me to use
the medium in a highly iterative, experimental way. My former career as a TV
commercials director making micro sixty-second advertising films trained me
to communicate emotional content and information using a highly condensed
aesthetic. As a reaction to the manipulative rhetoric of ads, I now passionately
advocate the Web 2.0 open-source filmmaking ethos of making personal

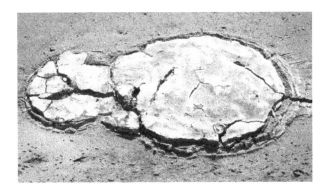

Figure 19.1 Still from *Codified Space* of an eroded road marking. Courtesy of the artist.

films publicly available via online streaming sites such as YouTube and Vimeo (*Codified Space* is available on Vimeo). The advantage of this online distribution platform is that viewers can watch films on small portable screens, which makes content highly accessible. Close-up framings of material details have a greater graphic impact on small screens than do long shots, hence there is a tendency to frame online micro-narratives predominantly in this way. Compact online cinema, then, can be seen to create its own perceptual aesthetic.

Codified Space deals with a seemingly mundane, functionless place—a derelict multistory car park, which, through its digitally mediated reconstruction and employment of close-up framings to reveal commonly overlooked details (see Figure 19.1), has the power to surprise.

The film invokes what sound theorist Michael Stocker refers to as a "cognitive reality shift" (2013, 52), by disrupting and reshaping our relationship to space, using a visual-sonic affective register. As a filmmaker, I am fascinated by the potential of cinematics to construct imaginative new spaces—ones that are narratively generative in nature invoking affective responses and triggering new thought patterns. I use writing in conjunction with my film practice as a way of stimulating theoretical and philosophical exploration of this potential.

Codified Space explores the nexus between the built environment and film, in imaginatively and experimentally attempting to transform ideologically coded attitudes and behaviors. French theorist Henri Lefebvre (1991, 49–53) argues that urban space is a social construction, which he terms "abstract space." Abstract space affects spatial practices and perceptions that are fundamental to the reproduction of society, and capitalism. Every society produces its own form of ideological space, which is defined and controlled by state power. Lefebvre writes:

> So long . . . as the only connection between workspaces, leisure spaces and living spaces is supplied by the agencies of political power and by their mechanisms of control—so long must the project of "changing life" . . . be taken up or abandoned according to the mood of the moment. (59–60)

Everyday urban experience could be revolutionized, Lefebvre asserts, by reflecting on the everyday realities of boredom, versus the illusory promises offered by capitalism. Without transforming our everyday lives, capitalism continues to inhibit real self-expression (ibid.). This I interpret as the need to develop an emotionally authentic and critically reflective engagement with the cityscape that surrounds us, such that we can learn to live and express ourselves creatively within it, rather than being controlled and depersonalized by it.

Codified Space sets out to poetically/politically recode the site of the derelict car park, using the formal elements of the film medium such as framing, movement, editing, and sound. Film by its inherent sequential nature can be said to narrativize space. I use "narrative" in the loose sense of the term to mean that it provides a visual structure that takes the viewer on a (digitally mediated) journey that starts in one place and ends in another. In *Codified Space* the journey is dynamically enhanced through the use of a slider, which, during the filming phase, enabled the choreographing of tracking, dollying, and rising shots that create a strong sense of embodied movement through three-dimensional geographic space. Through the juxtaposition of shots filmed at the macro and microscale—the film seeks to provide a holistic impression of the complex totality of an environment, conveying a palpable sense of its form, structure, scale, and activity.

Film captures a place's subtle ephemeral qualities—the changing pattern of light as it falls on its surfaces, its acoustic dimensionality; in other words its preconscious affective atmosphere. The derelict car park is then in a sense the character of the film, constitutive of both the foreground subject and the background context.

The car park as functional structure

The specific building featured in *Codified Space* is the seven-story, concrete and brick Anglia Square car park, (see Figure 19.2) located in the provincial city of Norwich

Figure 19.2 Still from *Codified Space* of the derelict car park facade. Courtesy of the artist.

(UK), a prime example of the 1970s Brutalism movement's aesthetic, which sought to create an architectural image that communicated strength, functionality, and an overt expression of materiality (McClelland and Stewart 2007, 12).

The monumental, modernist site—cathedral like in its proportions and scale—is situated in a once prosperous, but now economically deprived district of Norwich.

As a structure conceived and built solely for the containment and movement of cars, the functional genre of the multistory car park has been derisively described by the managing editor of the e-journal *Architectural Record*, Beth Broome, as "lurk[ing] somewhere in the vicinity of prisons and toll plazas" (2010). The car park acts as the symbolic container of the ideology of the car system and is a potent symbol of our global dependency on oil. Fraser and Kerr observe that at the urban scale, "the car has become the principal determinant of the human environment" (2002, 317). Shopping malls and car parks create a new pattern of planned, urban life consuming vast tracts of land that largely remain unused by people (325). The car park fits within Marc Augé's anthropological notion of "non-place," which he describes as space formed in relation to certain ends such as transport, transit, commerce, and leisure, which are defined partly by the words and texts they offer us in the form of codified instructional ideograms such as road signs (1995, 94–96).

In its derelict state, the car park represents the end-stage of the inexorable processes of "creative destruction," which economist Joseph Schumpeter (1942) conceived as the ceaseless devaluation and destruction of existing wealth, in

Figure 19.3 Still from *Codified Space* of parking bay marking. Courtesy of the artist.

order to make way for the creation of new wealth—in this case, new shopping malls and their associated car parks. The ground-level CCTV camera featured in *Codified Space* denotes the all-seeing surveillance that controls the space, and behavior within it. In his historical critique of the development of Los Angeles, Mike Davis argues that CCTV turns city spaces into prison-like structures designed to exclude undesirable influences. Davis states:

> This is the city of defensible spaces, fear and distrust, where the boundaries between creative destruction and destructive creation are no longer clear. (1990, 311–13)

French philosopher Michel Foucault notes that through CCTV surveillance the "basic functioning of society is penetrated . . . with disciplinary mechanisms" (1977, 209). In spatial and architectural terms, this has allowed a meshing of security and aesthetic concerns in the instrumental site of the car park.

Codified Space adopts the stance that a derelict car park need not be thought unimaginatively as simply a nonfunctioning instrumental space. Scrutinized closely as a singular site, it takes on an uncanny, atmospheric mood. Through its cinematic representation it suggests that commodified, functional places do not "die" but rather mutate in their form and meaning. For example, the film features the painted road surface markings that no longer serve their intended function to officially guide and orientate drivers—as heavily eroded shapes, which now offer indeterminate aesthetic meanings—where formerly they provided clear, semiotic instruction. Like the ancient Nazca lines of Peru, etched in the earth, which Cynthia Brown (2007, 167) speculates were used as giant astronomical calendars, these mutated road surface markings on the upper exposed level that face up to the heavens (see Figure 19.3) can be surrealistically recoded—using this anthropological association—as mysterious, sacred markings to be read by the gods. Similarly, the all-seeing panoptic gaze of the CCTV camera, featured in the film, is subverted into an absurdist act during the closing sequence, where it is observed monitoring rubbish blowing purposelessly in an alleyway. My intention here is to hint at the aesthetics inherent in all space expressed in part through lyrical movement, which stands in stark opposition to the conception of city space as solely serving a functional purpose.

The urban ecological mesh

An urban ecological conception of place provides another filmic lens through which to understand the derelict car park—shifting the frame of reference beyond the human, to evoke feelings of connection to nature. *Codified Space* presents the site as a strange, alien ecosystem. Nonhuman entities—animals, insects, plants, and microbes—interact undisturbed with the material structure, in a state of postapocalyptic recovery from the contaminants—petrol, motor oil, and heavy metals—previously leaked by cars onto its surfaces. The cinematic encounter with this place is intended to move us to think and feel more compassionately about the living web of this urban environment.

Through the compact narrative, we observe the soft lines of organic patterns, which reveal the influence of nature, and the way it is inextricably enmeshed with the hard geometric lines of the precast concrete forms and tarmac road surfaces. As geographer Alastair Bonnett notes, "Accepting that the city is a multi-species environment benefits us all by enriching, enlivening and, ironically humanizing our sense of place" (2014, 73). It is a place where we discover the extraordinary in the ordinary city.

Many of the natural processes and organisms inhabiting this concrete island are invisible to the naked eye—hidden, or too diminutive. To capture this activity, the film presents the car park at two spatial scales—the building scale and the granular scale of the road surface. Juxtaposing the larger, slower-changing macroscale and the smaller, faster-changing microscale aids the viewer in understanding their spatial and temporal relationships. The building decays over months, years, and decades while insects and hardy lichens change over the course of minutes and hours.

Figure 19.4 Still from *Codified Space* of pigeon excrement and feathers. Courtesy of the artist.

At the macroscale, a feral pigeon is observed in the film inhabiting an internal access stairway. Evidence of the inexorable processes of defecation, at the microscale, is splattered across the lino-floor in front of the defunct elevator shaft (see Figure 19.4), providing the viewer of the film with an intimate window into the creature's makeshift habitat.

Abandoned buildings are common nesting areas for pigeons, particularly roof spaces, according to Wendell Levi (2013), a leading authority on the subject, yet we are seldom aware of them. Also, at the microscale, the tiny bright red Bryobia spider mites that reproduce asexually in all female cloned populations, inhabit the territory of the cracks in the top deck road surface and painted direction markings, which are acutely observed through the close-up camera lens. It was only after several visits to the site, during which I sat in a state of quiet observation, that I in fact became aware of their existence beneath my feet.

Environmental theorist Richard Forman (2014, 34) suggests that scales are fractal in nature, with patterns repeated in similar form at different scales. At each scale these patterns are composed of distinct objects with boundaries (32). This is conveyed cinematically in the film, through the juxtaposition of mites in their cracks viewed from above, with macroscale pedestrians walking along a residential street between rows of terraced houses, viewed from a similarly high angle.

Codified Space provides the perceptual equipment to comprehend the intimate complexity of the car park's ecological phenomena at different scales through montage juxtaposition, revealing the hierarchical relationship between organisms and the urban surroundings. Thus the film may have an appeal to those drawn to the idea that decay and inertia will always overtake the hubris of late modernity with its unfaltering confidence in science and technology as a means to reorder the social and natural world (Scott 1999, 4).

The close-up scrutiny of the surface textures of the derelict car park stimulates the viewer's bodily sense of touch—through an affective visuality— which provides a vital connection to the lived sense of place. "Cinematic tactility" occurs not only at the skin or the screen, but traverses all the organs of the spectator's body, suggests film theorist Jennifer Barker (2009), using a phenomenological framework of analysis. By affectively encountering an image, close enough that figure and ground commingle, the viewer is confronted with their inseparability from the image, enabling a haptic visuality that challenges the paradigm of passive cinematic spectatorship. The high-definition digital image quality employed in the film brings a sharpness of detail that further heightens this sense of tactility, or haptics.

Sounding the territory

The sound design for *Codified Space* arose out of an urge to decouple the indexical link we normally associate between audio and visual reality, a linkage that sound theorist Michel Chion (1994) defines as causal sound. This has been replaced with an imaginary sound field, which establishes a sense of feral auditory life in order to affect a relationship of enchantment between the viewer and the temporal-spatial flow of the film.

Diegetic sounds were recorded at the site, and subsequently transfigured using the Spectral Gate filter that divides the original signal into two frequency ranges above and below the central frequency. The modulated, distorted sounds—though recorded at the site—take on a strange, mysterious, and unearthly quality, suggestive of morse code, which when anchored to the visual singularities of the spatial narrative, act to reconfigure their meaning as a kind of "contagious bio-electronic language" (La Belle 2010, 232) that expresses and defines the locales and boundaries of the territory.

Using Félix Guattari's understanding of art as viral, "not through representation but through affective contamination," (1995, 92–93) the intention in the film is to sonically "infect" the cochlea at a preconscious level. The eroded markings, graffiti, and organic life forms, in the film, are given a vocal register of dynamic, unworldly utterances that act as a metaphor for sentient spirits engaged in sonic exchange.

In creating cognitive dissonance between the derelict car park and its imaginary sound field, *Codified Space* enables us to enter into an emotional relationship with it, generating an energy that, Stocker argues,

> can work on us on a multitude of levels; from the cognitive to the subconscious; from the emotional to the physical. It is integrally woven into our experience of the sacred, wielding profound power to affect us, while remaining something we cannot grasp, are unable to see, and does not seem to affect the objects around us. (2013, 32)

Though we rely on visual cues to confirm our whereabouts, our experience of where we are is often more dependent on sound (2). This is confirmed in the film, for example, where we observe an agglomeration of bristling communication antennae atop an adjacent office block, which is experienced viscerally through the suddenly amplified, distorted acoustic energy of a radio signal making the viewer privy to sounds that fall outside the human audible range. The secret unworldly soundscape that unfolds affectively revitalizes our senses, and recodes our understanding of the derelict site.

Conclusion

Codified Space constructs a singular, poetic discourse of a derelict car park as a place that challenges the dominant understanding of the city as abstracted, rational, and controlled. It recodes and recasts this geography through the manipulation of light and sound and the creation of a narrative space that takes us on a temporal journey of juxtaposed relational images, which collectively reconstitute a sense of its totality, and imbue it with a resonant acoustic atmosphere. This mediated screen space offers the viewer the opportunity to encounter an expanded sense of spatiality that is transformative. Bonnett (2014, 297) notes that our basic human motivations are to seek freedom, escape, and creativity and that these desires are closely bound up with place: "We are a place making and place loving species," he asserts (3). By foregrounding the extraordinary, *Codified Space* invites us to appreciate the fact that derelict urban sites have considerable symbolic power, rendering them emotionally potent. In featuring the nonhuman life forms that inhabit this derelict site, the film raises our awareness of urban ecology, building in us a sense of empathy toward the environment. Without releasing and realizing our geographical thought and practice through imaginative ways of engagement with urban space, such as those explored and expressed by short independent films, we will be trapped in the limitations of a bland, utilitarian notion of the city as an efficient socioeconomic mechanism conceived by policymakers and shaped by detached urban planning, which produces sterile public spaces. A vibrant compact cinematics is essential to the continuation of a free-thinking, creative society.

Bibliography

Ackerman, McCarton. 2012. "Novelists Seek Help Fighting Internet Addiction." *The Fix.* Available at: https://www.thefix.com/content/novelists-internet-addiction-software90593 (accessed April 1, 2016).

Agar, Jon. 2013. *Constant Touch: A Global History of the Mobile Phone.* London: Icon Books.

Agre, Philip E. 1994. "*Surveillance* and *Capture*: Two Models of Privacy." *Information Society* 10 (2): 101–27.

Alexander, Neta. Forthcoming 2017. "Rage Against the Machine: Buffering, Noise, and 'Perpetual Anxiety' in the Age of Connected Viewing." *Cinema Journal* 56 (February 2).

Althousser, Louis. 1977. "Ideology and Ideological State Apparatuses (Notes towards an Investigation)." In *Lenin and Philosophy and Other Essays.* Trans. Ben Brewster. London: New Left Books. 127–86.

Alvaredo, Facundo, Anthony B. Atkinson, Thomas Piketty, and Emmanuel Saez. 2013. "The Top 1 Percent in International and Historical Perspective." *Journal of Economic Perspectives* 27 (3): 3–20.

Anderson, Benedict. 1983. *Imagined Communities: Reflections on the Origins and Spread of Nationalism.* Revised and extended edition. London: Verso.

Anderson, Joseph D. 1996. *The Reality of Illusion: An Ecological Approach to Cognitive Film Theory.* Carbondale and Edwardsville, US: Southern Illinois University Press.

Aristotle. 1990. *Aristotle on the Art of Poetry.* Trans. Ingram Bywater. Oxford: Oxford University Press.

Ascott, Justin. Dir. 2011. *Codified Space.* Online Video. Available at: https://vimeo.com/26260209 (accessed October 16, 2015).

Askill, Daniel. Dir. 2015. *Take Flight. The New York Times Magazine.* December 10. Available at: http://www.nytimes.com/interactive/2015/12/10/magazine/great-performers-take-flight.html (accessed December 28, 2015).

Augé, Marc. 1995. *Non-Places: Introduction to an Anthropology of Supermodernity.* Trans. John Howe. London: Verso.

Augé, Marc. 2002. *In the Metro.* Trans. Tom Conley. Minneapolis: University of Minnesota Press.

Austin, Matthew. 2005. *My Inner Short: Where r u?* UK: Blink Media. Available at: https://www.youtube.com/watch?v=GarSLZjqZAk (accessed February 26, 2016).

Badiou, Alain. 2013. *Cinema.* Ed. Antoine de Baecque. Trans. Susan Spitzer. Cambridge, MA: Polity.

Bal, Mieke. 2009. *Narratology: Introduction to the Theory of Narrative*. Third edition. Toronto: University of Toronto Press.

Bann, Stephen. 2013. "Nadar's Aerial View." In *Seeing From Above: The Aerial View in Visual Culture*. Eds. Mark Dorrian and Frederic Pousin. London: IB Tauris. 83–94.

Barker, Jennifer M. 2009. *The Tactile Eye: Touch and the Cinematic Experience*. London: University of California Press.

Baron, Robert A. 1990. "Conflict in Organizations." In *Psychology in Organizations. Integrating Science and Practice*. Eds. Kevin R. Murphy and Frank E. Saal. Hillside, NJ: Laurence Erlbaum Associates. 197–215.

Barthes, Roland. 1989 [orig. 1971]. "Style and Its Image." In *The Rustle of Language*. Trans. Richard Howard. Berkely and Los Angeles, CA: University of California press. 90–99.

Bastajian, Tina, and Seda Manavoğlu. *Coffee Deposits Topologies of Chance*. Available at: http://www.coffeedeposits.nl (accessed April 6, 2016).

Beairsto, Ric. 1998. *The Tyranny of Story. Audience Expectations and the Short Screenplay*. Vancouver: Vancouver Film School.

Beller, Jonathan. 2006. *The Cinematic Mode of Production: Attention Economy and the Society of the Spectacle*. Hanover, NH: Darthmouth College Press.

Benjamin, Walter. 1968. "The Work of Art in the Age of Mechanical Reproduction." In *Illuminations*. New York: Schocken Books. 217–51.

Benjamin, Walter. 1999. "Experience and Poverty." In *Selected Writings* 2: 1927–1934. Eds. Michael W. Jennings, Howard Eiland, and Gary Smith. Trans. Rodney Livingstone, et al. Cambridge, MA and London: Belknap of Harvard University Press. 731–36.

Benjamin, Walter. 2008. "The Work of Art in the Age of Its Technological Reproducibility. Second Version." In *The Work of Art in the Age of its Technological Reproducibility, and Other Writings on Media*. Eds. Michael William Jennings, Brigid Doherty, Thomas Y. Levin, and Edmund Jephcott. Trans. Edmund Jephcott, Rodney Livingstone, Howard Eiland, et al. Cambridge, MA: Harvard University Press. 19–55.

Bennett, M. Todd. 2016. *One World, Big Screen: Hollywood, the Allies, and World War II*. Chapel Hill: The University of North Carolina Press.

Bergson, Henri. 1998. *Creative Evolution*. Trans. Arthur Mitchell. New York: Dover.

Biró, Yvette, and Catherine Portuges. 1997. "Caryatids of Time: Temporality in the Cinema of Agnès Varda." *Performing Arts Journal* 19 (3): 1–10.

Blackmore, Tim. 2007. "The Speed Death of the Eye: The Ideology of Hollywood Film Special Effects." *Bulletin of Science Technology Society* 27 (5): 367–72.

Bolter, Jay David, and Richard Grusin. 1999. *Remediation: Understanding New Media*. Cambridge, MA: MIT Press.

Bolter, Jay David, Blair MacIntyre, Maribeth Gandy, and Petra Schweitzer. 2006. "New Media and the Permanent Crisis of Aura." *Convergence* 12 (1): 21–39.

Bonnett, Alastair. 2015. *Off the Map: Feral Places and What They Tell Us About the World*. London: Aurum Press Ltd.

Boothby, Richard. 2001. *Freud as Philosophy: Metapsychology After Lacan*. New York: Routledge.

Bordwell, David. 1985. *Narration in the Fiction Film*. Madison: University of Wisconsin Press.

Bordwell, David. 2002. "Intensified Continuity: Visual Style in Contemporary American Film." *Film Quarterly* 55 (3): 16–28.

Bottcher, Saul. 2013. "Basics of Fiction Writing: Narrative Tension." Available at: http://www.indiebooklauncher.com/resources-diy/basics-of-fiction-writing-narrative-tension.php (accessed February 10, 2016).

Bredehoft, Thomas A. 2006. "Comics, Architecture, Multidimensionality and Time: Chris Ware's Jimmy Corrigan: The Smartest Kid on Earth." *Modern Fiction Studies* 52 (4): 869–90.

Brooks, Cleanth. 1947. "The Heresy of Paraphrase." In *The Well Wrought Urn: Studies in the Structure of Poetry*. New York: Harvest Books.

Broome, Beth. 2010. *1111 Lincoln Road. Architectural Record*. [Online] Available at: http://www.architecturalrecord.com (accessed October 30, 2015).

Brown, Cynthia Stokes. 2007. *Big History*. New York: The New Press.

Brown, Wendy. 2015. *Undoing the Demos: Neoliberalism's Stealth Revolution*. New York: Zone.

Brownlow, Kevin. 1980. "Silent Films: What was the Right Speed?" *Sight and Sound* 49 (3, Summer): 164–67.

Buchan, Suzanne. 2013. "Introduction: Pervasive Animation." In *Pervasive Animation*. Ed. Suzanne Buchan. London: Routledge. 1–21.

Buchan, Suzanne, and Andres Janser. 2015. *Animierte Wunderwelten/Animated Wonderlands*. Zurich: Museum fur Gestaltung Zurich.

Bukatman, Scott. 2014. "Sculpture, Stasis, the Comics and Hellboy." *Critical Inquiry* 40 (3 Spring): 104–17.

Bull, Michael. 2005. "No Dead Air! The iPod and the Culture of Mobile Listening." *Leisure Studies* 24 (4): 343–55.

Bull, Michael. 2007. *Sound Moves: iPod Culture and Urban Experience*. London: Routledge.

Bull, Michael. 2013. "iPod Use: An Urban Aesthetics of Sonic Ubiquity." *Continuum: Journal of Media & Cultural Studies* 27 (4): 495–504.

Cameron, Allan. 2008. *Modular Narratives in Contemporary Cinema*. Houndmills, Basingstoke: Palgrave Macmillan.

Carels, Edwin. 2015. "Short Notice." In *Empedocles: European Journal for the Philosophy of Communication*. Special Issue: Short Film Experience. Eds. Pepita Hesselberth and Carlos M. Roos. 5 (1&2): 31–38.

Casetti, Francesco. 2015. *The Lumière Galaxy: Seven Key Words for the Cinema to Come*. New York: Columbia University Press.

Castells, Manuel. 2000. "Grassrooting the Space of Flows." In *Cities in the Telecommunication Age: The Fracturing of Geographies*. Eds. James O. Wheeler, Yuko Aoyama, and Barney Warf. London; New York: Routledge. 18–30.

Castells, Manuel. 2004. "An Introduction to the Information Age." In *The Information Society Reader*. Eds. Frank Webster with Raimo Blom, Erkki Karvonen, Harri Melin, Kaarle Nordenstreng, and Ensio Puoskari. London and New York: Routledge. 138–49.

Castro, Teresa. 2013. "Aerial Views and Cinematism, 1898-1939." In *Seeing From Above: The Aerial View in Visual Culture*. Eds. Mark Dorrian and Frederic Pousin. London: IB Tauris. 118–33.

Chatman, Seymour. 1971. "On Defining 'Form.'" *New Literary History* 2 (2, Winter): 217–28.

Chion, Michel. 1994. *Audio-Vision: Sound On Screen*. Ed. and Trans. Claudia Gorbman. New York: Columbia University Press.

Chion, Michel. 1995. *David Lynch*. Trans. Robert Julian. London: BFI.

Chion, Michel. 1999. *The Voice in Cinema*. Trans. Claudia Gorbman. New York: Columbia University Press.

Chun, Wendy. 2008. "On 'Sourcery,' or Code as Fetish." *Configurations* 16 (3): 299–324.

Chun, Wendy. 2011. *Programmed Visions: Software and Memory*. Cambridge, MA: MIT Press.

Chun, Wendy. 2016. *Updating to Remain the Same: Habitual New Media*. Cambridge, MA: MIT Press.

Clarke, M. J. 2013. *Transmedia Television: New Trends in Network Serial Production*. London: Bloomsbury.

Colburn, Jeff. 2016. "Writing Tension and Conflict." Available at: http://www.fictionaddiction.net/Writer-s-Toolbox/writing-tension-writing-conflict.html (accessed February 10, 2016).

Cooley, Heidi Rae. 2004. "It's All About the Fit: The Hand, the Mobile Screenic Device and Tactile Vision." *Journal of Visual Culture* 3 (2): 133–55.

Cooper, Pat, and Ken Dancyger. 2000. *Writing the Short Film*. Second Edition. Boston: Focal Press.

Corrigan, Timothy. 2016. "Still Speed: Cinematic Acceleration, Value, and Execution." *Cinema Journal* 47 (2): 119–25.

Crafton, Donald. 1982. *Before Mickey: The Animated Film 1898-1928*. Chicago: The University of Chicago Press.

Crafton, Donald. 2006. "Pie and Chase: Gag, Spectacle and Narrative in Slapstick Comedy." In *The Cinema of Attractions Reloaded*. Ed. Wanda Strauven. Amsterdam: Amsterdam University Press. 355–64.

Crang, Mike, and Steve Graham. 2007. "Sentient Cities: Ambient Intelligence and the Politics of Urban Space." *Information, Communication & Society* 10 (6): 789–817.

Crary, Jonathan. 1990. *Techniques of the Observer: On Vision and Modernity in the Nineteenth Century*. Cambridge, MA and London: MIT Press.

Crary, Jonathan. 1999. *Suspensions of Perception: Attention, Spectacle, and Modern Culture*. Cambridge, MA: MIT Press.

Creeber, Glen. 2013. *Small Screen Aesthetics: From Television to the Internet*. London: BFI.

Critchley, Simon. 2007. *Infinitely Demanding: Ethics of Commitment, Politics of Resistance*. London: Verso.

Crossover. 2015. Korsakow—not the linear causal way of thinking. Crossover (January 15). Available at: http://www.xolabs.co.uk/2015/01/15/korsakow-not-the-linear-causal-way-of-thinking/ (accessed April 6, 2016).

Cubitt, Sean. 2009. "Line and Colour in The Band Concert." *Animation: An Interdisciplinary Journal* 4 (1): 11–30.

Cubitt, Sean. 2014. *The Practice of Light: A Genealogy of Visual Technologies from Prints to Pixels*. Cambridge, MA: MIT Press.

Curtis, Scott. 2015. *The Shape of Spectatorship*. New York: Columbia University Press.

Dancyger, Ken, and Jeff Rush. 2002. *Alternative Scriptwriting: Successfully Breaking the Rules*. Boston: Focal Press.

Davis, Mike. 1990. *City of Quartz: Excavating the Future in Los Angeles*. London: Verso.

Dean, Jodi. 2009. *Democracy and Other Neoliberal Fantasies: Communicative Capitalism and Left Politics*. Durham, NC: Duke University Press.

Degen, Monica, Clare Melhuish, and Gilian Rose. 2015. "Producing Place Atmospheres Digitally: Architecture, Digital Visualisation Practices and the Experience Economy." *Journal of Consumer Culture*. Available at: http://joc.sagepub.com/content/early/201 5/02/27/1469540515572238.abstract (accessed January 17, 2016).

Delaney, Paul. 1999. "Who Paid for Modernism." In *The New Economic Criticism*. Eds. Martha Woodmansee and Paul Osten. London: Routledge. 335–51.

Deleuze, Gilles. 1990. *Negotiations: 1972-1990*. New York, NY: Columbia University Press.

Deleuze, Gilles, and Félix Guattari. 1977. *Anti-Oedipus: Capitalism and Schizophrenia*. Trans. Robert Hurley, Mark Seem, and Helen R. Lane. New York: Viking Press.

Deloitte. 2015. *Short Form Video: A Future, But Not the Future, of Television: TMT Predictions 2015*. Available at: http://www2.deloitte.com/global/en/pages/technology-media-and-telecommunications/articles/tmt-pred-short-form-video.html (accessed March 3, 2016).

Deren, Maya, et al. 1963. "Poetry and the Film: A Symposium." *Film Culture* 29: 55–63.

Doane, Mary Ann. 2002. *The Emergence of Cinematic Time: Modernity, Contingency and the Archive*. Cambridge, MA: Harvard University Press.

Doane, Mary Ann. 2009. "The Location of the Image: Cinematic Projection and Scale in Modernity." In *The Art of Projection*. Eds. Stan Douglas and Christopher Eamon. Stuttgart: Hatje Cantz. 151–66.

Dorrian, Mark. 2015. *Writing on the Image: Architecture, the City and the Politics of Representation*. London: IB Tauris.

Dorrian, Mark, and Frederic Pousin. Eds. 2013. *Seeing from Above: The Aerial View in Visual Culture*. London: IB Tauris.

Dulac, Nicolas, and André Gaudreault. 2006. "Circularity and Repetition at the Heart of Attraction: Optical Toys and the Emergence of a New Cultural Series." In *The Cinema of Attractions Reloaded*. Ed. Wanda Stauven. Amsterdam: University of Amsterdam Press. 227–44.

Duncan, Stephen V. 2006. *A Guide to Screenwriting Success: Writing for Film and Television*. Lanham, MD: Rowman and Littlefield.

Dunn, Nick, Paul Cureton, and Serena Pollastri. 2014. *A Visual History of the Future*. London: Foresight, Government Office for Science. Available at: https://www.gov.uk/government/publications/future-cities-a-visual-history-of-the-future (accessed January 17, 2016).

Dyer-Witheford, Nick. 2015. *Cyber-Proletariat: Global Labour in the Digital Vortex*. Toronto, Ontario and London: Pluto Press.

Eisenstein, Sergei. 1986. *Eisenstein on Disney*. Ed. Jay Leyda. Calcutta: Seagull Books.

Eisenstein, Sergei. 1988. *Writings, 1922-34*. London: British Film Institute.

Ekman, Ulrik. 2015. "Complexity of the Ephemeral—Snap Video Chats." In *Empedocles: European Journal for the Philosophy of Communication*. Special Issue: Short Film Experience. Eds. Pepita Hesselberth and Carlos M. Roos. 5 (1&2): 97–101.

Ellis, John. 1982. *Visible Fictions Cinema, Television, Video*. London: Routledge.

Elsaesser, Thomas. 2006. "Discipline through Diegesis: The Rube Film between Attraction and Integration." In *The Cinema of Attractions Reloaded*. Ed. Wanda Strauven. Amsterdam: Amsterdam University Press. 205–23.

Elsaesser, Thomas. 2013. "The 'Return' of 3-D: On Some of the Logics and Genealogies of the Image in the Twenty-First Century." *Critical Inquiry* 39 (2): 217–46.

Engberg, Maria. 2014. "Polyaesthetic Sights and Sounds: Media Aesthetics in The Fantastic Flying Books of Mr. Morris Lessmore, Upgrade Soul and The Vampyre of Time and Memory." *SoundEffects* 4 (1): 21–40.

Engell, Lorenz. 2013. "The Tactile and the Index: From the Remote Control to the Hand-Held Computer. Some Speculative Reflections on the Bodies of the Will." *NECSUS: European Journal of Media Studies* 2 (2): 323–36.

Eppink, Jason. 2014. "A Brief History of the Gif (So Far)." *Journal of Visual Culture* 13 (3): 298–306.

Ernst, Wolfgang. 2013. *Digital Memory and the Archive*. Minneapolis: University of Minnesota Press.

Feher, Michel. 2009. "Self-Appreciation; Or, The Aspirations of Human Capital." *Public Culture* (29): 21–41.

Fickers, Andreas. 1998. *Der "Transistor" als technisches und kulturelles Phänomen: die Transistorisierung der Radio- und Fernsehempfänger in der deutschen*

Rundfunkindustrie 1955 bis 1965. Bassum: Verlag für Geschichte der Naturwissenschaften und der Technik.

Field, Syd. 1994. *Screenplay: The Foundations of Screenwriting*. Third Edition. New York: Dell.

Fiore, Neil. 1989. *The Now Habit*. London and New York: Penguin.

Flattum, Jerry. 2013. "Conflict—The Foundation of Storytelling." *Script*. March 18. Available at: http://www.scriptmag.com/features/conflict-the-foundation-of-storytelling (accessed February 10, 2016).

Forman, Richard T. T. 2014. *Urban Ecology: Science of Cities*. Cambridge: Cambridge University Press.

Forster, E. M. 2002. *Aspects of the Novel*. New York: Rosetta Books.

Forster, Mark. 2007. *Do it Tomorrow*. London: Hodder and Stoughton.

Foucault, Michel. 1977. *Discipline and Punishment: The Birth of the Prison*. New York: Vintage.

Foucault, Michel. 1989. *The Archeology of Knowledge*. Trans. A. M. Sheridan Smith. Routledge Classics. London and New York: Routledge.

Fraser, Murray, and Joe Kerr. 2002. "Motopia: Cities Cars and Architecture." In *Autopia: Cars and Culture*. Eds. Peter Wollen and Joe Kerr. London: Reaktion Books Ltd. 315–26.

Freud, Sigmund. 1992. "Letter from September 22, 1907 (no. 130)." In *The Letters of Sigmund Freud*. Ed. Ernst L. Freud. Trans. Tania and James Stern. New York: Dover. 261–63.

Frick, Caroline. 2011. *Saving Cinema: The Politics of Preservation*. Oxford: Oxford University Press.

Froomkin, Dan. 2013. "It Can't Happen Here: Why is there so Little Coverage of Americans who are Struggling with Poverty?" *Neiman Reports*. March 12. Available at: http://niemanreports.org/articles/it-cant-happen-here-2/ (accessed February 17, 2016).

Fuchs, Christian. 2014. *Digital Labour and Karl Marx*. New York: Routledge.

Gaines, Jane. 2007. "Sad Songs of Nitrate: Women's Work in the Silent Film Archive." *Camera Obscura* 22 (3): 170–78.

Galloway, Alexander, and Eugene Thacker. 2007. *The Exploit: A Theory of Networks*. Minneapolis: University of Minnesota Press.

Gaudreault, André, and Philippe Gauthier. 2011. "Could Kinematography be Animation and Could Animation be Kinematography?" *Animation: An Interdisciplinary Journal* 6 (2): 85–91.

Genette, Gerard. 1997. *Paratexts: Thresholds of Interpretation*. Cambridge: Cambridge University Press.

Gibbs, Samuel. 2014. "Apple Urged to Stop using Harmful Chemicals in Its Factories" *The Guardian*. March 12, 2014. Available at: http://www.theguardian.com/technology/2014/mar/12/apple-harmful-chemicals-factories-labour (accessed April 6, 2016).

Gibson, James J. 1982 [orig. 1977]. "The Theory of Affordances." In *Perceiving, Acting, and Knowing: Toward an Ecological Psychology.* Eds. J. Bransford and R. Shaw. Hillsdale, NJ: Erlbaum. 67–82.

Gilbert, David. 2010. "The Three Ages of Aerial Vision: London's Aerial Iconography from Wenceslaus Hollar to Google Earth." *The London Journal* 35 (3): 289–99.

Gilens, Martin. 2003. "How the Poor Became Black The Racialization of American Poverty in the Mass Media." In *Race and the Politics of Welfare Reform.* Eds. Sanford F. Schram, Joe Soss, and Richard C. Fording. Ann Arbor: University of Michigan Press. 101–30.

Gillespie, Tarleton. 2003. "The Stories Tools Tell." In *New Media: Theories and Practices of Digitextuality.* Eds. Anna Everett and John T. Caldwell. New York: Routledge. 107–26.

Godmilow, Jill. 1991. "What's Wrong with the Liberal Documentary." *Peace Review* 11 (1): 91–98.

Goggin, Gerard. 2006. *Cell Phone Culture: Mobile Technology in Everyday Life.* New York and London: Routledge.

Goggin, Gerard, and Larissa Hjorth. Eds. 2014. *The Routledge Companion to Mobile Media.* London: Routledge.

Gopnik, Adam. 1986. "The Genius of George Herriman." *New York Review of Books* 33 (December 18): 19–28.

Grainge, Paul. Ed. 2011. *Ephemeral Media: Transitory Screen Culture from Television to YouTube.* London: BFI.

Grau, Oliver. 2003. *Virtual Art: From Illusion to Immersion.* Trans. Gloria Custance. Cambridge, MA: MIT Press.

Gray, Jonathan. 2010. *Show Sold Separately: Promos, Spoilers and Other Media Paratexts.* New York: NYU Press.

Gregg, Melissa. 2011. *Work's Intimacy.* New York: Wiley.

Greimas, Algirdas Julien, and Joseph Courtés. 1982. *Semiotics and Language: An Analytical Dictionary.* Bloomington: Indiana University Press.

Greimas, Algirdas Julien, and Joseph Courtés. 1986. *Sémiotique: dictionnaire raisonné de la théorie du language. Volume 2.* Paris: Hachette.

Guattari, Félix. 1995. *Chaosmosis: An Ethico-Aesthetic Paradigm.* Trans. Paul Bains and Julian Pefanis. Bloomington: Indiana University Press.

Gunning, Tom. 1981. "Dr. Jacobs' Dream Work: Ken Jacobs' The Doctor's Dream." *Millennium Film Journal* 10/11 (Fall–Winter): 210–18.

Gunning, Tom. 1984. "Non-Continuity, Continuity and Discontinuity: A Theory of Genres in Early Cinema." *Iris* 2 (March 1): 101–12.

Gunning, Tom. 1986. "The Cinema of Attraction: Early Film, Its Spectator and the Avant-Garde." *Wide Angle* 8 (3&4): 63–70.

Gunning, Tom. 1989. "Primitive Cinema, a Frame-up? Or The Trick's on Us." *Cinema Journal* 28 (2, Winter): 3–12.

Gunning, Tom. 1990. "The Cinema of Attractions: Early Film, Its Spectator and the Avant-Garde." In *Early Cinema: Space, Frame, Narrative*. Ed. Thomas Elsaesser. London: BFI. 58–59.

Gunning, Tom. 1995. "An Aesthetic of Astonishment." In *Viewing Positions: Ways of Seeing Film*. Ed. Linda Williams. New Brunswick, NJ: Rutgers University Press. 114–33.

Gunning, Tom. 1995. "Response to 'Pie and Chase.'" In *Classical Hollywood Comedy*. Eds. Henry Jenkins and Kristine Brunovska Karnick. New York and London: Routledge. 120–22.

Gunning, Tom. 2013. "The Transforming Image: The Roots of Animation in Metamorphosis and Motion." In *Pervasive Animation*. Ed. Scott Buchan. London: Routledge. 52–70.

Gunning, Tom. 2015. "Just Minutes to Go: The Short Film Experience." In *Empedocles: European Journal for the Philosophy of Communication*. Special Issue: Short Film Experience. Eds. Pepita Hesselberth and Carlos M. Roos. 5 (1&2): 65–73.

Gurevitch, Leon. 2015. "From Edison to Pixar: The Spectacular Screen and the Attention Economy from Celluloid to CG." *Journal of Media & Cultural Studies* 29 (3): 445–65.

Hampton, Ant. *Cue China (Elsewhere, Offshore)*. Available at: http://www.anthampton.com/cc.html (assessed April 6, 2016).

Harries, Dan. 2002 "Watching the Internet." In *The New Media Book*. Ed. Dan Harries. London: The British Film Institute. 171–83.

Hassan, Robert. 2007. "Network Time." In *24/7: Time and Temporality in the Network Society*. Eds. Robert Hassan and Ronald E. Purser. Stanford: Stanford University Press. 37–61.

Hastie, Amelie. 2007. "Eating in the Dark: A Theoretical Concession." *Journal of Visual Culture* 6 (2): 283–302.

Hauser & Wirth. 2009. "Pipilotti Rist." *Hauser & Wirth*. August 28. Available at: http://www.hauserwirth.com/exhibitions/323/pipilotti-rist/view/ (accessed February 26, 2016).

Heidegger, Martin. 1995. *The Fundamental Concepts of Metaphysics: World, Finitude, Solitude*. Trans. William McNeill and Nicholas Walker. Bloomington: Indiana University Press.

Heilmann, Till A. 2014. "'Tap, tap, flap, flap.' Ludic Seriality, Digitality, and the Finger." *Eludamos: Journal for Computer Game Culture* 8 (1): 33–46. Available at: http://www.eludamos.org/index.php/eludamos/article/viewArticle/vol8no1-3/8-1-3-html (accessed February 26, 2016).

Hesselberth, Pepita. 2012. "From Subject-Effect to Presence-Effect: A Deictic Approach to the Cinematic." *NECSUS: European Journal of Media Studies* 1 (2): 241–67.

Hesselberth, Pepita. 2014. *Cinematic Chronotopes: Here, Now, Me*. New York: Bloomsbury.

Hesselberth, Pepita, and Carlos M. Roos. 2015. "Short Film Experience: Introduction." *Empedocles: European Journal for the Philosophy of Communication* 5 (1&2): 3–12.

Holdsworth, Amy. 2016. "TV dinners." Keynote paper delivered at Material Cultures of Television Conference. University of Hull, UK. March 22nd.

Hollands, Robert G. 2008. "Will the Real Smart City Please Stand Up?" *City* 12 (3): 303–20.

Howard, David, and Mabley, Edward. 1993. *The Tools of Screenwriting. A Writer's Guide to the Craft and Elements of a Screenplay*. New York: St Martin's Press.

Hunter, Lew. 1994. *Screenwriting*. London: Robert Hale.

Huws, Ursula. 2014. *Labor in the Global Digital Economy: The Cybertariat Comes of Age*. New York: Monthly Review Press.

Jancovich, Mark. 1993. *The Cultural Politics of the New Criticism*. Cambridge University Press.

Jenkins, Henry, Sam Ford, and Joshua Green. 2013. *Spreadable Media: Creating Value and Meaning in a Networked Culture*. New York: NYU Press.

Johnson, Claudia Hunter. 2000. *Crafting Short Screenplays that Connect*. Boston: Focal Press.

Johnson, Eric. 2015. "Virtual Reality Is 'The Last Medium,' Says Filmmaker and VRSE CEO Chris Milk (Q&A)." *Re/code*. October 1. Available at: recode.net/2015/10/01/virtual-reality-is-the-last-medium-says-filmmaker-and-VRSE-ceo-chris-milk-qa/ (accessed December 28, 2015).

Joselit, David. 2007. *Feedback*. Cambridge, MA: MIT Press.

Juhasz, Alexandra. 2011. *Learning from YouTube*. MIT Press. Available at: http://vectors.usc.edu/projects/learningfromyoutube (accessed February 26, 2016).

Kendall, Tina. 2016. "Staying on, or Getting off (the Bus): Approaching Speed in Cinema and Media Studies." *Cinema Journal* 47 (2): 112–18.

Kernan, Lisa. 2004. *Coming Attractions: Reading American Movie Trailers*. Austin: University of Texas Press.

Kirp, David L. 2015. "What Do the Poor Need? Try Asking Them." *The New York Times*. August 8. Available at: http://www.nytimes.com/2015/08/09/opinion/sunday/david-l-kirp-what-do-the-poor-need-try-asking-them.html?_r=0 (accessed February 26, 2016).

Kittler, Friedrich. 1999. *Gramophone, Film, Typewriter*. Trans. Geoffrey Winthrop-Young and Michael Wutz. Writing Science. Stanford, CA: Stanford University Press.

Klein, Norman M. 1993. *Seven Minutes: The Life and Death of the Animated Cartoon*. London: Verso.

Klein, Norman M. 2000. "Animation and Animorphs: A Brief Disappearing Act." In *Meta Morphing: Transformation and the Culture of Quick Change*. Ed. Vivian Sobchack. Minneapolis: University of Minnesota Press. 21–40.

Klinger, Barbara. 2006. *Beyond the Multiplex: Cinema, New Technologies and the Home*. Berkeley: University of California Press.

Krauss, Rosalind. 1986. *The Originality of the Avant Garde and Other Modernist Myths*. Cambridge, MA: MIT Press.

Lacan, Jacques. 1967. *Le Séminaire XIV: La logique du fantasme, 1966-1967*. unpublished manuscript.

Lane, James D., Stefan J. Kasian, Justine E. Owens, and Gail R. Marsh. 1998. "Binaural Auditory Beats Affect Vigilance Performance and Mood." *Physiology and Behavior* 63 (2): 249–52.

Lanier, Jaron. 2006. "Digital Maoism: The Hazards of the New Online Collectivism." *Edge.org*. May 29. Available at: http://edge.org/conversation/digital-maoism-the-hazards-of-the-new-online-collectivism (accessed April 1, 2016).

Lanier, Jaron. 2013. *Who Owns the Future?* New York: Simon & Schuster.

Leadbetter, Charles, and Paul Miller. 2004. *The Pro-Am Revolution: How Enthusiasts Are Changing Our Economy and Society*. London: Demos.

Lefebvre, Henri. 1991. *The Production of Space*. Trans. Donald Nicholson-Smith. Oxford: Blackwell.

Levi, Wendell. 2013. *The Pigeon*. Sumter, SC: Wendell Levi Publishing Co.

Levinas, Emmanuel. 1969. *Totality and Infinity: An Essay on Exteriority*. Trans. Alphonso Lingis. Pittsburgh: Duquesne University Press.

Levinas, Emmanuel. 1989. "Reality and Its Shadow." In *The Levinas Reader*. Ed. Seán Hand. Trans. Alphonso Lingis. Oxford: Blackwell. 129–43.

"Lights, Camera, Action—Introducing the Nokia Shorts." 2003. *The British Independent Film Awards*. [Online] Available at: http://www.bifa.org.uk/press_release.php?id=1 (accessed June 10, 2006).

Lind, Maria, and Hito Steyerl. Eds. 2010. *The Greenroom Reconsidering the Documentary and Contemporary Art #1*. Berlin: Sternberg Press.

Lombard, Matthew, and Theresa Ditton. 1997. "At the Heart of It All: The Concept of Presence." *Journal of Computer-Mediated Communication* 3 (2). Available at: http://onlinelibrary.wiley.com/doi/10.1111/j.1083-6101.1997.tb00072.x/full (accessed December 28, 2015).

Lorey, Isabell. 2006. "Governmentality and Self-Precarization: On the Normalization of Cultural Producers." *Eipcp: Transversal Texts*. Trans. Lisa Rosenblatt and Dagmar Fink. Available at: http://eipcp.net/transversal/1106/lorey/en (accessed April 01, 2016).

Lupton, Deborah. 2016. *The Quantified Self*. Malden, MA: Polity.

Lütticken, Sven. 2009. "Viewing Copies: On the Mobility of the Moving Images." *e-flux journal #8*. Available at: http://www.e-flux.com/journal/viewing-copies-on-the-mobility-of-moving-images/ (accessed February 12, 2016).

Macarthur, John. 2013. "The Figure from Above: On the Obliqueness of the Plan in Urbanism and Architecture." In *Seeing from Above: The Aerial View in Visual Culture*. Eds. Mark Dorrian and Frederic Pousin. London: IB Tauris. 188–209.

Manovich, Lev. 2001. *The Language of New Media*. Cambridge, MA: MIT Press.

Manovich, Lev. 2009. "The Practice of Everyday (Media) Life: From Mass Consumption to Mass Cultural Production?" *Critical Inquiry* 32 (2): 319–31.

Manovich, Lev. 2013. *Software Takes Command*. London: Bloomsbury.

Marks, Laura U. 2002. *Touch: Sensuous Theory and Multisensory Media*. Minneapolis: University of Minnesota Press.

Martin, Adrian. 2008. "*Cléo From 5 to 7*: Passionate Time." *The Criterion Collection*. Available at: https://www.criterion.com/current/posts/499-cleo-from-5-to-7-passionate-time (accessed December 8, 2015).

Marx, Karl. 1976. *Capital: Vol. One*. Trans. Ben Fowkes. London: Penguin Books/*New Left Review*.

McCarthy, Anna. 2016. "Marx, Memory, Loss: Ways of Reading Capital." *Social Text* 128 (Summer): 105–26.

McClelland, Michael, and Graeme Stewart. 2007. *Concrete Toronto: A Guide To Concrete Architecture from the Fifties to the Seventies*. Toronto: Coach House Books.

McGowan, Todd. 2007. *The Impossible David Lynch*. New York: Columbia University Press.

McKee, Robert. 1997. *Story. Substance, Structure, Style and the Principles of Screenwriting*. New York: Regan Books.

McPherson, Tara. 2006. "Reload: Liveness, Mobility, and the Web." In *New Media, Old Media*. Eds. Wendy Hui Kyong Chun and Thomas Keenan. London: Routledge. 199–208.

Mellencamp, Patricia. 1988. "Last Seen in the Streets of Modernism." *East West Film Journal* 3 (1): 45–67.

Michelson, Annette. 1971. "Toward Snow (Part 1)." *Artforum* 9 (June): 30–37.

Michotte, Albert. 1955. "Perception and Cognition." *Acta Psychologica* 11: 69–91.

Milk, Chris. 2015a. *Clouds over Sidra*. Available at: http://VRSE.works/creators/chris-milk/work/the-united-nations-clouds-over-sidra/ (accessed December 28, 2015).

Milk, Chris. 2015b. "How Virtual Reality can Create the Ultimate Empathy Machine." Ted 2015. Available at: https://www.ted.com/talks/chris_milk_how_virtual_reality_can_create_the_ultimate_empathy_machine (accessed December 28, 2015).

Miller, James. 2014. "The Fourth Screen: Mediatization and the Smartphone." *Mobile Media & Communication* 2 (2): 209–26.

Miller, Nancy. 2007. "Minifesto for a New Age." *Wired* 15 (3). Available at: https://www.wired.com/2007/03/snackminifesto/ (accessed November 22, 2015).

"Mobile Film Making: The New Genre." 2006. *Mobile Film Makers 2006*. Available at: http://mfm06.notionage.com/insider/new_genre.html (accessed May 19, 2006).

Montello, Daniel R. 1993. "Scale and Multiple Psychologies of Space." In *Spatial Information Theory a Theoretical Basis for Gis: European Conference, Cosit'93 Marciana Marina, Elba Island, Italy September 19–22, 1993 Proceedings*. Eds. Andrew U. Frank and Irene Campari. Berlin, Heidelberg: Springer Verlag. 312–21.

Moore, Karenza, and Jason Rutter. 2004. "Understanding Consumers' Understanding of Mobile Entertainment." Proceedings of *Mobile Entertainment: User-centred Perspectives*. March 25–27, 2004. Available at: http://jasonrutter.co.uk/wp-content/

uploads/2015/05/Moore-Rutter-2004-MOBILE-ENTERTAINMENT-User-centred-Perspectives.pdf (accessed November 20, 2015).

Moretti, Franco. 1983. *Signs taken for Wonders: Studies in the Sociology of Literary Forms*. Trans. Susan Fischer, David Forgacs, and David Miller. London: Verso.

Moretti, Franco. 2013. *Distant Reading*. London, New York: Verso.

Morley, David. 1988. *Family Television: Cultural Power and Domestic Leisure*. Revised edition. Abington, Oxon; New York: Routledge.

Moseley, Roger, and Aya Saiki. 2014. "Nintendo's Art of Musical Play." In *Music in Video Games: Studying Play*. Eds. K. J. Donnelly, William Gibbons, and Neil Lerner. London: Routledge. 51–76.

Mouton, Janice. 2001. "From Feminine Masquerade to Flâneuse: Agnès Varda's Cléo in the City." *Cinema Journal* 40 (2): 3–16.

Moynihan, Tim. 2015. "The NYT Is About to Launch VR's Big Mainstream Moment." *Wired*. Oktober 21. Available at: http://www.wired.com/2015/10/the-nyts-new-project-will-be-vrs-first-mainstream-moment/ (accessed December 28, 2015).

Mulvey, Laura. 1975. "Visual Pleasure and Narrative Cinema." *Screen* 16 (3): 6–18.

Mulvey, Laura. 2006. *Death 24x a Second: Stillness and the Moving Image*. London: Reaktion Books.

Münsterberg, Hugo. 2002 [orig. 1916]. *Hugo Münsterberg on Film. The Photoplay: A Psychological Study and Other Writings*. Ed. Allan Langdale. New York: Routledge.

MuveeMobile. 2006. *Nokia*. Available at: http://www.muvee.com/website/mv_mobile_FAQ.php (accessed May 23, 2006).

Nafus, Dawn. Ed. 2016. *Quantified: Biosensing Technologies in Everyday Life*. Cambridge, MA: MIT Press.

Nancy, Jean-Luc. 2013. *The Pleasure in Drawing*. Trans. Philip Armstrong. New York: Fordham University Press.

National Center for Law and Economic Justice. 2015. "Poverty in the United States: A Snapshot, National Center for Law and Economic Justice." *Data from U. S. Census Bureau*. Available at: http://nclej.org/wp-content/uploads/2015/11/2014PovertyStats.pdf (accessed February 26, 2016).

Neff, Gina, and Dawn Nafus. 2016. *Self-Tracking*. Cambridge, MA: MIT Press.

Nelson, Roy Jay. 1983. "Reflections in a Broken Mirror: Varda's *Cléo de 5 à 7*." *The French Review* 56 (5): 735–43.

Nichols, Bill. 1988. "The Work of Culture in the Age of Cybernetic Systems." *Screen* 29 (1): 22–46.

Nichols, Bill. 2010. *Introduction to Documentary*. Second edition. Bloomington: Indiana University Press.

NLA. 2014. *Smarter London: How Digital Technologies are Shaping the City*. London: New London Architecture.

Nochimson, Martha. 1997. *The Passion of David Lynch: Wild at Heart in Hollywood*. Austin: University of Texas Press.

Nokia Future Applications. 2002. "One Day You'll be Able to Watch Videos on Your
  Mobiles." 2005. [TV Advertisement] Available at: https://www.creativeclub.co.uk/
  (ismati452yxirdqowexqsx55)/FrMain/search.aspx (accessed March 31, 2006).

Nordau, Max. 1892. *Entartung*. Berlin: Carl Dunder.

Norman, Donald A. 1990. *The Design of Everyday Things*. New York: Doubleday.

Oettermann, Stephan. 1997. *The Panorama: History of a Mass Medium*. Trans. Deborah
  Lucas Schneider. Cambridge, MA: MIT Press.

Ofcom. 2004. *The Communications Market 2004—Telecommunications*. Available at:
  http://stakeholders.ofcom.org.uk/binaries/research/cmr/telecoms.pdf (accessed
  December 10, 2015).

Olma, Sebastian. 2014. "Of Thumbs and Heads: A Comment on Michel Serres' 'Petite
  Poucette'." *Institute of Network Cultures*. July 12. Available at: http://networkcultures.
  org/mycreativity/2014/07/12/of-thumbs-and-heads-a-comment-on-michel-serres-
  petite-poucette/ (accessed February 26, 2016).

Palmer, R. Barton. Ed. 2010. *Larger Than Life: Movie Stars of the 1950s*. New Brunswick,
  NJ: Rutgers University Press.

Papini, Giovanni. 1907. "La filosofia del cinematografo." *La Stampa*, Turin (May 18): 1.

Parikka, Jussi. 2015a. *A Geology of Media*. Minneapolis: University of Minnesota Press.

Parikka, Jussi. 2015b. "Sites of Media Archaeology: Producing the Contemporary as a Shared
  Topic." *Journal of Contemporary Archaeology* 2 (1): 8–14. Available at: https://journals.
  equinoxpub.com/index.php/JCA/article/view/27110/pdf (accessed October 21, 2015).

Perlow, Leslie A. 2013. *Sleeping with Your Smartphone: How to Break the 24/7 Habit and
  Change the Way you Work*. Cambridge, MA: Harvard Business Review Press.

Perrault, Charles. 1842. *Mémoires, contes et autres oeuvres*. Paris: Librairie de Charles
  Gosselin.

Perrault, Charles. 1889. "Little Thumb." In *The Blue Fairy Book*. Ed. Andrew Lang.
  London: Longmans, Green, and Co. 231–41. Available at: http://www.pitt.
  edu/~dash/perrault08.html (accessed February 26, 2016).

Pew Research Center. 2014. *Beyond Red vs. Blue: The Political Typology*. June. Available
  at: http://www.people-press.org/files/2014/06/6-26-14-Political-Typology-release1.
  pdf (accessed March 27, 2016).

Pew Research Center. 2015. *State of the News Media*. April 29. Available at:
  http://www.journalism.org/files/2015/04/FINAL-STATE-OF-THE-NEWS-MEDIA1.
  pdf (accessed February 21, 2016).

Phillips, Andrea. 2012. *A Creator's Guide to Transmedia Storytelling*. New York:
  McGraw-Hill.

Poulaki, Maria. 2015a. "Brain Science and Film Theory: Reassessing the Place of
  Cognitive Discontinuity in Cinema." *Projections* 9 (1): 23–42.

Poulaki, Maria. 2015b. "Featuring Shortness in Online Loop Cultures." In *Empedocles:
  European Journal for the Philosophy of Communication*. Special Issue: Short Film
  Experience. Eds. Pepita Hesselberth and Carlos M. Roos. 5 (1&2): 91–96.

Powrie, Phil. 2011. "Heterotopic Spaces and Nomadic Gazes in Varda: From *Cléo de 5 à 7* to *Les Glaneurs et la glaneuse.*" *L'Esprit Créateur* 51 (1): 68–82.

Prouty, Richard. 2009. "A Turtle on a Leash." *One-Way Street*. Available at: http://onewaystreet.typepad.com/one_way_street/2009/10/a-turtle-on-a-leash.html (accessed February 12, 2016).

Puglisi, Becca. 2013. "Conflict vs Tension." Available at: http://writershelpingwriters.net/2013/11/conflict-vs-tension-2/ (accessed February 10, 2016).

Rabari, Chirag, and Michael Storper. 2014. "The Digital Skin of Cities: Urban Theory and Research in the Age of the Sensored and Metered City, Ubiquitous Computing and Big Data." *Cambridge Journal of Regions, Economy and Society* 8 (1): 27–42.

Rampley, Matthew. 2005. "Visual Practices in the Age of Industry." In *Exploring Visual Culture: Definitions, Concepts, Contexts*. Ed. Matthew Ramply. Edinburgh: Edinburgh University Press. 179–96.

Raskin, Richard. 2014. "On Short Film Storytelling." *Journal of Scandinavian Cinema* 4 (1): 29–34.

Rastegar, Roya. 2012. "Difference, Aesthetics and the Curatorial Crisis of Film Festivals." *Screen* 53 (3 Autumn): 310–17.

Read, Jason. 2014. "Distracted by Attention." *New Inquiry*. Available at: http://thenewinquiry.com/essays/distracted-by-attention/ (accessed February 12, 2016).

Repo, Petteri, Kaarina Hyvönen, Mika Pantzar, and Päivi Timonen. "Users Inventing Ways to Enjoy New Mobile Services—The Case of Watching Mobile Videos." *Proceedings of the 37th Hawaii International Conference on System Sciences*. Available at: https://www.computer.org/csdl/proceedings/hicss/2004/2056/04/205640096c.pdf (accessed March 10, 2006).

Richardson, Ingrid. 2005. "Mobile Techsoma: Some Phenomenological Reflections on Itinerant Media Devices." *The Fibre Culture Journal* 6. Available at: http://six.fibreculturejournal.org/fcj-032-mobile-technosoma-some-phenomenological-reflections-on-itinerant-media-devices/ (accessed November 20, 2015).

Roberts, Lisa. 2006. *Pocket Shorts*. Interview-Audio-cassette. May 25.

Rose, Max, and Frank R. Baumgartner. 2013. "Framing the Poor: Media Coverage and U.S. Poverty Policy, 1960-2008." *Policy Studies Journal* 41 (1): 22–53.

Rosler, Martha. 1989. "In Around, and Afterthoughts on Documentary Photography." In *The Context of Meaning: Critical Histories of Photography*. Ed. Richard Bolton. Cambridge, MA: MIT Press. 303–25.

Rossi, Uggo. 2015. "The Variegated Economics and the Potential Politics of the Smart City." *Territory, Politics, Governance*. Available at: https://www.academia.edu/10618544/The_variegated_economics_and_the_potential_politics_of_the_smart_city (accessed January 17, 2016).

Roustang, François. 2000. *How to Make a Paranoid Laugh, or, What Is Psychoanalysis?* Trans. Anne A. Vila. Philadelphia: University of Pennsylvania Press.

Salvation Army. 2012. *Perceptions of Poverty: The Salvation Army's Report to America.* May. Available at: http://salvationarmynorth.org/wpcontent/uploads/2012/10/2012S APovertyReportWEB.pdf (accessed February 21, 2016).

Sattler, Peter R. 2009. "Past Imperfect: Building Stories and the Art of Memory." In *The Comics of Chris Ware: Comics as a Way of Thinking.* Eds. David M. Ball and Martha B. Kuhlman. Jackson: The University of Mississippi Press. 206–21.

Schneider, Alexandra. 2004. *"Die Stars sind wir": Heimkino als filmische Praxis in der Schweiz der Dreissigerjahre.* Marburg: Schueren Verlag.

Schneider, Alexandra. 2014. "Au delà du dispositif le cinéma (re)trouve son enfance: A propos des films-tablets et films-mobiles d'enfants." Unpublished lecture presented at the international conference *Images, Histoire, Langage: Carte blanche à Jacques Aumont, Michel Marie et Roger Odin.* Paris, November 20–21.

Schneider, Alexandra, and Wanda Strauven. Forthcoming 2016. "The Kid Selfie as Self-Inscription: Re-Inventing an Emerging Media Practice." In *#SELFIE: Imag(in)ing the Self in Digital Media.* Eds. Jens Ruchatz, Sabine Wirth, and Julia Eckel. Leuven: Palgrave McMillan.

Scholz, Trebor. Ed. 2012. *Digital Labor: The Internet as Playground and Factory.* New York: Routledge.

Scholz, Trebor. 2016. *Uberworked and Underpaid.* Cambridge, UK; Malden, MA: Polity Press.

Schüll, Natasha Dow. 2012. *Addiction by Design: Machine Gambling in Las Vegas.* Princeton, NJ: Princeton University Press.

Schumpeter, Joseph A. 1942. *Capitalism, Socialism, and Democracy.* New York: Harper And Brothers.

Scott, James C. 1999. *Seeing Like A State: How Certain Schemes To Improve The Human Condition Have Failed.* New Haven: Yale University Press.

Segaran, Toby, and Jeff Hammerbacher. Eds. 2009. *Beautiful Data: The Stories Behind Elegant Data Solutions.* Beijing and Sebastopol, CA: O'Reilly Media.

Sekula, Allan. 1978. "Dismantling Modernism, Reinventing Documentary (Notes on the Politics of Representation)." *The Massachusetts Review* 19 (4): 859–83.

Serres, Michel. 2012. *Petite Poucette.* Paris: Le Pommier.

Serres, Michel. 2013. *Erfindet euch neu!: Eine Liebeserklärung an die vernetzte Generation.* Berlin: Suhrkamp.

Serres, Michel. 2015. *Thumbelina: The Culture and Technology of Millennials.* Lanhum, MD: Rowman & Littlefield International.

"Shane Meadows Launches Nokia Shorts 2005." 2005. *NokiaShortsRelease05. doc—Raindance Film Festival.* Available at: http://www.raindance.co.uk/Docs/ NokiaShortsRelease05.do (accessed December 10, 2015).

Shaviro, Steven. 2013. "Accelerationist Aesthetics: Necessary Inefficiency in Times of Real Subsumption." *e-flux journal* #46. Available at: http://www.e-flux.com/journal/ accelerationist-aesthetics-necessary-inefficiency-in-times-of-real-subsumption/ (accessed February 29, 2016).

Shifman, Limor. 2013. *Memes in Digital Culture*. Essential Knowledge. Cambridge, MA: MIT Press.

Shklovsky, Viktor. 1965. "Art as Technique." In *Russian Formalist Criticism: Four Essays*. Eds. Lee T. Lemon, Marion J. Reis, and Lee T. Lemon. Lincoln: University of Nebraska Press. 3–24.

"Short Form Video: A Future but not the Future, of Television." 2015. *Deloitte TMT Predictions* 2015. Available at: http://www.deloitte.co.uk/tmtpredictions/short-form-video-a-future-but-not-the-future-of-television/ (accessed December 13, 2015).

Smith, Jonas Heide. 2007. "The Road not Taken—The How's and Why's of Interactive Fiction." Available at: http://game-research.com/index.php/articles/the-road-not-taken-the-hows-and-whys-of-interactive-fiction/ (accessed February 10, 2016).

Smith, Tim J. 2005. *An Attentional Theory of Continuity Editing*. PhD diss., Institute for Communicating and Collaborative Systems School of Informatics. Edinburgh: University of Edinburgh. Available at: https://www.era.lib.ed.ac.uk/bitstream/handle/1842/1076/smith_ATOCE_0506.pdf?sequence=1&isAllowed=y (accessed March 9, 2016).

Soar, Matt. 2014. "Making (with) the Korsakow System: Database Documentaries as Articulation and Assemblage." In *New Documentary Ecologies: Emerging Platforms, Practices and Discourses*. Eds. Kate Nash, Craig Hight, and Catherine Summerhayes. London: Palgrave Macmillan. 154–73.

Söderström, Ola, Till Paasche, and Francisco Klauser. 2014. "Smart cities as corporate storytelling." *City* 18 (3): 307–20.

Spigel, Lynn. 1992. *Make Room for TV: Television and the Family Ideal in Post-war America*. Chicago: University of Chicago Press.

Stengers, Isabelle. 2005. "An Ecology of Practices." *Cultural Studies Review* 11 (1): 183–96.

Sterne, Jonathan. 2012. *MP3: The Meaning of a Format*. Durham, NC: Duke University Press.

Steyerl, Hito. 2003. "Politics of Truth, Documentarism in the Art Field, 'Reality Art.'" *Hefte für Gegenwartskunst*. March. Available at: http://www.springerin.at/dyn/heft_text.php?textid=1353&lang=en (accessed March 22, 2016).

Steyerl, Hito. 2006. "The Language of Things." *Transversal Texts*. eipcp—European Institute for Progressive Cultural Policies. June. Available at: http://eipcp.net/transversal/0606/steyerl/en (accessed February 27, 2016).

Steyerl, Hito. 2009. "In Defense of the Poor Image." *e-flux journal* #10. Available at: http://www.e-flux.com/journal/in-defense-of-the-poor-image/ (accessed January 12, 2016).

Stingelin, Martin, and Matthias Thiele. Eds. 2010. *Portable Media: Schreibszenen in Bewegung zwischen Peripatetik und Mobiltelefon*. Paderborn: Fink.

Stocker, Michael. 2013. *Hear Where We Are: Sound Ecology And Sense Of Place*. London: Springer.

Strauven, Wanda. 2016. "(Film) History Made by Nameless Children." In *A History of Cinema Without Names*. Eds. Diego Cavallotti, Federico Giordano, and Leonardo Quaresima. Milano: Mimesis International. 239–45.

Sykes, Andy. 2005. *Evil Fun with Zimmy*. UK: Blink Media. Available at: https://www.
    youtube.com/watch?v=4H5KuN08xAE&index=18&list=PL36F45C87E8FA3D7F
    (accessed February 26, 2016).

Tagg, Melissa. 2015. "Conflict Vs. Tension." Available at: http://www.thewritersalleyblog.
    com/2015/06/conflict-vs-tension-guest-post-by.html (accessed February 10, 2016).

Telotte, Jay P. 2008. *The Mouse Machine: Disney and Technology*. Urbana: University of
    Illinois Press.

Terranova, Tiziana. 2004. *Network Culture: Politics for the Information Age*. London and
    Ann Arbor, MI: Pluto Press.

Thalhofer, Florian. *Planet Galata*. Available at: http://www.planetgalata.com/. Assessed
    on April 6, 2016.

The Invisible Committee. 2015. "Fuck off, Google!" In *To Our Friends*. Cambridge, MA:
    MIT Press. 62–81.

Thomson, David. 2013. *The Big Screen: The Story of the Movies*. New York: Farrar, Straus
    and Giroux.

Thumim, Janet. Ed. 2002. *Small Screens, Big Ideas: Television in the 1950s*. London and
    New York: I. B. Tauris.

Tryon, Chuck. 2013. *On-Demand Culture: Digital Delivery and the Future of Movies*.
    New Brunswick, NJ: Rutgers University Press.

Ungar, Steven. 2008. *Cleo de 5 à 7*. London: BFI Publishing.

Valck, Marijke de. 2007. *Film Festivals: From European Geopolitics to Global Cinephilia*.
    Amsterdam: Amsterdam University Press.

Väliaho, Pasi. 2013. "Spellbound: Early Cinema's Transformational Spaces." *Space and
    Culture* 16 (2): 161–72.

Van Dijck, José. 2013. *The Culture of Connectivity: A Critical History of Social Media*.
    Oxford and New York: Oxford University Press.

Voci, Paola. 2010. *China on Video: Smaller-Screen Realities*. London: Routledge.

Walker, David. 2014. "Metabasis, Desis, and Lusis." Available at: http://hull-awe.org.uk/
    index.php?title=Metabasis,_desis,_and_lusis (accessed February 10, 2016).

Ware, Chris. 1994. *Acme Novelty Library 2: Quimby the Mouse*. Seattle: Fantagraphics.

Ware, Chris. 1994–95. *Acme Novelty Library 4: Sparky*. Seattle: Fantagraphics.

Ware, Chris. 2000. *Jimmy Corrigan the Smartest Kid on Earth*. New York: Pantheon.

Ware, Chris. 2003. *Quimby the Mouse*. Seattle: Fantagraphics.

Ware, Chris. 2012. *Building Stories*. New York: Pantheon.

Weiland, K. M. 2012. "What's the Difference Between Conflict and Tension?" Available
    at: http://www.helpingwritersbecomeauthors.com/conflict-and-tension/ (accessed
    February 10, 2016).

Wildemuth, Barbara M., Gary Marchionini, Meng Yang, Gary Geisler, Todd Wilkens,
    Anthony Hughes, and Richard Gruss. 2003. "How Fast Is Too Fast? Evaluating Fast
    Forward Surrogates for Digital Video." *Proceedings of the 3rd ACM/IEEE-CS Joint
    Conference on Digital Libraries* (JCDL). 221–30.

Wolf, Mark J. P. 2012. *Encyclopedia of Video Games: The Culture, Technology and Art of Gaming*. Santa Barbara: Greenwood Publishing.

Wollen, Peter. 2002. "Speed and the Cinema." In *Paris Hollywood: Writings on Film*. London: Verso. 264–74.

Wollen, Peter. 2004. "Godard and Counter Cinema: *Vent d'est*." In *Film Theory and Criticism*. Sixth edition. Eds. L. Braudy and M. Cohen. New York and Oxford: Oxford University Press. 525–33.

Woodward, Martin. 2015. *Brainwave Entrainment Plus: Make Binaural Beats & Isochronic Tones On Your PC for Hypnosis, Relaxation, Meditation & More!* Raleigh, NC: Lulu Press, Inc.

Yates, Frances A. 2009. *The Art of Memory*. London: Routledge.

Zielinski, Siegfried. 1999. *Audiovisions: Cinema and Television as Entr'actes in History*. Amsterdam: Amsterdam University Press.

Zielinski, Siegfried. 2006. *Deep Time of the Media: Toward an Archaeology of Hearing and Seeing by Technical Means*. Trans. Gloria Custance. Foreword Timothy Druckrey. Cambridge, MA: MIT Press.

Žižek, Slavoj. 2000. *The Ticklish Subject*. London: Verso.

Žižek, Slavoj. 2001. *Enjoy Your Symptom: Jacques Lacan In Hollywood and Out*. London: Routledge.

Index

238   *Index*

    151 n.1, 185, 198
VR film   170
vrse.com   167–8, 171

Walden, Kim Louise   *133–42*
Walker, David   35
Ware, Chris   153–64
Warhol, Andy   108
Wavelength   107
web 2.0   87, 114, 121 n.5, 199
Weiland, K. M.   29
While you are Waiting   137, 142 n.2
White, Richard   49
Wildemuth, Barbara M.   105
Wilder, Billy   60
Wilkenson Eyre   178

Wilson, Andrew   137, 142 n.4
Windows media player   104
Wolf, Mark J. P.   75
Wollen, Peter   41, 104, 110
Woodward, Martin   122 n.15
WVLNT   107

Xbox (console)   1

Yates, Frances A.   164 n.3
ying yang   29
Youtube   1, 66, 90, 97, 104, 111 n.1, 118,
    166, 171–2, 178, 200

Zepo   30, 35
Zielinski, Siegfried   13 n.3
Žižek, Slavoj   159

CPSIA information can be obtained
t www.ICGtesting.com
nted in the USA
W021507210119
69LV00016B/934/P